SHAKESPEAREAN
NEGOTIATIONS

SHAKESPEAREAN NEGOTIATIONS

*The Circulation of
Social Energy in
Renaissance England*

STEPHEN GREENBLATT

CLARENDON PRESS · OXFORD

Oxford University Press, Great Clarendon Street, Oxford OX2 6DP

Oxford New York

Athens Auckland Bangkok Bogota Bombay Buenos Aires
Calcutta Cape Town Dar es Salaam Delhi Florence Hong Kong
Istanbul Karachi Kuala Lumpur Madras Madrid Melbourne
Mexico City Nairobi Paris Singapore Taipei Tokyo Toronto Warsaw

and associated companies in
Berlin Ibadan

Oxford is a trade mark of Oxford University Press

Published in the United States by
Oxford University Press Inc., New York

© 1988 by the Regents of the University of California

First published 1988
First published in paperback 1990
Reprinted 1992, 1997

British Library Cataloguing in Publication Data
Greenblatt, Stephen J.
Shakespearean negotiations: the
circulation of social energy in
Renaissance England.
1. Shakespeare, William — Criticism and
interpretation
I. Title.
822´.3´3   PR2976
ISBN 0-19-812980-7 (Hbk)
ISBN 0-19-812227-6 (Pbk)

Printed and bound in Great Britain
on acid-free paper by
Biddles Ltd, Guildford and King's Lynn

Contents

To my mother and
to the memory of my father

Acknowledgments

This book argues that works of art, however intensely marked by the creative intelligence and private obsessions of individuals, are the products of collective negotiation and exchange. Why should works of criticism be any different? The chapters that follow have been written out of a sustained engagement with others who have been asking similar questions about Shakespeare and Renaissance literature: I want in particular to cite Stephen Orgel, Louis Montrose, Leah Marcus, Jonathan Goldberg, Steven Mullaney, Richard Strier, Jean Howard, Don Wayne, Harry Berger, Jr., Leonard Tennenhouse, Jonathan Crewe, Richard Helgerson, Jonathan Dollimore, Alan Sinfield, Margaret Ferguson, Frank Whigham, and Peter Stallybrass. I have also received important suggestions, encouragement, and valuable criticism from Ellen Greenblatt, Michael Baxandall, Louis Marin, Mitchell Breitwieser, Tzvetan Todorov, T. Walter Herbert, Jr., Sheila Cavanagh, Caroline Bynum, John Bender, Lisa Jardine, Roy Porter, Barbara Bowen, Lu Gu-Sun, Yang Zhou-Han, William Bouwsma, Gene Brucker, Hayden White, Joan DeJean, Neil Hertz, Ruth Leys, Timothy Bahti, Jane Newman, David Harris Sacks, Anne Middleton, Jonas Barish, John Coolidge, Donald Friedman, Joel Altman, Janet Adelman, Stephen Booth, Peter Brown, Doris Kretschmer, Deborah Willis, Paula Findlen, Stephanie Fay, Lindsay Kaplan, Jeffrey Knapp, and Oliver Arnold, and from many others at Berkeley and elsewhere who have responded to these materials when I presented them as lectures. I have a special intellectual and personal indebtedness to Natalie Zemon Davis, Elaine Scarry, David Miller, Susan Foster,

Michael Fried, and Robert Pinsky. And I am at once pleased and saddened to recall illuminating conversations with two brilliant colleagues who are now gone: Michel de Certeau and Michel Foucault.

The exchanges with which my study of Shakespeare is concerned are institutional as well as personal, and again my own book itself is scarcely exempt. Several of the chapters received helpful criticisms when I first presented them at academic conferences: "Reconstructing Individualism," at Stanford University; the Ninth Annual Symposium in English and American Literature, at the University of Alabama; "Drama, Theatre, and Society in Renaissance England," a Bronowski Colloquium at the University of California, San Diego; and a Gauss Colloquium on art history, at Princeton University. Moreover, parts of three chapters of the book have been published in the proceedings of these conferences or elsewhere: "Shakespeare and the Exorcists," in *After Strange Texts: The Role of Theory in the Study of Literature* (Papers from the Ninth Alabama Symposium), ed. Gregory S. Jay and David L. Miller (University: University of Alabama Press, 1984), pp. 101–23, and, in a different version, in *Shakespeare and the Question of Theory*, ed. Patricia Parker and Geoffrey Hartman (New York: Methuen, 1985), pp. 163–87; "Invisible Bullets" appeared first in *Glyph* 8 (1981): 40–61, then in revised versions in *Political Shakespeare: New Essays in Cultural Materialism*, ed. Jonathan Dollimore and Alan Sinfield (Manchester: Manchester University Press, 1985), pp. 18–47, and in *Shakespeare's "Rough Magic": Renaissance Essays in Honor of C. L. Barber*, ed. Peter Erickson and Coppélia Kahn (Newark: University of Delaware Press, 1985), pp. 276–302; finally, a portion of "Fiction and Friction" appeared in the collected papers of the Stanford Conference, *Reconstructing Individualism: Autonomy, Individuality, and the Self in Western Thought*, ed. David Wellberry and Thomas Heller (Stanford: Stanford University Press, 1986), pp. 30–52. None of these essays was "occasional" in origin or design; in bringing together revised and expanded versions of them in the present volume, along with material that has not before appeared in print, I hope that the larger project for which I have conceived and written them will become apparent.

The Guggenheim Foundation played a sustaining role in this project, as in my preparation of an earlier book. A senior fellowship at the Society for the Humanities at Cornell University was the occasion for my first researches into Renaissance demonological and medical texts, researches that I continued, with the generous assistance of my university's Class of 1932 Chair and a Humanities Research Fellowship, at the British Library, the Warburg Institute, and the Wellcome Institute in London and at the Bibliothèque Nationale and the Bibliothèque Mazarine in Paris.

The University of California at Berkeley has been for many years now an extraordinarily stimulating and rewarding place to work. My students, both undergraduate and graduate, have had a profound influence upon everything I have written. And at the center of my intellectual life at Berkeley is the group of colleagues who have worked together on the journal *Representations* and have shared ideas, argued, criticized, and given of themselves with remarkable generosity: Paul Alpers, Svetlana Alpers, Howard Bloch, Frances Ferguson, Joel Fineman, Catherine Gallagher, Denis Hollier, Lynn Hunt, Steven Knapp, Thomas Laqueur, Walter Michaels, Paul Rabinow, Michael Rogin, and Randolph Starn. I have been lucky in my friends.

A Note on Texts

Throughout this book, except where noted, I have used *The River-side Shakespeare*, ed. G. Blakemore Evans (Boston: Houghton Mif-flin, 1974). I have not, however, included the brackets with which the Riverside editors signal their adoption of variant readings.

In the body of my book, I have modernized spelling in quota-tions from Renaissance texts, since it seemed odd to cite Shake-speare in a modernized edition while leaving his contemporaries to look quaint and timeworn. In the footnotes, I have left titles and quotations the way I found them.

Chapter One

The Circulation of Social Energy

I began with the desire to speak with the dead.

This desire is a familiar, if unvoiced, motive in literary studies, a motive organized, professionalized, buried beneath thick layers of bureaucratic decorum: literature professors are salaried, middle-class shamans. If I never believed that the dead could hear me, and if I knew that the dead could not speak, I was nonetheless certain that I could re-create a conversation with them. Even when I came to understand that in my most intense moments of straining to listen all I could hear was my own voice, even then I did not abandon my desire. It was true that I could hear only my own voice, but my own voice was the voice of the dead, for the dead had contrived to leave textual traces of themselves, and those traces make themselves heard in the voices of the living. Many of the traces have little resonance, though every one, even the most trivial or tedious, contains some fragment of lost life; others seem uncannily full of the will to be heard. It is paradoxical, of course, to seek the living will of the dead in fictions, in places where there was no live bodily being to begin with. But those who love literature tend to find more intensity in simulations—in the formal, self-conscious miming of life—than in any of the other textual traces left by the dead, for simulations are undertaken in full awareness of the absence of the life they contrive to represent, and hence they may skillfully anticipate and compensate for the vanishing of the actual life that has empowered them. Conventional in my tastes, I found the most satisfying intensity of all in Shakespeare.

I wanted to know how Shakespeare managed to achieve such intensity, for I thought that the more I understood this achievement, the more I could hear and understand the speech of the dead.

The question then was how did so much life get into the textual traces? Shakespeare's plays, it seemed, had precipitated out of a sublime confrontation between a total artist and a totalizing society. By a total artist I mean one who, through training, resourcefulness, and talent, is at the moment of creation complete unto himself; by a totalizing society I mean one that posits an occult network linking all human, natural, and cosmic powers and that claims on behalf of its ruling elite a privileged place in this network. Such a society generates vivid dreams of access to the linked powers and vests control of this access in a religious and state bureaucracy at whose pinnacle is the symbolic figure of the monarch. The result of this confrontation between total artist and totalizing society was a set of unique, inexhaustible, and supremely powerful works of art.

In the book I have written something of this initial conception survives, but it has been complicated by several turns in my thinking that I had not foreseen. I can summarize those turns by remarking that I came to have doubts about two things: "total artist" and "totalizing society."

I did not, to be sure, doubt that the plays attributed to Shakespeare were in large part written by the supremely gifted alumnus of the Stratford grammar school. Nor did I cease to believe that Renaissance society was totalizing in intention. But I grew increasingly uneasy with the monolithic entities that my work had posited. No individual, not even the most brilliant, seemed complete unto himself—my own study of Renaissance self-fashioning had already persuaded me of this—and Elizabethan and Jacobean visions of hidden unity seemed like anxious rhetorical attempts to conceal cracks, conflict, and disarray. I had tried to organize the mixed motives of Tudor and Stuart culture under the rubric *power*, but that term implied a structural unity and stability of command belied by much of what I actually knew about the exercise of authority and force in the period.

If it was important to speak of power in relation to Renaissance literature—not only as the object but as the enabling condition of representation itself—it was equally important to resist the integration of all images and expressions into a single master discourse. For if Renaissance writers themselves often echoed the desire of princes and prelates for just such a discourse, brilliant critical and theoretical work in recent years by a large and diverse group of scholars had demonstrated that this desire was itself constructed out of conflicting and ill-sorted motives. Even those literary texts that sought most ardently to speak for a monolithic power could be shown to be the sites of institutional and ideological contestation.

But what does it mean to pull back from a notion of artistic completeness, on the one hand, and totalizing power, on the other? It can mean a return to the text itself as the central object of our attention. To speak of such a return has a salutary ring—there are days when I long to recover the close-grained formalism of my own literary training—but the referent of the phrase "the text itself" is by no means clear. Indeed in the case of Shakespeare (and of the drama more generally), there has probably never been a time since the early eighteenth century when there was less confidence in the "text." Not only has a new generation of textual historians undermined the notion that a skilled editorial weaving of folio and quarto readings will give us an authentic record of Shakespeare's original intentions, but theater historians have challenged the whole notion of the text as the central, stable locus of theatrical meaning. There are textual traces—a bewildering mass of them— but it is impossible to take the "text itself" as the perfect, unsubstitutable, freestanding container of all of its meanings.

The textual analyses I was trained to do had as their goal the identification and celebration of a numinous literary authority, whether that authority was ultimately located in the mysterious genius of an artist or in the mysterious perfection of a text whose intuitions and concepts can never be expressed in other terms.[1] The great attraction of this authority is that it appears to bind and fix the energies we prize, to identify a stable and permanent source of literary power, to offer an escape from shared contingency.

This project, endlessly repeated, repeatedly fails for one reason: there is no escape from contingency.

All the same, we do experience unmistakable pleasure and interest in the literary traces of the dead, and I return to the question how it is possible for those traces to convey lost life. Over the past several generations this question has been addressed principally by close reading of the textual traces, and I believe that sustained, scrupulous attention to formal and linguistic design will remain at the center of literary teaching and study. But in the essays that follow I propose something different: to look less at the presumed center of the literary domain than at its borders, to try to track what can only be glimpsed, as it were, at the margins of the text. The cost of this shift in attention will be the satisfying illusion of a "whole reading," the impression conveyed by powerful critics that had they but world enough and time, they could illuminate every corner of the text and knit together into a unified interpretive vision all of their discrete perceptions. My vision is necessarily more fragmentary, but I hope to offer a compensatory satisfaction: insight into the half-hidden cultural transactions through which great works of art are empowered.

I propose that we begin by taking seriously the collective production of literary pleasure and interest. We know that this production is collective since language itself, which is at the heart of literary power, is the supreme instance of a collective creation. But this knowledge has for the most part remained inert, either cordoned off in prefatory acknowledgments or diffused in textual analyses that convey almost nothing of the social dimension of literature's power. Instead the work seems to stand only for the skill and effort of the individual artist, as if whole cultures possessed their shared emotions, stories, and dreams only because a professional caste invented them and parceled them out. In literary criticism Renaissance artists function like Renaissance monarchs: at some level we know perfectly well that the power of the prince is largely a collective invention, the symbolic embodiment of the desire, pleasure, and violence of thousands of subjects, the instrumental expression of complex networks of dependency and fear, the agent rather than the maker of the social will. Yet we can scarcely write of prince or poet without accepting the fiction that power directly emanates from him and that society draws upon this power.[2]

The attempt to locate the power of art in a permanently novel, untranslatable formal perfection will always end in a blind alley, but the frustration is particularly intense in the study of the Shakespearean theater for two reasons. First, the theater is manifestly the product of collective intentions. There may be a moment in which a solitary individual puts words on a page, but it is by no means clear that this moment is the heart of the mystery and that everything else is to be stripped away and discarded. Moreover, the moment of inscription, on closer analysis, is itself a social moment. This is particularly clear with Shakespeare, who does not conceal his indebtedness to literary sources, but it is also true for less obviously collaborative authors, all of whom depend upon collective genres, narrative patterns, and linguistic conventions.[3] Second, the theater manifestly addresses its audience as a collectivity. The model is not, as with the nineteenth-century novel, the individual reader who withdraws from the public world of affairs to the privacy of the hearth but the crowd that gathers together in a public play space.[4] The Shakespearean theater depends upon a felt community: there is no dimming of lights, no attempt to isolate and awaken the sensibilities of each individual member of the audience, no sense of the disappearance of the crowd.

If the textual traces in which we take interest and pleasure are not sources of numinous authority, if they are the signs of contingent social practices, then the questions we ask of them cannot profitably center on a search for their untranslatable essence. Instead we can ask how collective beliefs and experiences were shaped, moved from one medium to another, concentrated in manageable aesthetic form, offered for consumption. We can examine how the boundaries were marked between cultural practices understood to be art forms and other, contiguous, forms of expression. We can attempt to determine how these specially demarcated zones were invested with the power to confer pleasure or excite interest or generate anxiety. The idea is not to strip away and discard the enchanted impression of aesthetic autonomy but to inquire into the objective conditions of this enchantment, to discover how the traces of social circulation are effaced.

I have termed this general enterprise—study of the collective making of distinct cultural practices and inquiry into the relations among these practices—a poetics of culture. For me the inquiry is bound up with a specific interest in Renaissance modes of aesthetic empowerment: I want to know how cultural objects, expressions, and practices—here, principally, plays by Shakespeare and the stage on which they first appeared—acquired compelling force. English literary theorists in the period needed a new word for that force, a word to describe the ability of language, in Puttenham's phrase, to cause "a stir to the mind"; drawing on the Greek rhetorical tradition, they called it *energia*.[5] This is the origin in our language of the term "energy," a term I propose we use, provided we understand that its origins lie in rhetoric rather than physics and that its significance is social and historical. We experience that energy within ourselves, but its contemporary existence depends upon an irregular chain of historical transactions that leads back to the late sixteenth and early seventeenth centuries.[6] Does this mean that the aesthetic power of a play like *King Lear* is a direct transmission from Shakespeare's time to our own? Certainly not. That play and the circumstances in which it was originally embedded have been continuously, often radically, refigured. But these refigurations do not cancel history, locking us into a perpetual present; on the contrary, they are signs of the inescapability of a historical process, a structured negotiation and exchange, already evident in the initial moments of empowerment. That there is no direct, unmediated link between ourselves and Shakespeare's plays does not mean that there is no link at all. The "life" that literary works seem to possess long after both the death of the author and the death of the culture for which the author wrote is the historical consequence, however transformed and refashioned, of the social energy initially encoded in those works.

But what is "social energy"? The term implies something measurable, yet I cannot provide a convenient and reliable formula for isolating a single, stable quantum for examination. We identify *energia* only indirectly, by its effects: it is manifested in the capacity of certain verbal, aural, and visual traces to produce, shape, and organize collective physical and mental experiences. Hence it is associated with repeatable forms of pleasure and interest, with the capacity to arouse disquiet, pain, fear, the beating of the heart, pity, laughter, tension, relief, wonder. In its aesthetic modes, social energy must have a minimal predictability—enough to make simple repetitions possible—and a minimal range: enough to reach out beyond a single creator or consumer to some community, however constricted. Occasionally, and we are generally interested in these occasions, the predictability and range will be far greater: large numbers of men and women of different social classes and divergent beliefs will be induced to explode with laughter or weep or experience a complex blend of anxiety and exaltation. Moreover, the aesthetic forms of social energy are usually characterized by a minimal adaptability—enough to enable them to survive at least some of the constant changes in social circumstance and cultural value that make ordinary utterances evanescent. Whereas most collective expressions moved from their original setting to a new place or time are dead on arrival, the social energy encoded in certain works of art continues to generate the illusion of life for centuries. I want to understand the negotiations through which works of art obtain and amplify such powerful energy.

If one longs, as I do, to reconstruct these negotiations, one dreams of finding an originary moment, a moment in which the master hand shapes the concentrated social energy into the sublime aesthetic object. But the quest is fruitless, for there is no originary moment, no pure act of untrammeled creation. In place of a blazing genesis, one begins to glimpse something that seems at first far less spectacular: a subtle, elusive set of exchanges, a network of trades and trade-offs, a jostling of competing representations, a negotiation between joint-stock companies. Gradually, these complex, ceaseless borrowings and lendings have come to seem to me more important, more poignant even, than the epiphany for which I had hoped.

The textual traces that have survived from the Renaissance and that are at the center of our literary interest in Shakespeare are the products of extended borrowings, collective exchanges, and mutual enchantments. They were made by moving certain things—principally ordinary language but also metaphors, ceremonies, dances, emblems, items of clothing, well-worn stories, and so forth—from one culturally demarcated zone to another. We need to understand not only the construction of these zones but also the process of movement across the shifting boundaries between them. Who decides which materials can be moved and which must remain in place? How are cultural materials prepared for exchange? What happens to them when they are moved?

But why are we obliged to speak of movement at all? Except in the most material instances—items of clothing, stage properties, the bodies of actors—nothing is literally moved onto the stage. Rather, the theater achieves its representations by gesture and language, that is, by signifiers that seem to leave the signifieds completely untouched. Renaissance writers would seem to have endorsed this intangibility by returning again and again to the image of the mirror; the purpose of playing, in Hamlet's conventional words, is "to hold as 'twere the mirror up to nature: to show virtue her feature, scorn her own image, and the very age and body of the time his form and pressure" (3.2.21–24). The mirror is the emblem of instantaneous and accurate reproduction; it takes nothing from what it reflects and adds nothing except self-knowledge.

Perhaps this is what the players actually thought they were doing, but it is worth considering how convenient and self-protective the image of the mirror must have seemed. Artists in a time of censorship and repression had ample reason to claim that they had taken nothing from the world they represented, that they had never dreamed of violating the distance demanded by their superiors, that their representations only reflected faithfully the world's own form. Yet even in Hamlet's familiar account, the word *pressure*—that is, impression, as with a seal or signet ring—should signal to us that for the Renaissance more is at stake in mirrors than an abstract and bodiless reflection. Both optics and mirror lore in the period suggested that something was actively passing back and forth in the production of mirror images, that accurate representation depended upon material emanation and exchange.[7] Only if we reinvest the mirror image with a sense of pressure as well as form can it convey something of its original strangeness and magic. And only with the recovery of this strangeness can we glimpse a whole spectrum of representational exchanges where we had once seen simple reflection alone. In some exchanges the object or practice mimed onstage seems relatively untouched by the representation; in others, the object or practice is intensified, diminished, or even completely evacuated by its encounter with the theater; in still others, it is marked as a prize—something "up for grabs"—in an unresolved struggle between competing representational discourses. The mistake is to imagine that there is a single, fixed, mode of exchange; in reality, there are many modes, their character is determined historically, and they are continually renegotiated.

The range of these modes is treated in detail in the chapters that follow, but it might be useful to note some of the more common types:

1. *Appropriation.* There seems to be little or no payment or recip-rocal understanding or quid pro quo. Objects appear to be in the public domain, hence in the category of "things indifferent" (adia-phora): there for the taking. Or, alternatively, objects appear to be vulnerable and defenseless, hence graspable without punishment or retaliation.

The prime example of adiaphora is ordinary language: for liter-ary art this is the single greatest cultural creation that may be appro-priated without payment. One of the simplest and most sublime instances is Lear's anguished "Never, never, never, never, never." But once we pass beyond the most conventional and familiar ex-pressions, we come upon instances of language use that are charged with potential dangers, powerful social charms that can-not be simply appropriated. And under certain circumstances even ordinary language may be surprisingly contested.

The prime example of the vulnerable is the lower classes, who may at most times be represented almost without restraint.

2. *Purchase.* Here something, most often money, is paid by the theater company for an object (or practice or story) that is staged. The clearest instances are properties and costumes. The invento-ries that have survived suggest that theater companies were pre-pared to pay a high price for objects with a high symbolic valence: "Item, 1 popes miter"; "Item, 3 Imperial crowns; 1 plain crown"; "Bought a doublet of white satin laid thick with gold lace, and pair of round paned hose of cloth of silver, the panes laid with gold lace . . . £7.00."[8] Some of the costumes were made directly for the players; others came via transactions that reveal the circuitous chan-nels through which social energy could be circulated: suits were given by gentlemen to their servants in lieu of cash payment (or in addition to such payment); the servants sold the clothes to the players; the players appeared onstage in clothes that might actually have belonged to members of the audience.

The companies did not pay for "rights" to stories, so far as I know—at least not in the modern sense—but the playwright or company did pay for the books used as sources (for example, Holinshed or Marguerite of Navarre or Giraldi Cinthio), and the playwright himself was paid.

3. *Symbolic Acquisition.* Here a social practice or other mode of social energy is transferred to the stage by means of representation. No cash payment is made, but the object acquired is not in the realm of things indifferent, and something is implicitly or explicitly given in return for it. The transferring agency has its purposes, which may be more or less overt; the theater picks up what it can get and gives in return what it must (for example, public celebration or humiliation). In chapter 4 I discuss the way the charismatic religious practice of exorcism, under attack by the official church, is brought on to the stage, where its power is at once exploited and marked out as a fraud: "Five fiends have been in poor Tom at once: of lust, as Obidicut; Hobbididence, prince of dumbness; Mahu, of stealing; Modo, of murder; Flibbertigibbet, of mopping and mowing, who since possesses chambermaids and waiting-women."

We can further distinguish three types of symbolic acquistion:

a. *Acquisition through Simulation.* The actor simulates what is already understood to be a theatrical representation. The most extreme instance is the theater's own self-representations—that is, simulations of actors performing plays, as in *The Spanish Tragedy, Hamlet, The Knight of the Burning Pestle,* or *The Roman Actor*— but many of the most resonant instances involve more complex simulations of the histrionic elements in public ceremonials and rituals. For example, as I shall show in chapter 5, the spectacular royal pardons that were understood by observers to be theatrical occasions were staged as theatrical occasions in plays such as *Measure for Measure.*

b. *Metaphorical Acquisition.* Here a practice (or a set of social energies) is acquired indirectly. For example, after 1606 players were forbidden to take the name of the Lord in vain—that is, every use of the words "God" or "Christ Jesus" or the "Holy Ghost" or the "Trinity" onstage, even in wholly pious contexts, would be subject to a £10 fine.[9] The regulation threatened to remove from the performances not simply a set of names but a whole range of powerful energies, rituals, and experiences. The players' simple and effective response, sanctioned by a long tradition, was to substitute for the interdicted words names like Jove and Jupiter, each a miniature metaphor for the Christian God. To take a slightly more complex example, when the fairies in *A Midsummer Night's Dream* "consecrate" the marriage beds with field-dew, they are, in a mode at once natural and magical, enacting (and appropriating to the stage) the Catholic practice of anointing the marriage bed with holy water.[10]

Metaphorical acquisition works by teasing out latent homologies, similitudes, systems of likeness, but it depends equally upon a deliberate distancing or distortion that precedes the disclosure of likeness. Hence a play will insist upon the difference between its representation and the "real," only to draw out the analogy or proportion linking them. The chorus in *Henry V* urgently calls attention to the difference between the theater's power to command the imagination of the audience and the prince's power to command his subjects, but as the play unfolds, those powers become revealingly confounded (see chapter 2). Or again, the strategies of the theater and the family, seemingly far removed, are revealed by *King Lear* to be mirrors of each other.[11]

c. *Acquisition through Synecdoche or Metonymy.* Here the theater acquires cultural energy by isolating and performing one part or attribute of a practice, which then stands for the whole (often a whole that cannot be represented). For example, as I argue in chapter 3, verbal chafing becomes in Shakespeare's comedies not only a sign but a vital instance of an encompassing erotic heat otherwise impossible to stage in the public theater.

Inquiries into the relation between Renaissance theater and society have been situated most often at the level of reflection: images of the monarchy, the lower classes, the legal profession, the church, and so forth. Such studies are essential, but they rarely engage questions of dynamic exchange. They tend instead to posit two separate, autonomous systems and then try to gauge how accurately or effectively the one represents the other. But crucial questions typically remain outside the range of this critical practice: How is it determined what may be staged? To what extent is the object of theatrical representation itself already a representation? What governs the degree of displacement or distortion in theatrical representation? Whose interests are served by the staging? What is the effect of representation on the object or practice represented?

Above all, how is the social energy inherent in a cultural practice negotiated and exchanged?

If we are to attempt an answer to these questions, it would be well to begin with certain abjurations:

1. There can be no appeals to genius as the sole origin of the energies of great art.

2. There can be no motiveless creation.

3. There can be no transcendent or timeless or unchanging representation.

4. There can be no autonomous artifacts.

5. There can be no expression without an origin and an object, a *from* and a *for*.

6. There can be no art without social energy.

7. There can be no spontaneous generation of social energy.

Bound up with these negations are certain generative principles:

1. Mimesis is always accompanied by—indeed is always produced by—negotiation and exchange.

2. The exchanges to which art is a party may involve money, but they may involve other currencies as well. Money is only one kind of cultural capital.

3. The agents of exchange may appear to be individuals (most often, an isolated artist is imagined in relation to a faceless, amorphous entity designated society or culture), but individuals are themselves the products of collective exchange. In the Renaissance theater this collective nature is intensified by the artists' own participation in versions of joint-stock companies. In such companies individual venturers have their own sharply defined identities and interests (and their own initial capital), but to succeed they pool their resources, and they own essential properties in common.

If there is no expressive essence that can be located in an aesthetic object complete unto itself, uncontaminated by interpretation, beyond translation or substitution—if there is no mimesis without exchange—then we need to analyze the collective dynamic circulation of pleasures, anxieties, and interests.[12] This circulation depends upon a separation of artistic practices from other social practices, a separation produced by a sustained ideological labor, a consensual classification. That is, art does not simply exist in all cultures; it is made up along with other products, practices, discourses of a given culture. (In practice, "made up" means inherited, transmitted, altered, modified, reproduced far more than it means invented: as a rule, there is very little pure invention in culture.) Now the demarcation is rarely, if ever, absolute or complete, nor can we account for it by a single theoretical formulation. We can think up various metaphors to describe the process: the building of a set of walls or fences to separate one territory from adjacent territories; the erection of a gate through which some people and objects will be allowed to pass and others prohibited; the posting of a sign detailing the acceptable code of behavior within the walled territory; the development of a class of functionaries who specialize in the customs of the demarcated zone; the establishment, as in a children's game, of ritualized formulas that can be endlessly repeated. In the case of the public theater of the late sixteenth and early seventeenth centuries, these metaphors were literalized: there was the actual construction of a building, the charging of admission to cross the threshold, the set of regulations governing what could and could not be presented on the stage, a set of tacit understandings (for example, no one was actually to be killed or tortured, no one was to have sex onstage, no one was really cursing or praying or conjuring, and so forth), the writing of scripts that could be screened ahead of time by the censors, rehearsals, the relative nonparticipation of the audience, the existence of theater companies of professional actors.

This literalization and institutionalization of the place of art makes the Renaissance theater particularly useful for an analysis of the cultural circulation of social energy, and the stakes of the analysis are heightened by the direct integration of Shakespeare's plays— easily the most powerful, successful, and enduring artistic expressions in the English language—with this particular mode of artistic production and consumption. We are not, that is, dealing with texts written outside the institution and subsequently attached to it or with encysted productions staged in a long-established and ideologically dormant setting but with literary creations designed in intimate and living relation to an emergent commercial practice. For the most part these creations seem intended at once to enhance the power of the theater as an institution and to draw upon the power this institution has already accumulated. The desire to enhance the general practice of which any particular work is an instance is close to the center of all artistic production, but in the drama this desire is present in a direct, even coarse, sense because of the overwhelming importance and immediacy of material interests. Shakespeare the shareholder was presumably interested not simply in a good return on an individual play but in the health and success of his entire company as it related both to those who helped regulate it and to its audience. Each individual play may be said to make a small contribution to the general store of social energy possessed by the theater and hence to the sustained claim that the theater can make on its real and potential audience.

If each play is bound up with the theater's long-term institutional strategy, it is nonetheless important to avoid the assumption that the relation between mode and individual performance is always harmonious. It is possible for a playwright to be in tension with his own medium, hostile to its presuppositions and conditions, eager to siphon off its powers and attack its pleasures. Ben Jonson's career makes this tension manifest, and one can even glimpse it at moments in Shakespeare's. We can say, perhaps, that an individual play mediates between the mode of the theater, understood in its historical specificity, and elements of the society out of which that theater has been differentiated. Through its representational means, each play carries charges of social energy onto the stage; the stage in its turn revises that energy and returns it to the audience.

Despite the wooden walls and the official regulations, the boundaries between the theater and the world were not fixed, nor did they constitute a logically coherent set; rather they were a sustained collective improvisation. At any given time, the distinction between the theater and the world might be reasonably clear and the boundaries might assume the quality of self-evidence, so that the very cataloging of distinctions might seem absurd: for example, *of course* the theater audience could not intervene in the action on stage, *of course* the violence could only be mimed. But one can think of theaters that swept away every one of the supposedly self-evident distinctions, and more important for our purposes, Renaissance players and audiences could think of such counter-examples.

In consequence, the ratio between the theater and the world, even at its most stable and unchallenged moments, was never *perfectly* taken for granted, that is, experienced as something wholly natural and self-evident. Forces both within and without the theater were constantly calling attention to theatrical practices that violated the established conventions of the English playhouse. When Protestant polemicists characterized the Catholic Mass as theater, the attack conjured up a theater in which (1) the playhouse disguised itself as a holy place; (2) the audience did not think of itself as an audience but as a community of believers; (3) the theatrical performance—with its elaborate costumes and rituals—not only refused to concede that it was an illusion but claimed to be the highest truth; (4) the actors did not fully grasp that they were actors but actually believed in the roles they played and in the symbolic actions they mimed; and (5) the spectacle demanded of the audience not a few pennies and the pleasant wasting of several hours but a lifelong commitment to the institution that staged the show. Similarly, the playwrights themselves frequently called attention in the midst of their plays to alternative theatrical practices. Thus, for example, the denouement of Massinger's *Roman Actor* (like that of Kyd's *Spanish Tragedy*) turns upon the staging of a mode of theater in which princes and nobles take part in plays and in which the killing turns out to be real. It required no major act of imagination for a Renaissance audience to conceive of either of these alternatives to the conventions of the public playhouse: both were fully operative in the period itself, in the form of masques and courtly entertainments, on the one hand, and public maimings and executions, on the other.

Thus the conventional distinction between the theater and the world, however firmly grasped at a given moment, was not one that went without saying; on the contrary, it was constantly said. This "saying" did not necessarily subvert the distinction; often, in fact, it had the opposite effect, shoring up and insisting upon the boundaries within which the public theater existed. Nor did recognizing alternatives necessarily make these boundaries seem "merely" arbitrary; attacks on illegitimate forms of theater tended to moralize the existing practice. But the consciousness in the sixteenth century, as now, of other ways to construe the relation between the theater and the world heightened awareness of the theater as a contingent practice, with a set of institutional interests, motives, and constraints and with the concomitant possibility of inadvertently or deliberately violating these very interests. This possibility, even if never put into practice, affected the relation of the theater both to social and political authorities and to its own sense of itself: even the theater's moments of docile self-regulation, the instances of its willingness to remain well within conventional limits, were marked out as strategies, institutional decisions taken to secure the material well-being of the playing company.

The sustained cultural representation of alternative theatrical practices was probably sufficient by itself to call attention to the specific interests, vulnerabilities, and objective social conditions of the public stage. Even without transgression or persecution, the theater would have been denied the luxury at times granted to privileged cultural institutions, particularly those that perform public rites and preserve cultural memory: the luxury of forgetting that its representatives have a concrete, material interest in the rituals they perform and the boundaries they observe. But in fact the theater in the sixteenth and seventeenth centuries constantly violated its interests and transgressed its boundaries. Indeed these boundaries were defined in relation to transgressions that were fully understood as such only after the fact, and the interests of the theater could be clearly understood only when they had been violated. The Tudor and Stuart regulations governing the public stage were confused, inconsistent, and haphazard, the products neither of a traditional, collective understanding nor of a coherent, rational attempt to regularize and define a new cultural practice. They were instead a jumble of traditional rules and offices designed to govern older, very different theatrical practices and a set of ordinances drawn up hastily in response to particular and local pressures. As a result, even the relatively peaceful and prosperous moments in the troubled life of a theater company had an air of improvisation rather than of established and settled fact.[13]

This institutional improvisation frames the local improvisations of individual playwrights. Hence Shakespeare's representational equipment included not only the ideological constraints within which the theater functioned as an institution but also a set of received stories and generic expectations, including, as his career progressed, those established by his own earlier plays. And though in many of his materials he worked within fairly well-defined boundaries—he could not, for example, have Prince Hal lose the battle of Agincourt—Shakespeare actually had at every point a surprising range of movement. The choices he made were not purely subjective or individual or disinterested, but they were choices: there are dozens of tellings of the Lear story—it is part of the ideology of the family in the late Middle Ages and Renaissance—yet in none of them, so far as I know, does Cordelia die in Lear's arms.

But if we grant the Elizabethan theater this provisional character, should we not say that its air of improvisatory freedom is countered by a still greater insistence on the contained and scripted nature of the represented actions? After all, theatrical performance is distinct from most other social practices precisely insofar as its character is predetermined and enclosed, as it forces its audience to grant that retrospective necessity was prospective: the formal necessity disclosed when one looks back on events that have already occurred was in fact the necessity disclosed in the existence, before the performance itself, of the script.[14] Life outside the theater is full of confusion, schemes imperfectly realized, arbitrary interference, unexpected and unpredictable resistances from the body. On the stage this confusion is at once mimed and revealed to be only scripted. Of course, we may say that even onstage there is no certainty: the actors may forget their lines or blurt them out before their cue or altogether refuse to perform, the clown may decide to improvise, individuals in the audience may abandon the voluntary submission expected of them and intervene in the performance, the scaffolding may collapse and force the cancellation of the show. But this absurd, almost entirely theoretical contingency only gives the touch of freedom that seasons that disclosure of necessity.

We could argue further that one of the ideological functions of the theater was precisely to create in its audience the sense that what seemed spontaneous or accidental was in fact fully plotted ahead of time by a playwright carefully calculating his effects, that behind experienced uncertainty there was design, whether the design of the human patriarchs—the fathers and rulers who unceasingly watched over the errant courses of their subjects—or the overarching design of the divine patriarch. The theater then would confirm the structure of human experience as proclaimed by those on top and would urge us to reconfirm this structure in our pleasure.

But if the improvisational provisionality of the theater is not necessarily subversive ideologically, neither is the hidden order of scripted performance necessarily orthodox. Not only can the audience withhold its confirmation of that order and refuse to applaud, but the order itself is marked out as theatrical and to that extent unreal. In applauding, the audience need only be confirming its own practical interests in the playhouse.

Can we speak, however, of "practical interests" in this context? Should we not say that the theater escapes from the network of practices that governs the circulation of social energy? The public theater would seem to be of no *use* to the audience at all in providing material or symbolic strategic advantage: the events depicted on the stage do not impinge directly on the practical arrangements of the members of the audience, and via the script an abstractness, an atemporality, is concealed behind the powerful illusion of unfolding life.

These special conditions, though important, do not constitute the theater as a place radically detached from the realm of social practice. In the first place, the theater does have obvious use-value for several classes of people: those who act, write for it, regulate it, provide costumes, build and maintain the playhouses, ferry customers across the river, pick pockets or pick up tricks during the performance, provide refreshment, sweep up after the crowd, and so forth. Only one group—the audience—appears to be excluded from practical activity, and an activity cannot become nonpractical because it excludes a social group, for then virtually all activities would become nonpractical. Second, the audience's pleasure is in some important senses useful. The Renaissance had theories, as we do, arguing on both physiological and psychological grounds for the practical necessity of recreation, and these were supplemented by explicitly political theories. An audience watching a play, Nashe suggested, would not be hatching a rebellion. Third, the practical usefulness of the theater depends largely on the illusion of its distance from ordinary social practice. The triumphant cunning of the theater is to make its spectators forget that they are participating in a practical activity, to invent a sphere that seems far removed from the manipulations of the everyday. Shakespeare's theater is powerful and effective precisely to the extent that the audience believes it to be nonuseful and hence nonpractical.[15] And this belief gives the theater an unusually broad license to conduct its negotiations and exchanges with surrounding institutions, authorities, discourses, and practices.

These negotiations were defined by the unequivocal *exclusion* of relatively little from the privileged space of the playhouse, even though virtually everything represented on the stage was at least potentially dangerous and hence could be scrutinized and censored. The Elizabethan theater could, within limits, represent the sacred as well as the profane, contemporary as well as ancient times, stories set in England as well as as those set in distant lands. Allusions to the reigning monarch, and even to highly controversial issues in the reign, were not necessarily forbidden (though the company had to tread cautiously); the outlawed practices and agents of the Catholic faith could be represented with considerable sympathy, along with Turks, Jews, witches, demons, fairies, wild men, ghosts. Above all—and the enabling agent of this range of representational resources—the language of the theater was astonishingly open: the most solemn formulas of the church and state could find their way onto the stage and mingle with the language of the marketplace, just as elevated verse could alternate in the same play with the homeliest of prose. The theater is marked off from the "outside world" and licensed to operate as a distinct domain, but its boundaries are remarkably permeable.

For the circulation of social energy by and through the stage was not part of a single coherent, totalizing system. Rather it was partial, fragmentary, conflictual; elements were crossed, torn apart, recombined, set against each other; particular social practices were magnified by the stage, others diminished, exalted, evacuated. What then is the social energy that is being circulated? Power, charisma, sexual excitement, collective dreams, wonder, desire, anxiety, religious awe, free-floating intensities of experience: in a sense the question is absurd, for everything produced by the society can circulate unless it is deliberately excluded from circulation. Under such circumstances, there can be no single method, no overall picture, no exhaustive and definitive cultural poetics.

I offer instead four chapters that may be read as separate essays. I had thought at first to weave them together, for their local concerns intersect and their general project is the same, but the whole point is that they do not sketch a unified field. Each chapter focuses on a erent one of the major genres in which Shakespeare worked. As many scholars have demonstrated, there is no exclusive, categorical force behind these generic distinctions, but they are useful markers of different areas of circulation, different types of negotiation: in the histories, a theatrical acquisition of charisma through the subversion of charisma; in the comedies, an acquisition of sexual excitement through the staging of transvestite friction; in the tragedies, an acquisition of religious power through the evacuation of a religious ritual; and in the romances, an acquisition of salutary anxiety through the experience of a threatening plenitude. None of these acquisitions exhausts the negotiation, for the genre itself or even for a particular play, and the social energies I have detected in one genre may be found in equal measure in another. Plays are made up of multiple exchanges, and the exchanges are multiplied over time, since to the transactions through which the work first acquired social energy are added supplementary transactions through which the work renews its power in changed circumstances. My principal interest is in the early exchanges—in understanding how the energies were first collected and deployed and returned to the culture from which they came—but there is no direct access to these exchanges, no pure moment when the energy was passed and the process began. We can reconstruct at least aspects of the conditions in which the theater acquired its remarkable power, but we do so under the terms of our own interests and pleasures and in the light of historical developments that cannot simply be stripped away.

I had dreamed of speaking with the dead, and even now I do not abandon this dream. But the mistake was to imagine that I would hear a single voice, the voice of the other. If I wanted to hear one, I had to hear the many voices of the dead. And if I wanted to hear the voice of the other, I had to hear my own voice. The speech of the dead, like my own speech, is not private property.

Chapter Two

⟨⟨❈⟩⟩

Invisible Bullets

In his notorious police report of 1593 on Christopher Marlowe, the Elizabethan spy Richard Baines informed his superiors that Marlowe had declared, among other monstrous opinions, that "Moses was but a Juggler, and that one Heriots being Sir W Raleighs man Can do more than he."[1] The "Heriots" cast for a moment in this lurid light is Thomas Harriot, the most profound Elizabethan mathematician, an expert in cartography, optics, and navigational science, an adherent of atomism, the first Englishman to make a telescope and turn it on the heavens, the author of the first original book about the first English colony in America, and the possessor throughout his career of a dangerous reputation for atheism.[2] In all of his extant writings, private correspondence as well as public discourse, Harriot professes the most reassuringly orthodox religious faith, but the suspicion persisted. When he died of cancer in 1621, one of his contemporaries, persuaded that Harriot had challenged the doctrinal account of creation *ex nihilo*, remarked gleefully that "a *nihilum* killed him at last: for in the top of his nose came a little red speck (exceeding small), which grew bigger and bigger, and at last killed him."[3]

Charges of atheism leveled at Harriot or anyone else in this period are difficult to assess, for such accusations were smear tactics, used with reckless abandon against anyone whom the accuser happened to dislike. At a dinner party one summer evening in 1593, Sir Walter Ralegh teased an irascible country parson named Ralph Ironside and found himself the subject of a state investigation; at the other end of the social scale, in the same Dorsetshire

parish, a drunken servant named Oliver complained that in the
Sunday sermon the preacher had praised Moses excessively but
had neglected to mention his fifty-two concubines, and Oliver too
found himself under official scrutiny.[4] Few, if any, of these investigations turned up what we would call atheists, even muddled or
shallow ones; the stance that seemed to come naturally to me as a
green college freshman in mid–twentieth-century America seems
to have been almost unthinkable to the most daring philosophical
minds of late sixteenth-century England.

The historical evidence is unreliable; even in the absence of social pressure, people lie readily about their most intimate beliefs.
How much more must they have lied in an atmosphere of unembar-
rassed repression. Still, there is probably more than politic concealment involved here. After all, treason was punished as harshly as
atheism, yet while the period abounds in documented instances of
treason in word and deed, there are virtually no professed atheists.[5] If ever there were a place to confirm that in a given social
construction of reality certain interpretations of experience are sanctioned and others excluded, it is here, in the boundaries that contained sixteenth-century skepticism. Like Machiavelli and Montaigne, Thomas Harriot professed belief in God, and there is no
justification in any of these cases for dismissing the profession of
faith as mere hypocrisy.

I am arguing not that atheism was literally unthinkable in the late
sixteenth century but rather that it was almost always thinkable only
as the thought of another. This is one of its attractions as a smear;
atheism is a characteristic mark of otherness—hence the ease with
which Catholics can call Protestant martyrs atheists and Protestants
routinely make similar charges against the pope.[6] The pervasiveness
and frequency of these charges, then, does not signal the existence
of a secret society of freethinkers, a School of Night, but rather
registers the operation of a religious authority, whether Catholic or
Protestant, that confirms its power by disclosing the threat of atheism. The authority is secular as well as religious, since atheism is
frequently adduced as a motive for heinous crimes, as if all men and
women would inevitably conclude that if God does not exist, everything is permitted. At Ralegh's 1603 treason trial, for example, Justice Popham solemnly warned the accused not to let "Harriot, nor
any such Doctor, persuade you there is no eternity in Heaven, lest

you find an eternity of hell-torments."[7] Nothing in Harriot's writings suggests that he held the position attributed to him here, but the charge does not depend upon evidence: Harriot is invoked as the archetypal corrupter, Achitophel seducing the glittering Absalom. If the atheist did not exist, he would have to be invented.

Yet atheism is not the only mode of subversive religious doubt, and we cannot discount the persistent rumors of Harriot's hetero-doxy by pointing to either his conventional professions of faith or the conventionality of the attacks upon him. Indeed I want to sug-gest that if we look closely at *A Brief and True Report of the New Found Land of Virginia* (1588), the only work Harriot published in his life-time and hence the work in which he was presumably the most cautious, we can find traces of material that could lead to the re-mark attributed to Marlowe, that "Moses was but a Juggler, and that one Heriots being Sir W Raleighs man Can do more than he." And I want to suggest further that understanding the relation be-tween orthodoxy and subversion in Harriot's text will enable us to construct an interpretive model that may be used to understand the far more complex problem posed by Shakespeare's history plays.

Those plays have been described with impeccable intelligence as deeply conservative and with equally impeccable intelligence as deeply radical. Shakespeare, in Northrop Frye's words, is "a born courtier," the dramatist who organizes his representation of En-glish history around the hegemonic mysticism of the Tudor myth; Shakespeare is also a relentless demystifier, an interrogator of ide-ology, "the only dramatist," as Franco Moretti puts it, "who rises to the level of Machiavelli in elaborating all the consequences of the separation of political praxis from moral evaluation."[8] The con-flict glimpsed here could be investigated, on a performance-by-performance basis, in a history of reception, but that history is shaped, I would argue, by circumstances of production as well as consumption. The ideological strategies that fashion Shakespeare's history plays help in turn to fashion the conflicting readings of the plays' politics. And these strategies are no more Shakespeare's invention than the historical narratives on which he based his plots. As we shall see from Harriot's *Brief and True Report*, in the discourse of authority a powerful logic governs the relation be-tween orthodoxy and subversion.

I should first explain that the apparently feeble wisecrack about Moses and Harriot finds its way into a police file on Marlowe because it seems to bear out one of the Machiavellian arguments about religion that most excited the wrath of sixteenth-century authorities: Old Testament religion, the argument goes, and by extension the whole Judeo–Christian tradition, originated in a series of clever tricks, fraudulent illusions perpetrated by Moses, who had been trained in Egyptian magic, upon the "rude and gross" (and hence credulous) Hebrews.[9] This argument is not actually to be found in Machiavelli, nor does it originate in the sixteenth century; it is already fully formulated in early pagan polemics against Christianity. But it seems to acquire a special force and currency in the Renaissance as an aspect of a heightened consciousness, fueled by the period's prolonged crises of doctrine and church governance, of the social function of religious belief.

Here Machiavelli's writings are important. *The Prince* observes in its bland way that if Moses' particular actions and methods are examined closely, they appear to differ little from those employed by the great pagan princes; the *Discourses* treats religion as if its primary function were not salvation but the achievement of civic discipline, as if its primary justification were not truth but expediency.[10] Thus Romulus's successor Numa Pompilius, "finding a very savage people, and wishing to reduce them to civil obedience by the arts of peace, had recourse to religion as the most necessary and assured support of any civil society" (*Discourses*, 146). For although "Romulus could organize the Senate and establish other civil and military institutions without the aid of divine authority, yet it was very necessary for Numa, who feigned that he held converse with a nymph, who dictated to him all that he wished to persuade the people to." In truth, continues Machiavelli, "there never was any remarkable lawgiver amongst any people who did not resort to divine authority, as otherwise his laws would not have been accepted by the people" (147).

From here it was only a short step, in the minds of Renaissance authorities, to the monstrous opinions attributed to the likes of Marlowe and Harriot. Kyd, under torture, testified that Marlowe had affirmed that "things esteemed to be done by divine power might have as well been done by observation of men," and the Jesuit Robert Parsons claimed that in Ralegh's "school of Atheism," "both Moses and our Savior, the old and the New Testament, are jested at."[11] On the eve of Ralegh's treason trial, some "hellish verses" were lifted from an anonymous tragedy written ten years earlier and circulated as Ralegh's own confession of atheism. At first the earth was held in common, the verses declare, but this golden age gave way to war, kingship, and property:

> Then some sage man, above the vulgar wise,
> Knowing that laws could not in quiet dwell,
> Unless they were observed, did first devise
> The names of Gods, religion, heaven, and hell
> . . . Only bug-bears to keep the world in fear.[12]

The attribution of these lines to Ralegh is instructive: the fictional text returns to circulation as the missing confessional language of real life. That fiction is unlikely to represent an observable attitude in the "real" world, though we can never altogether exclude that possibility; rather it stages a cultural conceit, the recurrent fantasy of the archcriminal as atheist. Ralegh already had a reputation as both a poet and a freethinker; perhaps one of his numerous enemies actually plotted to heighten the violent popular hostility toward him by floating under his name a forgotten piece of stage villainy.[13] But quite apart from a possible conspiracy, the circulation fulfills a strong cultural expectation. When a hated favorite like Ralegh was accused of treason, what was looked for was not evidence but a performance, a theatrical revelation of motive and an enactment of despair. If the motives for treason revealed in this performance could be various—ambition, jealousy, greed, spite, and so forth—what permitted the release of these motives into action would always be the same: atheism. No one who actually loved and feared God would allow himself to rebel against an anointed ruler, and atheism, conversely, would lead inevitably to treason. Since atheism was virtually always, as I have argued, the thought of the other, it would be difficult to find a first-person confession—except, of course, in fiction and above all in the theater. The soliloquy is lifted from its theatrical context and transformed into "verses" that the three surviving manuscripts declare were "devised by that Atheist and Traitor Ralegh as it is said." The last phrase may signal skepticism about the attribution, but such reservations do not count for much: the "hellish verses" are what men like Marlowe, Harriot, or Ralegh would have to think in their hearts.

Harriot does not voice any speculations remotely resembling the hypotheses that a punitive religion was invented to keep men in awe and that belief originated in a fraudulent imposition by cunning "jugglers" on the ignorant, but his recurrent association with the forbidden thoughts of the demonized other may be linked to something beyond malicious slander. If we look attentively at his account of the first Virginia colony, we find a mind that seems interested in the same set of problems, a mind, indeed, that seems to be virtually testing the Machiavellian hypotheses. Sent by Ralegh to keep a record of the colony and to compile a description of the resources and inhabitants of the area, Harriot took care to learn the North Carolina Algonquian dialect and to achieve what he calls a "special familiarity with some of the priests."[14] The Virginian Indians believe, Harriot writes, in the immortality of the soul and in otherworldly punishments and rewards for behavior in this world: "What subtlety soever be in the *Wiroances* and Priests, this opinion worketh so much in many of the common and simple sort of people that it maketh them have great respect to the Governors, and also great care what they do, to avoid torment after death and to enjoy bliss" (374).[15] The split between the priests and people implied here is glimpsed as well in the description of the votive images: "They think that all the gods are of human shape, and therefore they represent them by images in the forms of men, which they call Kewasowak. . . . The common sort think them to be also gods" (373). And the social function of popular belief is underscored in Harriot's note to an illustration showing the priests carefully tending the embalmed bodies of the former chiefs: "These poor souls are thus instructed by nature to reverence their princes even after their death" (De Bry, p. 72).

We have then, as in Machiavelli, a sense of religion as a set of beliefs manipulated by the subtlety of priests to help instill obedience and respect for authority. The terms of Harriot's analysis—"the common and simple sort of people," "the Governors," and so forth—are obviously drawn from the language of comparable social analyses of England; as Karen Kupperman has most recently demonstrated, sixteenth- and seventeenth-century Englishmen characteristically describe the Indians in terms that closely replicate their

own self-conception, above all in matters of *status*.[16] The great mass
of Indians are seen as a version of "the common sort" at home, just
as Harriot translates the Algonquian *weroan* as "great Lord" and
speaks of "the chief Ladies," "virgins of good parentage," "a young
gentlewoman," and so forth. There is an easy, indeed almost irresistible, analogy in the period between accounts of Indian and
European social structure, so that Harriot's description of the inward mechanisms of Algonquian society implies a description of
comparable mechanisms in his own culture.[17]

To this we may add a still more telling observation not of the
internal function of native religion but of the impact of European
culture on the Indians: "Most things they saw with us," Harriot
writes, "as mathematical instruments, sea compasses, the virtue of
the loadstone in drawing iron, a perspective glass whereby was
showed many strange sights, burning glasses, wildfire works,
guns, books, writing and reading, spring clocks that seem to go of
themselves, and many other things that we had, were so strange
unto them, and so far exceeded their capacities to comprehend the
reason and means how they should be made and done, that they
thought they were rather the works of gods than of men, or at the
leastwise they had been given and taught us of the gods" (375–76).
This delusion, born of what Harriot supposes to be the vast technological superiority of the European, caused the savages to doubt
that they possessed the truth of God and religion and to suspect
that such truth "was rather to be had from us, whom God so
specially loved than from a people that were so simple, as they
found themselves to be in comparison of us" (376).

Here, I suggest, is the very core of the Machiavellian anthropology that posited the origin of religion in an imposition of socially
coercive doctrines by an educated and sophisticated lawgiver on a
simple people. And in Harriot's list of the marvels—from wildfire
to reading—with which he undermined the Indians' confidence in
their native understanding of the universe, we have the core of the
claim attributed to Marlowe: that Moses was but a juggler and that
Ralegh's man Harriot could do more than he. The testing of this
hypothesis in the encounter of the Old World and the New was
appropriate, we may add, for though vulgar Machiavellianism implied that all religion was a sophisticated confidence trick, Machiavelli himself saw that trick as possible only at a radical point of

origin: "If any one wanted to establish a republic at the present time," he writes, "he would find it much easier with the simple mountaineers, who are almost without any civilization, than with such as are accustomed to live in cities, where civilization is already corrupt; as a sculptor finds it easier to make a fine statue out of a crude block of marble than out of a statue badly begun by another."[18] It was only with a people, as Harriot says, "so simple, as they found themselves to be in comparison of us," that the imposition of a coercive set of religious beliefs could be attempted.

In Harriot, then, we have one of the earliest instances of a significant phenomenon: the testing upon the bodies and minds of non–Europeans or, more generally, the noncivilized, of a hypothesis about the origin and nature of European culture and belief. In encountering the Algonquian Indians, Harriot not only thought he was encountering a simplified version of his own culture but also evidently believed that he was encountering his own civilization's past.[19] This past could best be investigated in the privileged anthropological moment of the initial encounter, for the comparable situations in Europe itself tended to be already contaminated by prior contact. Only in the forest, with a people ignorant of Christianity and startled by its bearers' technological potency, could one hope to reproduce accurately, with live subjects, the relation imagined between Numa and the primitive Romans, Moses and the Hebrews. The actual testing could happen only once, for it entails not detached observation but radical change, the change Harriot begins to observe in the priests who "were not so sure grounded, nor gave such credit to their traditions and stories, but through conversing with us they were brought into great doubts of their own" (375).[20] I should emphasize that I am speaking here of events as reported by Harriot. The history of subsequent English–Algonquian relations casts doubt on the depth, extent, and irreversibility of the supposed Indian crisis of belief. In the *Brief and True Report,* however, the tribe's stories begin to *collapse* in the minds of their traditional guardians, and the coercive power of the European beliefs begins to show itself almost at once in the Indians' behavior: "On a time also when their corn began to wither by reason of a drought which happened extraordinarily, fearing that it had come to pass by reason that in some thing they had displeased us, many would come to us and desire us to pray to our God of England, that he would preserve their corn, promising that when it was ripe we also should be partakers of their fruit" (377). If we remember that the English, like virtually all sixteenth-century Europeans in the New World, resisted or were incapable of provisioning themselves and in consequence depended upon the Indians for food, we may grasp the central importance for the colonists of this dawning Indian fear of the Christian God.

As early as 1504, during Columbus's fourth voyage, the natives, distressed that the Spanish seemed inclined to settle in for a long visit, refused to continue to supply food. Knowing from his almanac that a total eclipse of the moon was imminent, Columbus warned the Indians that God would show them a sign of his displeasure; after the eclipse, the terrified Indians resumed the supply. But an eclipse would not always be so conveniently at hand. John Sparke, who sailed with Sir John Hawkins in 1564–65, noted that the French colonists in Florida "would not take the pains so much as to fish in the river before their doors, but would have all things put in their mouths."[21] When the Indians wearied of this arrangement, the French turned to extortion and robbery, and before long there were bloody wars. A similar situation seems to have arisen in the Virginia colony: despite land rich in game and ample fishing grounds, the English nearly starved to death when the exasperated Algonquians refused to build fishing weirs and plant corn.[22]

It is difficult to understand why men so aggressive and energetic in other regards should have been so passive in the crucial matter of feeding themselves. No doubt there were serious logistic problems in transporting food and equally serious difficulties adapting European farming methods and materials to the different climate and soil of the New World, yet these explanations seem insufficient, as they did even to the early explorers themselves. John Sparke wrote that "notwithstanding the great want that the Frenchmen had, the ground doth yield victuals sufficient, if they would have taken pains to get the same; but they being soldiers, desired to live by the sweat of other mens brows" (Hakluyt 10:56). This remark bears close attention: it points not to laziness or negligence but to an occupational identity, a determination to be nourished by the labor of others weaker, more vulnerable, than oneself. This self-conception was not, we might add, exclusively military: the hallmark of power and wealth in the sixteenth century was to be waited on by others. "To live by the sweat of other men's brows" was the enviable lot of the gentleman; indeed in England it virtually defined a gentleman. The New World held out the prospect of such status for all but the poorest cabin boy.[23]

But the prospect could not be realized through violence alone, even if the Europeans had possessed a monopoly of it, because the relentless exercise of violence could actually reduce the food supply. As Machiavelli understood, physical compulsion is essential but never sufficient; the survival of the rulers depends upon a supplement of coercive belief. The Indians must be persuaded that the Christian God is all-powerful and committed to the survival of his chosen people, that he will wither the corn and destroy the lives of savages who displease him by disobeying or plotting against the English. Here is a strange paradox: Harriot tests and seems to confirm the most radically subversive hypothesis in his culture about the origin and function of religion by imposing his religion—with its intense claims to transcendence, unique truth, inescapable coercive force—on others. Not only the official purpose but the survival of the English colony depends upon this imposition. This crucial circumstance licensed the testing in the first place; only as an agent of the English colony, dependent upon its purposes and committed to its survival, is Harriot in a position to disclose the power of human achievements—reading, writing, perspective glasses, gunpowder, and the like—to appear to the ignorant as divine and hence to promote belief and compel obedience.

Thus the subversiveness that is genuine and radical—sufficiently disturbing so that to be suspected of it could lead to imprisonment and torture—is at the same time contained by the power it would appear to threaten. Indeed the subversiveness is the very product of that power and furthers its ends. One may go still further and suggest that the power Harriot both serves and embodies not only produces its own subversion but is actively built upon it: the project of evangelical colonialism is not set over against the skeptical critique of religious coercion but battens on the very confirmation of that critique. In the Virginia colony, the radical undermining of Christian order is not the negative limit but the positive condition for the establishment of that order. And this paradox extends to the production of Harriot's text: *A Brief and True Report*, with its latent heterodoxy, is not a reflection upon the Virginia colony or even a simple record of it—it is not, in other words, a privileged withdrawal into a critical zone set apart from power—but a continuation of the colonial enterprise.

By October 1586, rumors were spreading in England that Virginia offered little prospect of profit, that the colony had been close to starvation, and that the Indians had turned hostile. Harriot accordingly begins his report with a descriptive catalog in which the natural goods of the land are turned into social goods, that is, into "merchantable commodities": "Cedar, a very sweet wood and fine timber; whereof if nests of chests be there made, or timber thereof fitted for sweet and fine bedsteads, tables, desks, lutes, virginals, and many things else, . . . [it] will yield profit" (329–30).[24] The inventory of these commodities is followed by an inventory of edible plants and animals, to prove to readers that the colony need not starve, and then by the account of the Indians, to prove that the colony could impose its will on them. The key to this imposition, as we have seen, is the coercive power of religious belief, and the source of the power is the impression made by advanced technology upon a "backward" people.

Hence Harriot's text is committed to record what I have called his confirmation of the Machiavellian hypothesis, and hence too the potential subversiveness of this confirmation is invisible not only to those on whom the religion is supposedly imposed but also to most readers and quite possibly to Harriot himself. It may be that Harriot was demonically conscious of what he was doing— that he found himself situated exactly where he could test one of his culture's darkest fears about its own origins, that he used the Algonquians to do so, and that he wrote a report on his own findings, a coded report, since as he wrote to Kepler years later, "our situation is such that I still may not philosophize freely."[25] But this is not the only Harriot we can conjure up. A scientist of the late sixteenth century, we might suppose, would have regarded the natives' opinion that English technology was god-given—indeed divine—with something like corroboratory complacency. It would, as a colleague from whom I borrow this conjecture remarked, "be just like an establishment intellectual, or simply a well-placed Eliza-

bethan bourgeois, to accept that his superior 'powers'—moral, technological, cultural—were indeed signs of divine favor and that
therefore the superstitious natives were quite right in their perception of the need to submit to their benevolent conquerors."[26]

Now Harriot does not in fact express such a view of the ultimate
origin of his trunk of marvels—and I doubt that he held the view in
this form—but it is significant that in the next generation Bacon,
perhaps recalling Harriot's text or others like it, claims in *The New
Organon* that scientific discoveries "are as it were new creations,
and imitations of God's works" that may be justly regarded *as if*
they were manifestations not of human skill but of divine power:
"Let a man only consider what a difference there is between the life
of men in the most civilized province of Europe, and in the wildest
and most barbarous districts of New India; he will feel it to be great
enough to justify the saying that 'man is a god to man,' not only in
regard to aid and benefit, but also by a comparison of condition.
And this difference comes not from soil, not from climate, not from
race, but from the arts."[27] From this perspective the Algonquian
misconception of the origin and nature of English technology
would be evidence not of the power of Christianity to impose itself
fraudulently on a backward people but of the dazzling power of
science and of the naive literalism of the ignorant, who can conceive of this power only as the achievement of actual gods.[28]

Thus, for all his subtlety and his sensitivity to heterodoxy,
Harriot might not have grasped fully the disturbing implications of
his own text. The plausibility of a picture of Harriot culturally insu-
lated from the subversive energies of his own activity would seem
to be enhanced elsewhere in *A Brief and True Report* by his account
of his missionary efforts:

Many times and in every town where I came, according as I was able, I
made declaration of the contents of the Bible; that therein was set forth the
true and only God, and his mighty works, that therein was contained the
true doctrine of salvation through Christ, with many particularities of
Miracles and chief points of religion, as I was able then to utter, and
thought fit for the time. And although I told them the book materially and
of itself was not of any such virtue, as I thought they did conceive, but
only the doctrine therein contained; yet would many be glad to touch it, to
embrace it, to kiss it, to hold it to their breasts and heads, and stroke over
all their body with it; to show their hungry desire of that knowledge which
was spoken of. (376–77)

Here the heathens' confusion of material object and religious doctrine does not seem to cast doubts upon the truth of the Holy Book;
rather it signals precisely the naive literalism of the Algonquians
and hence their susceptibility to idolatry. They are viewed with a
touch of amusement, as Spenser in the *Faerie Queene* views the
"salvage nation" who seek to worship Una herself rather than the
truth for which she stands:

> During which time her gentle wit she plyes,
> To teach them truth, which worshipt her in vaine,
> And made her th'Image of Idolatryes;
> But when their bootlesse zeale she did restraine
> From her own worship, they her Asse would worship fayn.
>   (1.6.19)[29]

Harriot, for his part, is willing to temper the view of the savage as
idolater by reading the Algonquian fetishism of the book as a promising sign, an allegory of "their hungry desire of that knowledge
which was spoken of." Such a reading, we might add, conveniently supports the claim that the English would easily dominate
and civilize the Indians and hence advances the general purpose of
A Brief and True Report.

The apparent religious certainty, cultural confidence, and national self-interest here by no means rule out the possibility of what
I have called demonic consciousness—we can always postulate
that Harriot found ever more subtle ways of simultaneously recording and disguising his dangerous speculations—but the essential
point is that we need no such biographical romance to account for
the apparent testing and confirmation of the Machiavellian hypothesis: the colonial power produced the subversiveness in its
own interest, as I have argued, and *A Brief and True Report*, appro-
priately, was published by the great Elizabethan exponent of missionary colonialism, the Reverend Richard Hakluyt.

The thought that Christianity served to shore up the authority of
the colonists would not have struck Hakluyt or the great majority of
his readers as subversive. On the contrary, the role of religion in
preserving the social order was a commonplace that all parties vied
with each other in proclaiming. The suggestion that religions should
be ranked according to their demonstrated ability to control their
adherents would have been unacceptable, however, and the sugges-

tion that reinforcing civil discipline must be the real origin and ultimate purpose of Christianity would have been still worse. These
were possible explanations of the religion of another—skeptical arguments about ideological causality always work against beliefs one
does not hold—but as we might expect from the earlier discussion of
atheism, the application of this explanation to Christianity itself
could be aired, and sternly refuted, only as the thought of another.
Indeed a strictly functionalist explanation even of false religions was
rejected by Christian theologians of the period. "It is utterly vain,"
writes Calvin, "for some men to say that religion was invented by
the subtlety and craft of a few to hold the simple folk in thrall by this
device and that those very persons who originated the worship of
God for others did not in the least believe that any God existed." He
goes on to concede "that in order to hold men's minds in greater
subjection, clever men have devised very many things in religion by
which to inspire the common folk with reverence and strike them
with terror. But they would never have achieved this if men's minds
had not already been imbued with a firm conviction about God,
from which the inclination toward religion springs as from a seed."[30]
Similarly, Hooker argues, "lest any man should here conceive, that
it greatly skilleth not of what sort our religion be, inasmuch as heathens, Turks, and infidels, impute to religion a great part of the same
effects which ourselves ascribe thereunto," that the good moral effects of false religions result from their having religious—that is,
Christian—truths "entwined" in them.[31]

This argument, which derives from the early chapters of the Epistle to the Romans, is so integral to what John Coolidge has called the
Pauline Renaissance in England that Harriot's account of the Algonquians would have seemed, even for readers who sensed something
odd about it, closer to confirmation than to subversion of religious
orthodoxy. Yet it is misleading, I think, to conclude without qualification that the radical doubt implicit in Harriot's account is *entirely*
contained. After all, Harriot was hounded through his whole life by
charges of atheism, and, more tellingly, the remark attributed to
Marlowe suggests that a contemporary could draw the most dangerous conclusions from the Virginia report. Both of these signs of
slippage are compromised by their links to the society's well-
developed repressive apparatus: rumors, accusations, police reports. But if we should be wary of naively accepting a version of

reality proffered by the secret police, we cannot at the same time dismiss that version altogether. There is a perversely attractive, if bleak, clarity in such a dismissal—in deciding that subversive doubt was totally produced and totally contained by the ruling elite—but the actual evidence is tenebrous. We simply do not know what was thought in silence, what was written and then carefully burned, what was whispered by Harriot to Ralegh. Moreover, the "Atlantic Republican tradition," as Pocock has argued, does grow out of the "Machiavellian moment" of the sixteenth century, and that tradition, with its transformation of subjects into citizens, its subordination of transcendent values to capital values, does ultimately undermine, in the interests of a new power, the religious and secular authorities that had licensed the American enterprise in the first place.[32] In Harriot's text the relation between orthodoxy and subversion seems, at the same interpretive moment, to be both perfectly stable and dangerously volatile.

We can deepen our understanding of this apparent paradox if we consider a second mode of subversion and its containment in Harriot's account. Alongside the *testing* of a subversive interpretation of the dominant culture, we find the *recording* of alien voices or, more precisely, of alien interpretations. The occasion for this recording is another consequence of the English presence in the New World, not in this case the threatened extinction of the tribal religion but the threatened extinction of the tribe: "There was no town where we had any subtle device practiced against us," Harriot writes, "but that within a few days after our departure from every such town, the people began to die very fast, and many in short space; in some towns about twenty, in some forty, in some sixty and in one six score, which in truth was very many in respect of their numbers. The disease was so strange, that they neither knew what it was, nor how to cure it; the like by report of the oldest man in the country never happened before, time out of mind" (378).[33] Harriot is writing, of course, about the effects of measles, smallpox, or perhaps simply influenza on people with no resistance to them, but a conception of the biological basis of epidemic disease lies far, far in the future. For the English the deaths must be a moral phenomenon—this notion for them is as irresistible as the notion of germs for ourselves—and hence the "facts" as they are observed are already moralized: the deaths occurred only "where they used some practice against us," that is, where the Indians conspired secretly against the English. And with the wonderful self-validating circularity that characterizes virtually all powerful constructions of reality, the evidence for these secret conspiracies is precisely the deaths of the Indians.[34]

It is not surprising that Harriot seems to endorse the idea that God protects his chosen people by killing off untrustworthy Indians; what is surprising is to find him interested in the Indians' own anxious speculations about the unintended biological warfare that was destroying them. Drawing upon his special familiarity with the priests, he records a remarkable series of conjectures, almost all of which assume—correctly, as we now know—a link between the Indians' misfortune and the presence of the strangers. "Some people," observing that the English remained healthy while the Indians died, "could not tell," Harriot writes, "whether to think us gods or men"; others, seeing that the members of the first colony were all male, concluded that they were not born of women and therefore must be spirits of the dead returned to mortal form. Some medicine men learned in astrology blamed the disease on a recent eclipse of the sun and on a comet—a theory Harriot considers seriously and rejects—while others shared the prevailing English view and said "that it was the special work of God" on behalf of the colonists. And some who seem in historical hindsight eerily prescient prophesied "that there were more of [the English] generation yet to come, to kill theirs and take their places." The supporters of this theory even worked out a conception of the disease that in some features resembles our own: "Those that were immediately to come after us [the first English colonists], they imagined to be in the air, yet invisible and without bodies, and that they by our entreaty and for the love of us did make the people to die . . . by shooting invisible bullets into them" (380).

For a moment, as Harriot records these competing theories, it may seem to us as if there were no absolute assurance of God's national interest, as if the drive to displace and absorb the other had given way to conversation among equals, as if all meanings were provisional, as if the signification of events stood apart from power. Our impression is intensified because we know that the theory that would ultimately triumph over the moral conception of epidemic disease was already present, at least metaphorically, in the conversation.[35] In the very moment that the moral conception is busily authorizing itself, it registers the possibility (indeed from our vantage point, the inevitability) of its own destruction.

But why, we must ask ourselves, should power record other voices, permit subversive inquiries, register at its very center the transgressions that will ultimately violate it? The answer may be in part that power, even in a colonial situation, is not monolithic and hence may encounter and record in one of its functions materials that can threaten another of its functions; in part that power thrives on vigilance, and human beings are vigilant if they sense a threat; in part that power defines itself in relation to such threats or simply to that which is not identical with it. Harriot's text suggests an intensification of these observations: English power in the first Virginia colony *depends* upon the registering and even the production of potentially unsettling perspectives. "These their opinions I have set down the more at large," Harriot tells the "Adventurers, Favorers, and Wellwishers" of the colony to whom his report is addressed, "that it may appear unto you that there is good hope that they may be brought through discreet dealing and government to the embracing of the truth, and consequently to honor, obey, fear, and love us" (381). The recording of alien voices, their preservation in Harriot's text, is part of the process whereby Indian culture is constituted as a culture and thus brought into the light for study, discipline, correction, transformation. The momentary sense of instability or plenitude—the existence of other voices—is produced by the monological power that ultimately denies the possibility of plenitude, just as the subversive hypothesis about European religion is tested and confirmed only by the imposition of that religion.

We may add that the power of which we are speaking is in effect an allocation method—a way of distributing to some and denying to others critical resources (here primarily corn and game) that prolong life. In a remarkable study of the "tragic choices" societies make in allocating scarce resources (for example, kidney machines) or in determining high risks (for example, the military draft), Guido Calabresi and Philip Bobbitt observe that by complex mixtures of approaches, societies attempt to avert "tragic results, that is, results which imply the rejection of values which are proclaimed to be fundamental." Although these approaches may succeed for a time, it will eventually become apparent that some sacrifice of fundamental values has taken place, whereupon "fresh mixtures of methods will be tried, structured . . . by the shortcomings of the approaches they replace." These too will in time give way to others in a "strategy of successive moves," an "intricate game" that reflects the simultaneous perception of an inherent flaw and the determination to "forget" that perception in an illusory resolution.[36] Hence the simple operation of any systematic order, any allocation method, inevitably risks exposing its own limitations, even (or perhaps especially) as it asserts its underlying moral principle.

This exposure is most intense at moments when a comfortably established ideology confronts unusual circumstances, when the moral value of a particular form of power is not merely assumed but explained. We may glimpse such a moment in Harriot's account of a visit from the colonists' principal Indian ally, the chief Wingina. Wingina, persuaded that the disease ravaging his people was indeed the work of the Christian God, had come to request that the English ask their God to direct his lethal magic against an enemy tribe. The colonists tried to explain that such a prayer would be "ungodly," that their God was indeed responsible for the disease but that in this as in all things, he would act only "according to his good pleasure as he had ordained" (379). Indeed, if men asked God to make an epidemic, he probably would not do it; the English could expect such providential help only if they made sincere "petition for the contrary," that is, for harmony and good fellowship in the service of truth and righteousness.

The problem with these assertions is not that they are self-consciously wicked (in the manner of Richard III or Iago) but that they are dismayingly moral and logically coherent; or rather, what is unsettling is one's experience of them, the nasty sense that they are at once irrefutable ethical propositions and pious humbug with which the English conceal from themselves the rapacity and aggression, or simply the horrible responsibility, implicit in their very presence. The explanatory moment manifests the self-validating, totalizing character of Renaissance political theology—its ability to account for almost every occurrence, even (or above all) apparently perverse or contrary occurrences—and at the same time confirms for us the drastic disillusionment that extends from Machiavelli to its definitive expression in Hume and Voltaire. In his own way, Wingina himself clearly thought his lesson in Christian ethics was polite nonsense. When the disease spread to his enemies, as it did shortly thereafter, he returned to the English to thank them—I presume with the Algonquian equivalent of a sly wink—for their friendly help, for "although we satisfied them not in promise, yet in deeds and effect we had fulfilled their desires" (379). For Harriot, this "marvellous accident," as he calls it, is another sign of the colony's great expectations.

Once again a disturbing vista—a skeptical critique of the function of Christian morality in the New World—is glimpsed only to be immediately closed off. Indeed we may feel at this point that subversion scarcely exists and may legitimately ask ourselves how our perception of the subversive and orthodox is generated. The answer, I think, is that the term *subversive* for us designates those elements in Renaissance culture that contemporary audiences tried to contain or, when containment seemed impossible, to destroy and that now conform to our own sense of truth and reality. That is, we find "subversive" in the past precisely those things that are *not* subversive to ourselves, that pose no threat to the order by which we live and allocate resources: in Harriot's *Brief and True Report*, the function of illusion in the establishment of religion, the displacement of a providential conception of disease by one focused on "invisible bullets," the exposure of the psychological and material interests served by a certain conception of divine power. Conversely, we identify as principles of order and authority in Renaissance texts what we would, if we took them seriously, find subversive for ourselves: religious and political absolutism, aristocracy of birth, demonology, humoral psychology, and the like. That we do not find such notions subversive, that we complacently identify them as principles of aesthetic or political order, replicates the process of containment that licensed the elements we call subversive in Renaissance texts: that is, our own values are sufficiently strong for us to contain alien forces almost effortlessly. What we find in Harriot's *Brief and True Report* can best be described by adapting a remark about the possibility of hope that Kafka once made to Max Brod: There is subversion, no end of subversion, only not for us.

ii

Shakespeare's plays are centrally, repeatedly concerned with the production and containment of subversion and disorder, and the three practices that I have identified in Harriot's text—testing, recording, and explaining—all have their recurrent theatrical equivalents, above all in the plays that meditate on the consolidation of state power.

These equivalents are not unique to Shakespeare; they are the signs of a broad institutional appropriation that is one of the root sources of the theater's vitality. Elizabethan playing companies contrived to absorb, refashion, and exploit some of the fundamental energies of a political authority that was itself already committed to histrionic display and hence was ripe for appropriation. But if he was not alone, Shakespeare nonetheless contrived to absorb more of these energies into his plays than any of his fellow playwrights. He succeeded in doing so because he seems to have understood very early in his career that power consisted not only in dazzling display—the pageants, processions, entries, and progresses of Elizabethan statecraft—but also in a systematic structure of relations, those linked strategies I have tried to isolate and identify in colonial discourse at the margins of Tudor society. Shakespeare evidently grasped such strategies not by brooding on the impact of English culture on far-off Virginia but by looking intently at the world immediately around him, by contemplating the queen and her powerful friends and enemies, and by reading imaginatively the great English chroniclers. And the crucial point is less that he *represented* the paradoxical practices of an authority deeply complicit in undermining its own legitimacy than that he *appropriated* for the theater the compelling energies at once released and organized by these practices.

The representation of a self-undermining authority is the principal concern of *Richard II*, which marks a brilliant advance over the comparable representation in the *Henry VI* trilogy, but the full appropriation for the stage of that authority and its power is not achieved until 1 *Henry IV*. We may argue, of course, that in this play there is little or no "self-undermining" at all: emergent authority in 1 *Henry IV*—that is, the authority that begins to solidify around the figure of Hal—is strikingly different from the enfeebled command of Henry VI or the fatally self-wounded royal name of Richard II. "Who does not all along see," wrote Upton in the mid–eighteenth century, "that when prince Henry comes to be king he will assume a character suitable to his dignity?" My point is not to dispute this interpretation of the prince as, in Maynard Mack's words, "an ideal image of the potentialities of the English character,"[37] but to observe that such an ideal image involves as its positive condition the constant production of its own radical subversion and the powerful containment of that subversion.

We are continually reminded that Hal is a "juggler," a conniving hypocrite, and that the power he both serves and comes to embody is glorified usurpation and theft.[38] Moreover, the disenchantment makes itself felt in the very moments when Hal's moral authority is affirmed. Thus, for example, the scheme of Hal's redemption is carefully laid out in his soliloquy at the close of the first tavern scene, but as in the act of *explaining* that we have examined in Harriot, Hal's justification of himself threatens to fall away at every moment into its antithesis. "By how much better than my word I am," Hal declares, "By so much shall I falsify men's hopes" (1.2.210–11). To falsify men's hopes is to exceed their expectations, and it is also to disappoint their expectations, to deceive men, to turn hopes into fictions, to betray.

At issue are not only the contradictory desires and expectations centered on Hal in the play—the competing hopes of his royal father and his tavern friends—but our own hopes, the fantasies continually aroused by the play of innate grace, limitless playfulness, absolute friendship, generosity, and trust. Those fantasies are symbolized by certain echoing, talismanic phrases ("when thou art king," "shall we be merry?" "a thousand pound"), and they are bound up with the overall vividness, intensity, and richness of the theatrical practice itself. Yeats's phrase for the quintessential Shakespearean effect, "the emotion of multitude," seems particularly applicable to 1 *Henry IV* with its multiplicity of brilliant characters, its intensely differentiated settings, its dazzling verbal wit, its mingling of high comedy, farce, epic heroism, and tragedy. The play awakens a dream of superabundance, which is given its irresistible embodiment in Falstaff.

But that dream is precisely what Hal betrays or rather, to use his own more accurate term, "falsifies." He does so in this play not by a

decisive act of rejection, as at the close of 2 *Henry IV*, but by a more
subtle and continuous draining of the plenitude. "This chair shall be
my state," proclaims Falstaff, improvising the king's part, "this dagger my sceptre, and this cushion my crown." Hal's cool rejoinder
cuts deftly at both his real and his surrogate father: "Thy state is
taken for a join'd-stool, thy golden sceptre for a leaden dagger, and
thy precious rich crown for a pitiful bald crown" (2.4.378–82). Hal is
the prince and principle of falsification—he is himself a counterfeit
companion, and he reveals the emptiness in the world around him.
"Dost thou hear, Hal?" Falstaff implores, with the sheriff at the
door. "Never call a true piece of gold a counterfeit. Thou art essentially made, without seeming so" (2.4.491–93). The words, so oddly
the reverse of the ordinary advice to beware of accepting the counterfeit for reality, attach themselves to both Falstaff and Hal: do not
denounce me to the law for I, Falstaff, am genuinely your adoring
friend and not merely a parasite; and also, do not think of yourself,
Hal, as a mere pretender, do not imagine that your value depends
upon falsification.

The "true piece of gold" is alluring because of the widespread
faith that it has an intrinsic value, that it does not depend upon the
stamp of authority and hence cannot be arbitrarily duplicated or
devalued, that it is indifferent to its circumstances, that it cannot be
robbed of its worth. This is the fantasy of identity that Falstaff holds
out to Hal and that Hal empties out, as he empties out Falstaff's
pockets. "What hast thou found?" "Nothing but papers, my lord"
(2.4.532–33).[39] Hal is an anti-Midas: everything he touches turns to
dross. And this devaluation is the source of his own sense of value, a
value not intrinsic but contingent, dependent upon the circulation
of counterfeit coin and the subtle manipulation of appearances:

> And like bright metal on a sullen ground,
> My reformation, glitt'ring o'er my fault,
> Shall show more goodly and attract more eyes
> Than that which hath no foil to set it off.
> I'll so offend, to make offense a skill,
> Redeeming time when men think least I will.
>
> (1.2.212–17)

Such lines, as Empson remarks, "cannot have been written without bitterness against the prince," yet the bitterness is not incom-
patible with an "ironical acceptance" of his authority.[40] The dreams

of plenitude are not abandoned altogether—Falstaff in particular has an imaginative life that overflows the confines of the play itself—but the daylight world of *1 Henry IV* comes to seem increasingly one of counterfeit, and hence one governed by Bolingbroke's cunning (he sends "counterfeits" of himself out onto the battlefield) and by Hal's calculations. A "starveling"—fat Falstaff's word for Hal—triumphs in a world of scarcity. Though we can perceive at every point, through our own constantly shifting allegiances, the potential instability of the structure of power that has Henry IV and his son at the pinnacle and Robin Ostler, who "never joy'd since the price of oats rose" (2.1.12–13), near the bottom, Hal's "redemption" is as inescapable and inevitable as the outcome of those practical jokes the madcap prince is so fond of playing. Indeed, the play insists, this redemption is not something toward which the action moves but something that is happening at every moment of the theatrical representation.

The same yoking of the unstable and the inevitable may be seen in the play's acts of *recording*, that is, the moments in which we hear voices that seem to dwell outside the realms ruled by the potentates of the land. These voices exist and have their apotheosis in Falstaff, but their existence proves to be utterly bound up with Hal, contained politically by his purposes as they are justified aesthetically by his involvement. The perfect emblem of this containment is Falstaff's company, marching off to Shrewsbury: "discarded unjust servingmen, younger sons to younger brothers, revolted tapsters, and ostlers trade-fall'n, the cankers of a calm world and a long peace" (4.2.27–30). As many a homily would tell us, these are the very types of Elizabethan subversion—the masterless men who rose up periodically in desperate protests against their social superiors. A half century later they would swell the ranks of the New Model Army and be disciplined into a revolutionary force. But here they are pressed into service as defenders of the established order, "good enough to toss," as Falstaff tells Hal, "food for powder, food for powder" (4.2.65–66). For power as well as powder, and we may add that this food is produced as well as consumed by the great.

Shakespeare gives us a glimpse of this production in the odd little scene in which Hal, with the connivance of Poins, reduces the puny tapster Francis to the mechanical repetition of the word "Anon":

Prince:	Nay, but hark you, Francis: for the sugar thou gavest me, 'twas a pennyworth, was't not?
Francis:	O Lord, I would it had been two!
Prince:	I will give thee for it a thousand pound. Ask me when thou wilt, and thou shalt have it.
Poins:	(*Within*) Francis!
Francis:	Anon, anon.
Prince:	Anon, Francis? No, Francis; but tomorrow, Francis; or, Francis, a' Thursday; or indeed, Francis, when thou wilt.

(2.4.58–67)

The Bergsonian comedy in such a moment resides in Hal's exposing a drastic reduction of human possibility: "That ever this fellow should have fewer words than a parrot," he says at the scene's end, "and yet the son of a woman!" (2.4.98–99). But the chief interest for us resides in Hal's producing the very reduction he exposes. The fact of this production, its theatrical demonstration, implicates Hal not only in the linguistic poverty upon which he plays but in the poverty of the five years of apprenticeship Francis has yet to serve: "Five year!" Hal exclaims, "by'r lady, a long lease for the clinking of pewter" (2.4.45–46). And as the prince is implicated in the production of this oppressive order, so is he implicated in the impulse to abrogate it: "But, Francis, darest thou be so valiant as to play the coward with thy indenture, and show it a fair pair of heels and run from it?" (2.4.46–48).

It is tempting to think of this particular moment—the prince awakening the apprentice's discontent—as linked darkly with some supposed uneasiness in Hal about his own apprenticeship.[41] The momentary glimpse of a revolt against authority is closed off at once, however, with a few obscure words calculated to return Francis to his trade without enabling him to understand why he must return to it:

Prince:	Why then your brown bastard is your only drink! for look you, Francis, your white canvas doublet will sully. In Barbary, sir, it cannot come to so much.
Francis:	What, sir?
Poins:	(*Within*) Francis!
Prince:	Away, you rogue, dost thou not hear them call?

(2.4.73–79)

If Francis takes the earlier suggestion, robs his master and runs away, he will find a place for himself, the play implies, only as one of the "revolted tapsters" in Falstaff's company, men as good as dead long before they march to their deaths as upholders of the crown. Better that he should follow the drift of Hal's deliberately mystifying words and continue to clink pewter. As for the prince, his interest in the brief exchange, beyond what we have already sketched, is suggested by his boast to Poins moments before Francis enters: "I have sounded the very base-string of humility. Sirrah, I am sworn brother to a leash of drawers, and can call them all by their christen names, as Tom, Dick, and Francis" (2.4.5–8). The prince must sound the base-string of humility if he is to play all of the chords and hence be the master of the instrument, and his ability to conceal his motives and render opaque his language offers assurance that he himself will not be played on by another.

I have spoken of such scenes in *1 Henry IV* as resembling what in Harriot's text I have called *recording*, a mode that culminates for Harriot in a glossary, the beginnings of an Algonquian–English dictionary, designed to facilitate further acts of recording and hence to consolidate English power in Virginia. The resemblance may be seen most clearly perhaps in Hal's own glossary of tavern slang: "They call drinking deep, dyeing scarlet, and when you breathe in your watering, they cry 'hem!' and bid you play it off. To conclude, I am so good a proficient in one quarter of an hour, that I can drink with any tinker in his own language during my life" (2.4.15–20). The potential value of these lessons, the functional interest to power of recording the speech of an "under-skinker" and his mates, may be glimpsed in the expressions of loyalty that Hal laughingly recalls: "They take it already upon their salvation, that . . . when I am King of England I shall command all the good lads in Eastcheap" (2.4.9–15).

It may be objected that there is something slightly absurd in likening such moments to aspects of Harriot's text; *1 Henry IV* is a play, not a tract for potential investors in a colonial scheme, and the only values we may be sure Shakespeare had in mind, the argument would go, are theatrical values. But theatrical values do not exist in a realm of privileged literariness, of textual or even institutional self-referentiality. Shakespeare's theater was not isolated by its wooden walls, nor did it merely reflect social and ideological forces that lay entirely outside it: rather the Elizabethan and Jacobean theater was itself a *social event* in reciprocal contact with other social events.

One might add that 1 *Henry IV* itself insists upon the impossibility of sealing off the interests of the theater from the interests of power. Hal's characteristic activity is playing or, more precisely, theatrical improvisation—his parts include his father, Hotspur, Hotspur's wife, a thief in buckram, himself as prodigal, and himself as penitent—and he fully understands his own behavior through most of the play as a role that he is performing. We might expect that this role playing gives way at the end to his true identity: "I shall hereafter," Hal has promised his father, "Be more myself" (3.2.92–93). With the killing of Hotspur, however, Hal clearly does not reject all theatrical masks but rather replaces one with another. "The time will come," Hal declares midway through the play, "That I shall make this northren youth exchange / His glorious deeds for my indignities" (3.2.144–46); when that time *has* come, at the play's close, Hal hides with his "favors" (that is, a scarf or other emblem, but the word *favor* also has in the sixteenth century the sense of "face") the dead Hotspur's "mangled face" (5.4.96), as if to mark the completion of the exchange.

Theatricality, then, is not set over against power but is one of power's essential modes. In lines that anticipate Hal's promise, the angry Henry IV tells Worcester, "I will from henceforth rather be myself, / Mighty and to be fear'd, than my condition" (1.3.5–6). "To be oneself" here means to perform one's part in the scheme of power rather than to manifest one's natural disposition, or what we would normally designate as the very core of the self. Indeed it is by no means clear that such a thing as a natural disposition exists in the play except as a theatrical fiction: we recall that in Falstaff's hands the word *instinct* becomes histrionic rhetoric, an improvised excuse for his flight from the masked prince. "Beware instinct—the lion will not touch the true prince. Instinct is a great matter; I was now a coward on instinct. I shall think the better of myself, and thee, during my life; I for a valiant lion, and thou for a true prince" (2.4.271–75). Both claims—Falstaff's to natural valor, Hal's to legitimate royalty—are, the lines darkly imply, of equal merit.

Again and again in 1 *Henry IV* we are tantalized by the possibility of an escape from theatricality and hence from the constant pressure of improvisational power, but we are, after all, in the theater, and our pleasure depends upon there being no escape, and our applause ratifies the triumph of our confinement. The play operates in the manner of its central character, charming us with its visions of breadth and solidarity, "redeeming" itself in the end by betraying our hopes, and earning with this betrayal our slightly anxious admiration. Hence the odd balance in this play of spaciousness—the constant multiplication of separate, vividly realized realms—and militant claustrophobia: the absorption of all of these realms by a power at once vital and impoverished. The balance is almost perfect, as if Shakespeare had somehow reached through in *1 Henry IV* to the very center of the system of opposed and interlocking forces that held Tudor society together.

iii

When we turn, however, to the plays that continue the chronicle of Hal's career, *2 Henry IV* and *Henry V*, we find not only that the forces balanced in the earlier play have pulled apart—the claustrophobia triumphant in *2 Henry IV*, the spaciousness triumphant in *Henry V*[42]—but that from this new perspective the familiar view of *1 Henry IV* as a perfectly poised play must be revised. What appeared as "balance" may on closer inspection seem like radical instability tricked out as moral or aesthetic order; what appeared as clarity may seem now like a conjurer's trick concealing confusion in order to buy time and stave off the collapse of an illusion.[43] Not waving but drowning.

In *2 Henry IV* the characteristic operations of power are less equivocal than they had been in the preceding play: there is no longer even the lingering illusion of distinct realms, each with its own system of values, its soaring visions of plenitude, and its bad dreams. There is manifestly a single system now, one based on predation and betrayal. Hotspur's intoxicating dreams of honor are dead, replaced by the cold rebellion of cunning but impotent schemers. The warm, roistering noise overheard in the tavern—noise that seemed to signal a subversive alternative to rebellion—turns out to be the sound of a whore and a bully beating a customer to death. And Falstaff, whose earlier larcenies were gilded by fantasies of innate grace, now talks of turning diseases to commodity (1.2.248).

Only Prince Hal seems in this play less meanly calculating, subject now to fits of weariness and confusion, though this change serves less to humanize him (as Auerbach argued in a famous essay) than to make it clear that the betrayals are systematic. They happen to him and for him. He need no longer soliloquize his intention to "falsify men's hopes" by selling his wastrel friends: the sale will be brought about by the structure of things, a structure grasped in this play under the twinned names of time and necessity. So too there is no longer any need for heroic combat with a dangerous, glittering enemy like Hotspur (the only reminder of whose voice in this play is Pistol's parody of Marlovian swaggering); the rebels are deftly, if ingloriously, dispatched by the false promises of Hal's younger brother, the primly virtuous John of Lancaster. To seal his lies, Lancaster swears fittingly "by the honor of my blood" (4.2.55)—the cold blood, as Falstaff observes of Hal, that he inherited from his father.

The recording of alien voices—the voices of those who have no power to leave literate traces of their existence—continues in this play, but without even the theatrical illusion of princely complicity. The king is still convinced that his son is a prodigal and that the kingdom will fall to ruin after his death—perhaps he finds a peculiar consolation in the thought—but it is no longer Hal alone who declares (against all appearances) his secret commitment to disciplinary authority. Warwick assures the king that the prince's interests in the good lads of Eastcheap are entirely what they should be:

> The Prince but studies his companions
> Like a strange tongue, wherein, to gain the language,
> 'Tis needful that the most immodest word
> Be look'd upon and learnt, which once attain'd,
> Your Highness knows, comes to no further use
> But to be known and hated. So, like gross terms,
> The Prince will in the perfectness of time
> Cast off his followers, and their memory
> Shall as a pattern or a measure live,
> By which his Grace must mete the lives of other,
> Turning past evils to advantages.
>
> (4.4.68–78)

At first the language analogy likens the prince's low-life excursions to the search for proficiency: perfect linguistic competence, the "mastery" of a language, requires the fullest possible vocabulary. But the darkness of Warwick's words—"to be known and hated"—immediately pushes the goal of Hal's linguistic researches beyond proficiency. When in *1 Henry IV* Hal boasts of his mastery of tavern slang, we are allowed for a moment at least to imagine that we are witnessing a social bond, the human fellowship of the extremest top and bottom of society in a homely ritual act of drinking together. The play may make it clear, as I have argued, that well-defined political interests are involved, but these interests may be bracketed, if only briefly, for the pleasure of imagining what Victor Turner calls "communitas"—a union based on the momentary breaking of the hierarchical order that normally governs a community.[44] And even when we pull back from this spacious sense of union, we are permitted for much of the play to take pleasure at least in Hal's surprising skill, the proficiency he rightly celebrates in himself.

To learn another language is to acknowledge the existence of another people and to acquire the ability to function, however crudely, in another social world. Hal's remark about drinking with any tinker in his own language suggests, if only jocularly, that for him the lower classes are virtually another people, an alien tribe—immensely more populous than his own—within the kingdom. That this perception extended beyond the confines of Shakespeare's play is suggested by the evidence that middle- and upper-class English settlers in the New World regarded the American Indians less as another race than as a version of their own lower classes; one man's tinker is another man's Indian.[45]

If Hal's glossary initially seems to resemble Harriot's practical word list in the *Brief and True Report*, with its Algonquian equivalents for *fire, food, shelter*, Warwick's account of Hal's intentions suggests a deeper resemblance to a different kind of glossary, one more specifically linked to the attempt to understand and control the lower classes. I refer to the sinister glossaries appended to sixteenth-century accounts of criminals and vagabonds. "Here I set before the good reader the lewd, lousy language of these loitering lusks and lazy lorels," announces Thomas Harman as he introduces (with a comical flourish designed to display his own rhetorical gifts) what he claims is an authentic list, compiled at great personal cost.[46] His pamphlet, *A Caveat for Common Cursitors*, is the fruit, he declares, of personal research, difficult because his informants are "marvellous subtle and crafty." But "with fair flattering words, money, and good cheer," he has learned much about their ways, "not without faithful promise made unto them never to discover their names or anything they showed me" (82). Harman cheerfully goes on to publish what they showed him, and he ends his work not only with a glossary of "peddler's French" but with an alphabetical list of names, so that the laws made for "the extreme punishment" of these wicked idlers may be enforced.

It is not clear that Harman's subjects—upright men, doxies, Abraham men, and the like—bear any more relation to social reality than either Doll Tearsheet or Mistress Quickly.[47] Much of the *Caveat*, like the other cony-catching pamphlets of the period, has the air of a jest book: time-honored tales of tricksters and rogues, dished out as realistic observation. (It is not encouraging that the rogues' term for the stocks in which they were punished, according to Harman, is "the harmans.") But Harman is concerned to convey at least the impression of accurate observation and recording— clearly, this was among the book's selling points—and one of the principal rhetorical devices he uses to do so is the spice of betrayal: he repeatedly calls attention to his solemn promises never to reveal anything he has been told, for his breaking of his word assures the accuracy and importance of what he reveals.

A middle-class Prince Hal, Harman claims that through dissembling he has gained access to a world normally hidden from his kind, and he will turn that access to the advantage of the kingdom by helping his readers to identify and eradicate the dissemblers in their midst. Harman's own personal interventions—the acts of detection and apprehension he proudly reports (or invents)—are not enough; only his book can fully expose the cunning sleights of the rogues and thereby induce the justices and shrieves to be more vigilant and punitive. Just as theatricality is thematized in the *Henry IV* plays as one of the crucial agents of royal power, so in *A Caveat for Common Cursitors* (and in much of the cony-catching literature of the period in England and France) printing is represented in the text itself as a force for social order and the detection of criminal fraud. The printed book can be widely disseminated and easily revised, so that the vagabonds' names and tricks may be known before they themselves arrive at an honest citizen's door; as if this mobility were not tangible enough, Harman claims that when his pamphlet was only halfway printed, his printer helped him apprehend a particularly sly "counterfeit crank"—a pretended epileptic. In Harman's account the printer turns detective, first running down the street to apprehend the dissembler, then on a subsequent occasion luring him "with fair allusions" (116) and a show of charity into the hands of the constable. With such lurid tales Harman literalizes the power of the book to hunt down vagabonds and bring them to justice.

The danger of such accounts is that the ethical charge will reverse itself, with the forces of order—the people, as it were, of the book—revealed as themselves dependent on dissembling and betrayal and the vagabonds revealed either as less fortunate and well-protected imitators of their betters or, alternatively, as primitive rebels against the hypocrisy of a cruel society. Exactly such a reversal seems to occur again and again in the rogue literature of the period, from the doxies and morts who answer Harman's rebukes with unfailing, if spare, dignity to the more articulate defenders of vice elsewhere who insist that their lives are at worst imitations of the lives of the great:

Though your experience in the world be not so great as mine [says a cheater at dice], yet am I sure ye see that no man is able to live an honest man unless he have some privy way to help himself withal, more than the world is witness of. Think you the noblemen could do as they do, if in this hard world they should maintain so great a port only upon their rent? Think you the lawyers could be such purchasers if their pleas were short, and all their judgements, justice and conscience? Suppose ye that offices would be so dearly bought, and the buyers so soon enriched, if they counted not pillage an honest point of purchase? Could merchants, without lies, false making their wares, and selling them by a crooked light, to deceive the chapman in the thread or colour, grow so soon rich and to a baron's possessions, and make all their posterity gentlemen?[48]

Though these reversals are at the very heart of the rogue literature, it would be as much of a mistake to regard their intended effect as subversive as to regard in a similar light the comparable passages—most often articulated by Falstaff—in Shakespeare's his-

tories. The subversive voices are produced by and within the affir-
mations of order; they are powerfully registered, but they do not
undermine that order. Indeed, as the example of Harman—so
much cruder than Shakespeare—suggests, the order is neither possible nor fully convincing without both the presence and perception of betrayal.

This dependence on betrayal does not prevent Harman from
leveling charges of hypocrisy and deep dissembling at the rogues
and from urging his readers to despise and prosecute them. On the
contrary, Harman's moral indignation seems paradoxically heightened by his own implication in the deceitfulness that he condemns,
as if the rhetorical violence of the condemnation cleansed him of
any guilt. His broken promises are acts of civility, necessary strategies for securing social well-being. The "rowsy, ragged rabblement
of rakehells" has put itself outside the bounds of civil conversation;
justice consists precisely in taking whatever measures are necessary to eradicate them. Harman's false oaths are the means of
identifying and ridding the community of the purveyors of false
oaths. The pestilent few will "fret, fume, swear, and stare at this
my book," in which their practices, disclosed after they had received fair promises of confidentiality, are laid open, but the majority will band together in righteous reproach: "The honourable will
abhor them, the worshipful will reject them, the yeomen will
sharply taunt them, the husbandmen utterly defy them, the labour-
ing men bluntly chide them, the women with clapping hands cry
out at them" (84). To like reading about vagabonds is to hate them
and to approve of their ruthless betrayal.

"The right people of the play," a gifted critic of 2 *Henry IV*
observes, "merge into a larger order; the wrong people resist or
misuse that larger order."[49] True enough, but like Harman's community of vagabond-haters, the "larger order" of the Lancastrian
state in this play seems to batten on the breaking of oaths. Shakespeare does not shrink from any of the felt nastiness implicit in this
sorting out of the right people and the wrong people; he takes the
discursive mode that he could have found in Harman and a hundred other texts and intensifies it, so that the founding of the
modern state, like the self-fashioning of the modern prince, is
shown to be based upon acts of calculation, intimidation, and de-

ceit. And these acts are performed in an entertainment for which audiences, the subjects of this very state, pay money and applaud.

There is, throughout 2 *Henry IV*, a sense of constriction that is only intensified by the obsessive enumeration of details: "Thou didst swear to me upon a parcel-gilt goblet, sitting in my Dolphin chamber, at the round table by a sea-coal fire, upon Wednesday in Wheeson week . . ." (2.1.86–89). We may find, in Justice Shallow's garden, a few twilight moments of release from this oppressive circumstantial and strategic constriction, but Falstaff mercilessly deflates them—and the puncturing is so wonderfully adroit, so amusing, that we welcome it: "I do remember him at Clement's Inn, like a man made after supper of a cheese-paring. When 'a was naked, he was for all the world like a fork'd redish, with a head fantastically carv'd upon it with a knife" (3.2.308–12).

What remains is the law of nature: the strong eat the weak. Yet this is not quite what Shakespeare invites the audience to affirm through its applause. Like Harman, Shakespeare refuses to endorse so baldly cynical a conception of the social order; instead actions that should have the effect of radically undermining authority turn out to be the props of that authority. In this play, even more cruelly than in 1 *Henry IV*, moral values—justice, order, civility—are secured through the apparent generation of their subversive contraries. Out of the squalid betrayals that preserve the state emerges the "formal majesty" into which Hal at the close, through a final, definitive betrayal—the rejection of Falstaff—merges himself.

There are moments in *Richard II* when the collapse of kingship seems to be confirmed in the discovery of the physical body of the ruler, the pathos of his creatural existence:

> throw away respect,
> Tradition, form, and ceremonious duty,
> For you have but mistook me all this while.
> I live with bread like you, feel want,
> Taste grief, need friends: subjected thus,
> How can you say to me I am a king?
> (3.2.172–77)

By the close of 2 *Henry IV* such physical limitations have been absorbed into the ideological structure, and hence justification, of kingship. It is precisely because Prince Hal lives with bread that we can understand the sacrifice that he and, for that matter, his father have made. Unlike Richard II, Henry IV articulates this sacrifice not as a piece of histrionic rhetoric but as a private meditation, the innermost thoughts of a troubled, weary man:

> Why rather, sleep, liest thou in smoky cribs,
> Upon uneasy pallets stretching thee,
> And hush'd with buzzing night-flies to thy slumber,
> Than in the perfum'd chambers of the great,
> Under the canopies of costly state,
> And lull'd with sound of sweetest melody?
>
> (3.1.9–14)

Who knows? Perhaps it is even true; perhaps in a society in which the overwhelming majority of men and women had next to nothing, the few who were rich and powerful did lie awake at night. But we should understand that this sleeplessness was not a well-kept secret: the sufferings of the great are one of the familiar themes in the literature of the governing classes in the sixteenth century.[50] Henry IV speaks in soliloquy, but as is so often the case in Shakespeare, his isolation only intensifies the sense that he is addressing a large audience: the audience of the theater. We are invited to take measure of his suffering, to understand—here and elsewhere in the play—the costs of power. And we are invited to understand these costs in order to ratify the power, to accept the grotesque and cruelly unequal distribution of possessions: every-thing to the few, nothing to the many. The rulers earn, or at least pay for, their exalted position through suffering, and this suffering ennobles, if it does not exactly cleanse, the lies and betrayals upon which this position depends.

As so often, Falstaff parodies this ideology, or rather—and more significantly—presents it as humbug *before* it makes its appearance as official truth. Called away from the tavern to the court, Falstaff turns to Doll and Mistress Quickly and proclaims sententiously: "You see, my good wenches, how men of merit are sought after. The undeserver may sleep when the man of action is call'd on" (2.4.374–77). Seconds later this rhetoric—marked out as something with which to impress whores and innkeepers to whom one owes money one does not intend to pay—recurs in the speech and, by convention of the soliloquy, the innermost thoughts of the king.

This staging of what we may term anticipatory, or proleptic, parody is a major structural principle of Shakespeare's play. Its effect is not (as with straightforward parodies) to ridicule the claims of high seriousness but rather to mark them as slightly suspect and to encourage guarded skepticism. Thus in the wake of Falstaff's burlesque of the weariness of the virtuous, the king's insomniac pathos reverberates hollowness as well as poignancy. At such moments *2 Henry IV* seems to be testing and confirming a dark and disturbing hypothesis about the nature of monarchical power in England: that its moral authority rests upon a hypocrisy so deep that the hypocrites themselves believe it. "Then (happy) low, lie down!/Uneasy lies the head that wears a crown" (3.1.30–31): so the old pike tells the young dace. But the old pike actually seems to believe in his own speeches, just as he may believe that he never really sought the crown, "But that necessity so bow'd the state/ That I and greatness were compell'd to kiss" (3.1.73–74). Our privileged knowledge of the network of state betrayals and privileged access to Falstaff's cynical wisdom can make this opaque hypocrisy transparent. Yet even with *2 Henry IV*, where the lies and the self-serving sentiments are utterly inescapable, where the illegitimacy of legitimate authority is repeatedly demonstrated, where the whole state seems—to adapt More's phrase—a conspiracy of the great to enrich and protect their interests under the name of commonwealth, even here the state, watchful for signs of sedition on the stage, was not prodded to intervene. We may choose to attribute this apparent somnolence to incompetence or corruption, but the linkages I have sketched between the history plays and the discursive practices represented by Harriot and Harman suggest another explanation. Once again, though in a still more iron-age spirit than at the close of *1 Henry IV*, the play appears to ratify the established order, with the new-crowned Henry V merging his body into "the great body of our state," with Falstaff despised and rejected, and with Lancaster—the coldhearted betrayer of the rebels—left to admire his still more coldhearted brother: "I like this fair proceeding of the King's" (5.5.97).[51]

The mood at the close remains, to be sure, an unpleasant one— the rejection of Falstaff has been one of the nagging "problems" of Shakespeare criticism—but the discomfort only serves to verify Hal's claim that he has turned away his former self. If there is frustration at the harshness of the play's end, the frustration confirms a carefully plotted official strategy whereby subversive perceptions are at once produced and contained:

> My father is gone wild into his grave;
> For in his tomb lie my affections,
> And with his spirits sadly I survive,
> To mock the expectation of the world,
> To frustrate prophecies, and to rase out
> Rotten opinion. . . .
>
> (5.2.123–28)

iv

The first part of *Henry IV* enables us to feel at moments that we are like Harriot, surveying a complex new world, testing upon it dark thoughts without damaging the order that those thoughts would seem to threaten. The second part of *Henry IV* suggests that we are still more like the Indians, compelled to pay homage to a system of beliefs whose fraudulence only confirms their power, authenticity, and truth. The concluding play in the series, *Henry V,* insists that we have all along been both colonizer and colonized, king and subject. The play deftly registers every nuance of royal hypocrisy, ruthlessness, and bad faith—testing, in effect, the proposition that successful rule depends not upon sacredness but upon demonic violence—but it does so in the context of a celebration, a collective panegyric to "This star of England," the charismatic leader who purges the commonwealth of its incorrigibles and forges the martial national state.

By yoking together diverse peoples—represented in the play by the Welshman Fluellen, the Irishman Macmorris, and the Scotsman Jamy, who fight at Agincourt alongside the loyal Englishmen—Hal symbolically tames the last wild areas in the British Isles, areas that in the sixteenth century represented, far more powerfully than any New World people, the doomed outposts of a vanishing tribalism.[52] We might expect then that in *Henry V* the mode that I have called recording would reach its fullest flowering, and in a sense it does. The English allies are each given a distinct accentual notation—" 'a utt'red as prave words at the pridge as you shall see in a summer's day"; "By Chrish law, 'tish ill done! The work ish give over"; "It sall be vary gud, gud feith, gud captens bath, and I sall quit you with gud leve"—a notation that helped determine literary representations of the stock Welshman, Irishman, and Scotsman for centuries to come. But their distinctness is curiously formal, a collection of mechanistic attributes recalling the heightened but static individuality of Jonson's humorous grotesques.

The verbal tics of such characters interest us because they represent not what is alien but what is predictable and automatic. They give pleasure because they persuade an audience of its own mobility and complexity; even a spectator gaping passively at the play's sights and manipulated by its rhetoric is freer than these puppets jerked on the strings of their own absurd accents. Only Fluellen (much of the time an exuberant, bullying prince-pleaser) seems at one moment to articulate perceptions that lie outside the official line, and he arrives at these perceptions not through his foreignness but through his relentless pursuit of classical analogies. Teasing out a Plutarch-like parallel between Hal and "Alexander the Pig"—"There is a river in Macedon, and there is also moreover a river at Monmouth," and so forth—Fluellen reaches the observation that Alexander "did, in his ales and his angers, look you, kill his best friend, Clytus." Gower quickly intervenes: "Our King is not like him in that; he never kill'd any of his friends." But Fluellen persists: "as Alexander kill'd his friend Clytus, being in his ales and his cups; so also Harry Monmouth, being in his right wits and his good judgments, turn'd away the fat knight with the great belly doublet. He was full of jests, and gipes, and knaveries, and mocks—I have forgot his name." Gower provides it: "Sir John Falstaff" (4.7.26–51).

The moment is potentially devastating. The comparison with drunken Alexander focuses all our perceptions of Hal's sober cold-bloodedness, from his rejection of Falstaff—"The King has kill'd his heart" (2.1.88)—to his responsibility for the execution of his erstwhile boon companion Bardolph. The low-life characters in the earlier plays had been the focus of Hal's language lessons, but as Warwick had predicted, the prince studied them as "gross terms," no sooner learned than discarded.

The discarding in *Henry V* is not an attractive sight but is perfectly consistent with the practice we have analyzed in Harman's *Caveat*. Indeed in a direct recollection of the cony-catching litera-

ture, Fluellen learns that Pistol, whom he had thought "as valiant a
man as Mark Antony" (3.6.13–14), is "a rogue, that now and then
goes to the wars, to grace himself at his return into London under
the form of a soldier" (3.6.67–69). "You must learn to know such
slanders of the age," remarks Gower in a line that could serve as
Harman's epigraph, "or else you may be marvellously mistook"
(3.6.79–81). And how does Fluellen learn that Pistol is one of the
slanders of the age? What does Pistol do to give himself away? He
passionately pleads that Fluellen intervene to save Bardolph, who
has been sentenced to die for stealing a "pax of little price." "Let
gallows gape for dog, let man go free," rages Pistol, "And let not
hemp his windpipe suffocate" (3.6.42–43). Fluellen refuses; Bardolph hangs; and this attempt to save his friend's life marks Pistol
as a "rascally, scald, beggarly, lousy, pragging knave" (5.1.5–6). By
contrast, Hal's symbolic killing of Falstaff—which might have been
recorded as a bitter charge against him—is advanced by Fluellen as
the climactic manifestation of his virtues. No sooner is it mentioned
than the king himself enters in triumph, leading his French prisoners. This entrance, with its military "Alarum" followed by a royal
"Flourish," is the perfect emblematic instance of a potential disso-
nance being absorbed into a charismatic celebration. The betrayal
of friends does not subvert but rather sustains the moral authority
and the compelling glamour of power. That authority, as the play
defines it, is precisely the ability to betray one's friends without
stain.

   If neither the English allies nor the low-life characters seem to
fulfill adequately the role of aliens whose voices are "recorded,"
Henry V apparently gives us a sustained, even extreme, version of
this practice in the dialogue of the French characters, dialogue that is
in part presented untranslated in the performance. This dialogue
includes even a language lesson, the very emblem of "recording" in
the earlier plays. Yet like the English allies, the French enemies say
remarkably little that is alien or disturbing in relation to the central
voice of authority in the play. To be sure, several of the French
nobles contemptuously dismiss Hal as "a vain, giddy, shallow, humorous youth" (2.4.28), but these terms of abuse are outmoded; it is
as if news of the end of 1 *Henry IV* or of its sequel had not yet crossed
the Channel. Likewise, the easy French assumption of cultural and

social superiority to the English—"The emptying of our fathers' luxury, / Our scions, put in wild and savage stock" (3.5.6–7)—is voiced only to be deflated by the almost miraculous English victory. The glamour of French aristocratic culture is not denied (see, for example, the litany of noble names beginning at 3.5.40), but it issues in overweening self-confidence and a military impotence that is explicitly thematized as sexual impotence. The French warriors "hang like roping icicles / Upon our houses' thatch," while the English "Sweat drops of gallant youth in our rich fields!" (3.5.23–25). In consequence, complains the Dauphin,

> Our madams mock at us, and plainly say
> Our mettle is bred out, and they will give
> Their bodies to the lust of English youth.
> (3.5.28–30)

Thus the affirmation of French superiority is immediately reprocessed as an enhancement of English potency. By the play's close, with a self-conscious gesture toward the conventional ending of a comedy, the sexualized violence of the invasion is transfigured and tamed in Hal's wooing of Princess Katherine: "I love France so well that I will not part with a village of it; I will have it all mine. And, Kate, when France is mine and I am yours, then yours is France and you are mine" (5.2.173–76). Acknowledgment of the other has now issued in the complete absorption of the other.

As for the language lesson, it is no longer Hal but the French princess who is the student. There is always a slight amusement in hearing one's own language spoken badly, a gratifying sense of possessing effortlessly what for others is a painful achievement. This sense is mingled at times with a condescending encouragement of the childish efforts of the inept learner, at times with delight at the inadvertent absurdities or indecencies into which the learner stumbles. (I spent several minutes in Bergamo once convulsing passersby with requests for directions to the Colleone Chapel. It was not until much later that I realized that I was pronouncing it the "Coglioni"—"Balls"—Chapel.) In *Henry V* the pleasure is intensified because the French princess is by implication learning English as a consequence of the successful English invasion, an invasion graphically figured as a rape. And the pleas-

ing sense of national and specifically male superiority is crowned
by the comic spectacle of the obscenities into which the princess is
inadvertently led.[53]

If the subversive force of "recording" is substantially reduced in
Henry V, the mode I have called explaining is by contrast intensified
in its power to disturb. The war of conquest that Henry V launches
against the French is depicted as carefully founded on acts of "explaining." The play opens with a notoriously elaborate account of
the king's genealogical claim to the French throne, and, as in the
comparable instances in Harriot, this ideological justification of English policy is an unsettling mixture of "impeccable" reasoning (once
its initial premises are accepted) and gross self-interest.[54] In the ideological apologies for absolutism, the self-interest of the monarch and
the interest of the nation are identical, and both in turn are secured
by God's overarching design. Hence Hal's personal triumph at Agincourt is represented as the nation's triumph, which in turn is represented as God's triumph. When the deliciously favorable kill ratio—
ten thousand French dead compared to twenty-nine English[55]—is
reported to the king, he immediately gives "full trophy, signal, and
ostent," as the Chorus later puts it, to God: "Take it, God, / For it is
none but thine!" (4.8.11–12).

Hal evidently thinks this explanation of the English victory—this
translation of its cause and significance from human to divine
agency—needs some reinforcement:

> And be it death proclaimed through our host
> To boast of this, or take that praise from God
> Which is his only.
>
> (4.8.114–116)

By such an edict God's responsibility for the slaughter of the
French is enforced, and with it is assured at least the glow of divine
approval over the entire enterprise, from the complex genealogical
claims to the execution of traitors, the invasion of France, the
threats leveled against civilians, the massacre of the prisoners. Yet
there is something disconcerting as well as reinforcing about this
draconian mode of ensuring that God receive credit: with a strategic circularity at once compelling and suspect, God's credit for the
killing can be guaranteed only by the threat of more killing. The
element of compulsion would no doubt predominate if the audi-

ence's own survival were at stake—the few Elizabethans who openly challenged the theological pretensions of the great found themselves in deep trouble—but were the stakes this high in the theater? Was it not possible inside the playhouse walls to question certain claims elsewhere unquestionable?

A few years earlier, at the close of *The Jew of Malta*, Marlowe had cast a witheringly ironic glance, worthy of Machiavelli, at the piety of the triumphant: Ferneze's gift to God of the "trophy, signal, and ostent" of the successful betrayal of Barabas is the final bitter joke of a bitter play. Shakespeare does not go so far. But he does take pains to call attention to the problem of invoking a God of battles, let alone enforcing the invocation by means of the death penalty. On the eve of Agincourt, the soldier Williams had responded unenthusiastically to the disguised king's claim that his cause was good:

But if the cause be not good, the King himself hath a heavy reckoning to make, when all those legs, and arms, and heads, chopp'd off in a battle, shall join together at the latter day and cry all, "We died at such a place"— some swearing, some crying for a surgeon, some upon their wives left poor behind them, some upon the debts they owe, some upon their children rawly left. I am afeard there are few die well that die in a battle; for how can they charitably dispose of any thing, when blood is their argument? (4.1.134–43)

To this the king replies with a string of awkward "explanations" designed to show that "the King is not bound to answer the particular endings of his soldiers" (4.1.155–56)—as if death in battle were a completely unforeseen accident or, alternatively, as if each soldier killed were being punished by God for a hidden crime or, again, as if war were a religious blessing, an "advantage" to a soldier able to "wash every mote out of his conscience" (4.1.179–80). Not only are these explanations mutually contradictory, but they cast long shadows on the king himself. For in the wake of this scene, as the dawn is breaking, Hal pleads nervously with God not to think—at least "not to-day"—upon the crime from which he has benefited: his father's deposition and killing of Richard II. The king calls attention to all the expensive and ingratiating ritual acts that he has instituted to compensate for the murder of the divinely anointed ruler—reinterment of the corpse, five hundred poor "in yearly pay" to plead twice daily for pardon, two chantries where priests say mass for Richard's soul—and he promises to do more.

Yet in a moment that anticipates Claudius's inadequate repentance of old Hamlet's murder, inadequate since he is "still possess'd/Of those effects" for which the crime was committed (*Hamlet* 3.3.53–54), Hal acknowledges that these expiatory rituals and even "contrite tears" are worthless:

> Though all that I can do is nothing worth,
> Since that my penitence comes after all,
> Imploring pardon.
>
> (4.1.303–5)[56]

If by nightfall Hal is threatening to execute anyone who denies God full credit for the astonishing English victory, the preceding scenes would seem to have fully exposed the ideological and psychological mechanisms behind such compulsion, its roots in violence, magical propitiation and bad conscience. The pattern disclosed here is one we have glimpsed in *2 Henry IV*: we witness an anticipatory subversion of each of the play's central claims. The archbishop of Canterbury spins out an endless public justification for an invasion he has privately confessed would relieve financial pressure on the church; Hal repeatedly warns his victims that they are bringing pillage and rape upon themselves, but he speaks as the head of the invading army that is about to pillage and rape them; Gower claims that the king has ordered the killing of the prisoners in retaliation for the attack on the baggage train, but we have just been shown that the king's order preceded that attack.[57] Similarly, Hal's meditation on the sufferings of the great—"What infinite heart's ease/Must kings neglect, that private men enjoy!" (4.1.236–37)—suffers from his being almost single-handedly responsible for a war that by his own earlier account and that of the enemy is causing immense civilian misery. And after watching a scene in which anxious, frightened troops sleeplessly await the dawn, it is difficult to be fully persuaded by Hal's climactic vision of the "slave" and "peasant" sleeping comfortably, little knowing "What watch the King keeps to maintain the peace" (4.1.283).

This apparent subversion of the monarch's glorification has led some critics since Hazlitt to view the panegyric as bitterly ironic or to argue, more plausibly, that Shakespeare's depiction of Henry V is radically ambiguous.[58] But in the light of Harriot's *Brief and True Report*, we may suggest that the subversive doubts the play continually awakens originate paradoxically in an effort to intensify the power of the king and his war. The effect is bound up with the reversal that we have noted several times—the great events and speeches all occur twice: the first time as fraud, the second as truth. The intimations of bad faith are real enough, but they are deferred—deferred until after Essex's campaign in Ireland, after Elizabeth's reign, after the monarchy itself as a significant political institution. Deferred indeed even today, for in the wake of full-scale ironic readings and at a time when it no longer seems to matter very much, it is not at all clear that *Henry V* can be successfully performed as subversive.

The problem with any attempt to do so is that the play's central figure seems to feed on the doubts he provokes. For the enhancement of royal power is not only a matter of the deferral of doubt: the very doubts that Shakespeare raises serve not to rob the king of his charisma but to heighten it, precisely as they heighten the theatrical interest of the play; the unequivocal, unambiguous celebrations of royal power with which the period abounds have no theatrical force and have long since fallen into oblivion. The charismatic authority of the king, like that of the stage, depends upon falsification.

The audience's tension, then, enhances its attention; prodded by constant reminders of a gap between real and ideal, the spectators are induced to make up the difference, to invest in the illusion of magnificence, to be dazzled by their own imaginary identification with the conqueror. The ideal king must be in large part the invention of the audience, the product of a will to conquer that is revealed to be identical to a need to submit. *Henry V* is remarkably self-conscious about this dependence upon the audience's powers of invention. The prologue's opening lines invoke a form of theater radically unlike the one that is about to unfold: "A kingdom for a stage, princes to act, / And monarchs to behold the swelling scene!" (3–4). In such a theater-state there would be no social distinction between the king and the spectator, the performer and the audience; all would be royal, and the role of the performance would be to transform not an actor into a king but a king into a god: "Then should the warlike Harry, like himself, / Assume the port of Mars" (5–6). This is in effect the fantasy acted out in royal masques, but Shakespeare is intensely aware that his play is not a courtly entertainment, that his actors are "flat unraised spirits," and that his spectators are hardly monarchs—"gentles all," he calls them, with fine flattery.[59] "Let us," the prologue begs the audience, "On your imaginary forces work. . . . For 'tis your thoughts that now must deck our kings" (17–18, 28). This "must" is cast in the form of an appeal and an apology—the consequence of the miserable limitations of "this unworthy scaffold"—but the necessity extends, I suggest, beyond the stage: all kings are "decked" out by the imaginary forces of the spectators, and a sense of the limitations of king or theater only excites a more compelling exercise of those forces.

Power belongs to whoever can command and profit from this exercise of the imagination, hence the celebration of the charismatic ruler whose imperfections we are invited at once to register and to "piece out" (Prologue, 23). Hence too the underlying complicity throughout these plays between the prince and the playwright, a complicity complicated but never effaced by a strong counter-current of identification with Falstaff. In Hal, Shakespeare fashions a compelling emblem of the playwright as sovereign "juggler," the minter of counterfeit coins, the genial master of illusory subversion and redemptive betrayal. To understand Shakespeare's conception of Hal, from rakehell to monarch, we need in effect a poetics of Elizabethan power, and this in turn will prove inseparable, in crucial respects, from a poetics of the theater. Testing, recording, and explaining are elements in this poetics, which is inseparably bound up with the figure of Queen Elizabeth, a ruler without a standing army, without a highly developed bureaucracy, without an extensive police force, a ruler whose power is constituted in theatrical celebrations of royal glory and theatrical violence visited upon the enemies of that glory. Power that relies on a massive police apparatus, a strong middle-class nuclear family, an elaborate school system, power that dreams of a panopticon in which the most intimate secrets are open to the view of an invisible authority—such power will have as its appropriate aesthetic form the realist novel;[60] Elizabethan power, by contrast, depends upon its privileged visibility. As in a theater, the audience must be powerfully engaged by this visible presence and at the same time held at a respectful distance from it. "We princes," Elizabeth told a deputation of Lords and Commons in 1586, "are set on stages in the sight and view of all the world."[61]

Royal power is manifested to its subjects as in a theater, and the subjects are at once absorbed by the instructive, delightful, or terrible spectacles and forbidden intervention or deep intimacy. The play of authority depends upon spectators—"For 'tis your thoughts that now must deck our kings"—but the performance is made to seem entirely beyond the control of those whose "imaginary forces" actually confer upon it its significance and force. These matters, Thomas More imagines the common people saying of one such spectacle, "be king's games, as it were stage plays, and for the more part played upon scaffolds. In which poor men be but the lookers-on. And they that wise be will meddle no farther."[62] Within this theatrical setting, there is a notable insistence upon the paradoxes, ambiguities, and tensions of authority, but this apparent production of subversion is, as we have already seen, the very condition of power. I should add that this condition is not a theoretical necessity of theatrical power in general but a historical phenomenon, the particular mode of this particular culture. "In sixteenth century England," writes Clifford Geertz, comparing Elizabethan and Majapahit royal progresses, "the political center of society was the point at which the tension between the passions that power excited and the ideals it was supposed to serve was screwed to its highest pitch. . . . In fourteenth century Java, the center was the point at which such tension disappeared in a blaze of cosmic symmetry."[63]

It is precisely because of the English form of absolutist theatricality that Shakespeare's drama, written for a theater subject to state censorship, can be so relentlessly subversive: the form itself, as a primary expression of Renaissance power, helps to contain the radical doubts it continually provokes. Of course, what is for the state a mode of subversion contained can be for the theater a mode of containment subverted: there are moments in Shakespeare's career—*King Lear* is the greatest example[64]—when the process of containment is strained to the breaking point. But the histories consistently pull back from such extreme pressure. Like Harriot in the New World, the Henry plays confirm the Machiavellian hypothesis that princely power originates in force and fraud even as they draw their audience toward an acceptance of that power. And we are free to locate and pay homage to the plays' doubts only because they no longer threaten us.[65] There is subversion, no end of subversion, only not for us.

Chapter Three

Fiction and Friction

In September 1580, as he passed through a small French town on his way to Switzerland and Italy, Montaigne was told an unusual story that he duly recorded in his travel journal. It seems that seven or eight girls from a place called Chaumont-en-Bassigni plotted together "to dress up as males and thus continue their life in the world."[1] One of them set up as a weaver, "a well-disposed young man who made friends with everybody," and moved to a village called Montier-en-Der. There the weaver fell in love with a woman, courted her, and married. The couple lived together for four or five months, to the wife's satisfaction, "so they say." But then, Montaigne reports, the transvestite was recognized by someone from Chaumont; "the matter was brought to justice, and she was condemned to be hanged, which she said she would rather undergo than return to a girl's status; and she was hanged for using illicit devices to supply her defect in sex." The execution, Montaigne was told, had taken place only a few days before.

I begin with this story because in *Twelfth Night* Shakespeare almost, but not quite, retells it. It is one of those shadow stories that haunt the plays, rising to view whenever the plot edges toward a potential dilemma or resolution that it in fact eschews. If we dwell on these shadow stories, we shall be accused of daydreaming (a serious charge, for some reason, against literary critics); the plays insist only that we register them in passing as we take in (or are taken in by) the events that "actually" happen. What if Olivia had succeeded in marrying Orsino's page Cesario? And what if the scandal of a marriage contracted so far beneath a countess's station were

66

topped by a still greater scandal: the revelation that the young groom was in fact a disguised girl? Such a marriage—if we could still call it one—would make some sense in a play that had continually tantalized its audience with the spectacle of homoerotic desire: Cesario in love with "his" master Orsino, Orsino evidently drawn toward Cesario, Antonio passionately in love with Sebastian, Olivia aroused by a page whose effeminacy everyone remarks. But how could the play account for such desire, or rather, since an account is neither called for nor tendered, how could the play extricate itself from the objectification of illicit desire in a legal marriage?

The case recorded by Montaigne, let us recall, did not set off a psychological examination—the "scientia sexualis" that Foucault finds at the heart of the modern history of sexuality—but a legal proceeding, a trial issuing in a condemnation not, it seems, for deception but for the use of prohibited sexual devices, devices that enable a woman to take the part of a man.[2] So too at the critical moment of misunderstanding in *Twelfth Night*, when Olivia urges the apparently timorous Cesario to take up his new status as her husband, the issue is defined not in psychological but in legal terms. A priest is brought in to testify to the procedural impeccability of the ceremony he has performed:

> A contract of eternal bond of love,
> Confirm'd by mutual joinder of your hands,
> Attested by the holy close of lips,
> Strength'ned by interchangement of your rings,
> And all the ceremony of this compact
> Seal'd in my function, by my testimony.
>
> (5.1.156–61)

This legal validity would clash violently with the gross impropriety of a homosexual coupling; presumably, there would have to be a ceremony of undoing to resolve the scandal. But then, of course, Olivia does not succeed; she actually marries Viola's twin who is, as it happens, a male. At the moment that Cesario discloses what lies beneath the "masculine usurp'd attire"—"I am Viola"—her twin Sebastian frees Olivia from the scandalous shadow story:

> So comes it, lady, you have been mistook;
> But Nature to her bias drew in that.
>
> (5.1.259–60)

What happened in Montier-en-Der was against nature; in *Twelfth Night* events pursue their natural curve, the curve that assures the proper mating of man and woman. To be matched with someone of one's own sex is to follow an unnaturally straight line; heterosexuality, as the image of nature drawing to her bias implies, is bent. Shakespeare's metaphor is from the game of bowls; the "bias" refers not only to the curve described by the bowl as it rolls along the pitch but also to the weight implanted in the bowl to cause it to swerve. Something off-center, then, is implanted in nature—in Olivia's nature, in the nature that more generally governs the plot of the comedy—that deflects men and women from their ostensible desires and toward the pairings for which they are destined.

This deflection can be revealed only in movement. As befits a play intended for performance, the metaphor for nature invokes not simply internal structure but a structure whose realization depends upon temporal unfolding, or *rolling*. An enacted imbalance or deviation is providential, for a perfect sphere would roll straight to social, theological, legal disaster: success lies in a strategic, happy swerving. The swerving is not totally predictable because the bowl will encounter obstacles, or "rubs," that will make its course erratic; if sometimes frustrating, these rubs are also part of the pleasure and excitement of the game. Licit sexuality in *Twelfth Night*—the only craving that the play can represent as capable of finding satisfaction—depends upon a movement that deviates from the desired object straight in one's path toward a marginal object, a body one scarcely knows. Nature is an *unbalancing* act.

Swerving is not a random image in the play; it is one of the central structural principles of *Twelfth Night*, a principle that links individual characters endowed with their own private motivations to the larger social order glimpsed in the ducal court and the aristocratic household.[3] The play's initiatory design invites the audience to envisage the unification of court and household through the marriage of their symbolic heads, Orsino and Olivia. This uniting, at once a social and psychological consummation, is blocked only by a vow that must be broken in the interest of both the political and the natural order of things. To intensify the narrative pressure behind this design, the play insists upon the perfect eligibility of Olivia: she is not only a great heiress but, in the wake of the deaths of her father and only brother, the sole ruler of her fortunes. Courtship need not be represented, as for example in *The Taming of the Shrew* and *Much Ado about Nothing*, as (at least in part) a negotiation with the father or male guardian; the countess Olivia is a prize encumbered only by her devotion to her brother's memory. (Her uncle, who could have filled the role of her guardian, is a hopeless sot whose own candidate for his niece's hand is suitable only to be bilked and mocked.) The lady richly left was a major male wish-fulfillment fantasy in a culture where the pursuit of wealth through marriage was an avowed and reputable preoccupation. Here the fantasy is at its most dreamlike because it focuses not on a widow—the only group whose members actually corresponded on infrequent occasion to this daydream—but on "a virtuous maid" (1.2.36).[4]

The maid, however, is strong-willed and refuses perversely to submit to the erotic dance that would lead to the legitimate male appropriation of her person and her "dirty lands" (2.4.82). Indeed she appears to enjoy ruling her household—controlling access to her person, taking pleasure in her jester, managing her manager Malvolio, dispensing rewards and punishments. One extraordinary woman in the period provided, of course, a model for such a career, lived out to its fullest—the virgin queen, aging and heirless and very dangerous. The queen had at once mobilized, manipulated, and successfully resisted decades of anxious male attempts to see her married; but this was a career that Elizabeth herself, let alone her male subjects, could not tolerate in any woman of lesser station.

There is then a powerful logic—social, political, economic, erotic—to the eligible, perfectly independent male ruler of the land taking possession of this eligible, perfectly independent maiden prize. The linked elements of this logic are suggested by Orsino's anticipation of the time

> when liver, brain, and heart,
> These sovereign thrones, are all supplied, and fill'd
> Her sweet perfections with one self king!
>
> (1.1.36–38)

All that stands in the way, the play makes clear in its opening moments, is the extravagant irrationality of her vow:

> The element itself, till seven years' heat,
> Shall not behold her face at ample view;
> But like a cloistress she will veiled walk,

And water once a day her chamber round
With eye-offending brine; all this to season
A brother's dead love, which she would keep fresh
And lasting in her sad remembrance.

(1.1.25–31)

Olivia's swerving from this vow—absurdly ambitious in its projected duration, comically ritualized, perversely wedded to misery—is entirely predictable.[5] Indeed, in lines that play on the stan-
dard theological term for marital intercourse—"to pay the debt"—
Orsino takes her mourning less as an impediment to his love than
as an erotic promissory note:

O, she that hath a heart of that fine frame
To pay this debt of love but to a brother,
How will she love when the rich golden shaft
Hath kill'd the flock of all affections else
That live in her.

(1.1.32–36)[6]

The surprise for Orsino is that the swerving, when it comes, is
not in his direction. That it is not depends upon a series of events
that the play also represents as swervings: a shipwreck that keeps
Viola and Sebastian from reaching their destination, the blocking of
Viola's initial intention to serve Olivia, Viola's relatively unmoti-
vated decision to disguise herself in men's clothing, the mistaking
of Sebastian for the disguised Viola, and so forth. These apparently
random accidents are at once zany deflections of direction, intention, and identity and comically predictable drives toward a resolution no less conventional than the one for which Orsino had
longed. The plot initially invoked by Shakespeare's play is dis-
placed by another, equally familiar, plot—the plot of cross-dressing
and cross-coupling that had become a heavily overworked convention of Italian and Spanish comedy.[7]

Swerving in *Twelfth Night*, then, is at once a source of festive
surprise and a time-honored theatrical method of achieving a conventional, reassuring resolution. No one but Viola gets quite what
she or he consciously sets out to get in the play, and Viola gets
what she wants only because she is willing to submit herself to the
very principle of deflection: "I am not that I play" (1.5.184). She
embraces a strategy that the play suggests is not simply an accident

of circumstance but an essential life-truth: you reach a desired or at least desirable destination not by pursuing a straight line but by following a curved path. This principle underlies Sebastian's explanation of Olivia's mistake: "Nature to her bias drew in that."

Sebastian glosses his own image with the comment, "You would have been contracted to a maid" (5.1.261); that is, he invites Olivia to contemplate what would have happened had nature *not* drawn to her bias.[8] The line seems to call forth its complement—"But now you are contracted to a man"—yet characteristically *Twelfth Night* does not give us such a sensible and perfectly predictable turn. Instead Sebastian concludes by renewing the paradox after it had seemed resolved:

> Nor are you therein, by my life, deceiv'd,
> You are betroth'd both to a maid and man.
> (5.1.262–63)

A man because Sebastian has beneath his apparel what Cesario lacks—"Pray God defend me!" cries Cesario before the duel with Sir Andrew, "A little thing would make me tell them how much I lack of a man" (3.4.302–3); a maid because the term, by a quibble whose several sixteenth-century examples the OED records, could be applied to a male virgin.[9] Its use here refers wittily not only to Sebastian's virginity but to the homosexual coupling that Olivia has narrowly escaped. Only by not getting what she wants has Olivia been able to get what she wants and, more important, to want what she gets.

Nature has triumphed. The sexes are sorted out, correctly paired, and dismissed to bliss—or will be as soon as Viola changes her clothes. And nature's triumph is society's triumph, for the same clarification that keeps marriage from being scandalized by gender confusion keeps it from being scandalized by status confusion: no sooner has Sebastian explained to Olivia that he is both a maid and man than Orsino adds, as if he were in no way changing the subject, "Be not amaz'd, right noble is his blood." This is the first mention of the twins' nobility—previously we had only heard Cesario's declaration, "I am a gentleman"—and Orsino's knowledge must stem from the same source that settled the question of identity: the name of the father.[10] Throughout the play we have been allowed to think that Viola and Sebastian are beneath Olivia's station—hence the spectral doubling of Malvolio's dream of social climbing—and consequently that the play's festive inversions have been purchased at the cost of the more perfect social alliance between the duke and the countess. Now, through the magical power of the name of the father, we learn that the threat to the social order and the threat to the sexual order were equally illusory. All's well that ends well.

"The most fundamental distinction the play brings home to us," remarks C. L. Barber in his well-known essay on *Twelfth Night*, "is the difference between men and women. . . . Just as the saturnalian reversal of social roles need not threaten the social structure, but can serve instead to consolidate it, so a temporary, playful reversal of sexual roles can renew the meaning of the normal relation. One can add that with sexual as with other relations, it is when the normal is secure that playful aberration is benign. This basic security explains why there is so little that is queazy in all Shakespeare's handling of boy actors playing women, and playing women pretending to be men."[11] Perhaps. Yet however acute these remarks may be as a humane vision of life, we must question them as a summary judgment of Shakespearean comedy in general and of *Twelfth Night* in particular. At that play's end, Viola is still Cesario—"For so you shall be," says Orsino, "while you are a man" (5.1.386)—and Olivia, strong-willed as ever, is betrothed to one who is, by his own account, both "a maid and man." At the risk of intensifying our sense of the "queazy" (a category that might reward some inquiry), I would suggest that *Twelfth Night* may not finally bring home to us the fundamental distinction between men and women; not only may the distinction be blurred, but the home to which it is supposed to be brought may seem less securely ours, less cozy and familiar, than we have come to expect.

But how can we unsettle the secure relation between the normal and the aberrant? How can we question the nature that like a weighted bowl so providentially draws to her bias and resolves the comic predicaments? I propose that we examine the bowl more carefully, search out the off-center weight implanted in it, analyze why it follows the curve of gender. To do so we must historicize Shakespearean sexual nature, restoring it to its relation of negotiation and exchange with other social discourses of the body. For this task it is essential to break away from the textual isolation that is the primary principle of formalism and to move outside the charmed circle of a particular story and its variants. How can we do this? How but by swerving?

ii

In 1601 in a small town near Rouen, a thirty-two-year-old widowed mother of two, Jeane le Febvre, had a very odd experience. For nearly five weeks she had been sharing her bed (not at all an odd experience) with a fellow servant, a woman in her early twenties who was recuperating from a long illness. Then one evening, while they were doing the laundry together, the bedmate, Marie le Marcis, whispered that she was in fact a man—a claim she (or rather he) graphically demonstrated—and precipitously proposed marriage. Jeane at first refused, but during the following weeks the two fell in love.

The couple did not intend to keep their relationship clandestine; they wished to get their parents' permission and have a proper wedding, sanctified by the church. Indeed, despite the wildly irregular circumstances in which they found themselves, they seem to have been immediately caught up in the ordinary social problems and strategies that attended marriage negotiations in the Renaissance. Jeane had been raised in the Reformed faith; Marie, though he had been converted to that faith by an employer, wished now to return, as his mother had long been urging, to the Catholic church. We may assume that Marie's parents were gratified, but there is no record of their reaction either to Marie's return to Catholicism or, strangely enough, to the revelation that their daughter was a son. We are told, however, that they strenuously objected to his decision to marry a penniless widow with two small children. The dutiful son at first consented not to see Jeane, but finding the separation unendurable, he returned to his beloved's bed. There, after making vows to one another, they consummated their passion—three or four times, we are told, on the first night alone.[12]

Not content with secret vows and private pleasures, Marie and Jeane remained steadfast in their desire for the public confirmation of a wedding. But to acquire this confirmation, Marie le Marcis needed to acquire a new sexual identity in the eyes of the community; he had been baptized, named, dressed, and brought up as a girl. Accordingly, he changed his clothing, asked that he be called Marin le Marcis, and publicly declared his matrimonial intentions. Not surprisingly (though the lovers themselves appear to have been surprised), there was an immediate public scandal; the two were arrested, tried, and condemned, Marin to be burned alive, Jeane to watch the execution, then to be beaten and banished from Normandy. (After an appeal for mercy, the sentence was humanely moderated: Marin was only to be strangled to death, Jeane merely to be whipped.) The crime of which they were convicted was sodomy, for both the wife and the mother of the man in whose household the couple had served testified that Marie le Marcis had regularly had her menstrual period ["ses purgations naturelles"] (194), and a medical examination revealed no signs of masculinity. The accused maintained that as a consequence of the terror of imprisonment, his penis had retracted, but the court dismissed his claim. Marie, it was charged, was not a man but a "tribade"—a homosexual seductress who had, with her unnaturally enlarged clitoris, abused the all-too-willing Jeane.

Marin appealed his conviction to the Parlement of Rouen, which appointed a panel of doctors, surgeons, and midwives to renew the medical examination. One of the doctors, Jacques Duval, had a learned interest in hermaphroditism, to which he saw this case as allied, and consequently he pursued the examination much further than his colleagues. Where they were willing to stay on the surface, Duval, recalling that Aristotle had reproached philosophers who foolishly held themselves aloof from those things vulgarly thought to be indecent, was determined to probe. This determination was rewarded: responding to his finger's pressure was "a male organ, rather large and hard" (403); a second examination left no doubt, for the friction of the doctor's touch caused Marin to ejaculate, and the semen, he reports, was not thin and watery like a woman's but, like a man's, thick and white (404–5).

On the strength of Duval's expert testimony (with which the rest of the medical panel did not concur), the lovers' conviction was overturned. Marin and Jeane were released. The court evidently remained guardedly skeptical: Marin was ordered to wear women's clothes until he reached the age of twenty-five and was forbidden, on pain of death, to have sexual relations during this time with either sex. What would happen thereafter—whether Marin would be allowed to marry Jeane or be forced to remain Marie—the court left undecided. Perhaps at the trial's end the judges had not the vaguest idea what Marin's sex really was. In any case, they did not feel certain enough to let him either marry or burn. If customary procedures for determining the gender of hermaphrodites were followed, at the end of the probationary period Marin would be permitted to choose once and for all a sexual identity.[13] Case closed.

This cheerfully grotesque story is recounted in a long book—Duval's *On Hermaphrodites, Childbirth, and the Medical Treatment of Mothers and Children*—and I want to propose that we may understand this book not as bizarre static on the margins of normative individualism—sexless, colorless, and above all cultureless—but as part of the particular and contingent discourse out of which historically specific subjects were fashioned, represented, and communally incorporated.

On Hermaphrodites participates in a larger field of sexual discourse—a field that in the early modern period includes marriage manuals; medical, theological, and legal texts; sermons; indictments and defenses of women; and literary fictions. Rarely is any one text in this field decisively important—for even the strongest tradition generates counter-traditions—but taken as a whole, a culture's sexual discourse plays a critical role in the shaping of identity. It does so by helping to implant in each person a system of dispositions and orientations that governs individual improvisations, to implant, in other words, the defining off-center weight: "But nature to her bias drew in that."[14]

The concrete individual exists only in relation to forces that pull against spontaneous singularity and that draw any given life, however peculiarly formed, toward communal norms. Even Marin le Marcis's highly original improvisation, we might note, had the most conventional of goals: a publicly recognized name and gender, an officially sanctioned marriage. Indeed the drive to be reabsorbed into the communal is sufficiently strong in his case to make us doubt that individualism, in the sense of freestanding and irreducible particularity, had any meaning or value to Marin or anyone involved with him. It has been traditional, since Jakob Burckhardt, to trace the origins of autonomous individuality to the Renaissance, but the material under consideration here suggests that individual identity in the early modern period served less as a final goal

than as a way station on the road to a firm and decisive identification with normative structures.

Of these structures, the most powerful appear to have been those
governing sexual identity. Male writers of the period regarded gender as an enduring sign of distinction, both in the sense of privilege
and in the sense of differentiation. A man in Renaissance society had
symbolic and material advantages that no woman could hope to
attain, and he had them by virtue of separating himself, first as a
child and then as an adult, from women. All other significant differential indices of individual existence—social class, religion, language, nation—could, at least in imagination, be stripped away,
only to reveal the underlying natural fact of sexual difference. The
Renaissance delighted in stories of the transformation of individuals
out of all recognition—the king confused with the beggar, the great
prince reduced to the condition of a wild man, the pauper changed
into a rich lord.[15] Only the primary differentiation given by God
himself—"male and female he made them"—would seem to have
been exempt from this swirling indeterminacy. Even here, of
course, confusion was possible, for as the many stories of cross-
dressing suggest, apparel may deceive the eyes of the most skilled
observer. But beneath the apparel the body itself cannot lie—or so
we might expect.

Yet in Renaissance stories, paradoxically, the apparently fragile
and mutable social codes are almost always reinscribed—despite
his savage upbringing, the true prince reveals his noble nature—
while sexual difference, the foundation of all individuation, turns
out to be unstable and artificial at its origin. To help us understand
this paradox let us return to Duval's fascination with hermaphrodites. This fascination was not, for the late sixteenth century, eccen-
tric but was an instance of a widespread cultural concern with
prodigies. Prodigies could be viewed both as signs—monitory mes-
sages to be read by those who understood the art of divination—
and as wonders—marvelous instances of the inexhaustible variety
of things. Prodigies challenge the conventional classification of
things, but they do not make classification itself impossible. On the
contrary, as the voluminous accounts of monsters, earthquakes,
eclipses, unnaturally heavy rains, physical deformities, and so
forth affirm, these marvels give men a sense of the dynamic order
of nature that constantly produces those differences—the grada-

tions and distinctions and variations—by which men define themselves and their social and natural environment. Where the modern structuralist understanding of the world tends to sharpen its sense of individuation by meditating upon the normative, the Renaissance tended to sharpen its sense of the normative by meditating upon the prodigious.[16]

The presence of both male and female sexual organs in a single person is a resonant instance of that Renaissance meditation. Hermaphroditism was at once a bizarre anomaly, violating the most basic of natural categories, and a sign of the natural order whose underlying structure made possible the very generativity that produced the anomaly.[17] It is fitting then that Duval's book, in which the strange case of Marin le Marcis occupies so important a place, is not a mere compilation of the bizarre but a serious medical treatise on fertility, the care of pregnant women, and the safe delivery of babies. Discourse on hermaphroditism and discourse on normal sexuality and childbirth do not conflict for Duval; on the contrary, they are the same discourse, for the knowledge that enables one to understand the monstrous conjunction in one individual of the male and female sexes is the identical knowledge that enables one to understand the normal experience of sexual pleasure and the generation of healthy offspring.

Duval's task, as he understands it, is to display and explain the hidden riches of the human organs of generation and particularly of the womb, which he sees, in effect, as a fantastic treasure house to which he has acquired the key (159). But why should the case of Marin le Marcis seem to give him this precious key? The answer lies in the event that saved Marin's life: empowered by the court of law, the physician reaches in behind the woman's secret fold of flesh and feels with his finger's end a swelling penis.

Marin is an oddity, but for Duval his body encodes in its strangeness a universal natural paradox: on the one hand, a single individual is in reality double, since all bodies contain both male and female elements; on the other hand, there are not two radically different sexual structures but only one—outward and visible in the man, inverted and hidden in the woman. Neither of these beliefs is unique to Duval; on the contrary, they reflect ancient anatomical wisdom, which Renaissance physicians at once elaborated and challenged. Like many of his peers, Duval is in the awkward position of accepting beliefs with which he is not altogether comfortable; the case of Marin le Marcis serves him by simultaneously reaffirming and marginalizing these beliefs.

At least since the time of Galen it had been widely thought that both males and females contained both male and female elements (Duval goes so far as to posit male and female seed [327]); the predominance, rather than the exclusion, of one or the other helped, along with the original position of the seed in the womb and other factors, to determine sexual identity and to make possible a harmonious accord between sex and gender. Predominance was never—or at least rarely—absolute, nor, in the opinion of most, was it established in final and definitive form in the womb. On the contrary, virtually all males experienced a transition during childhood from a state close to that of females—indeed often called "effeminate"—to one befitting an adult man. Conversely, if less frequently, the predominance of the appropriate female characteristics could take some time to establish itself. Where the female elements were dominant but still insufficiently strong, the woman would be a virago; similarly, a man in whom male seed was weaker than it should be was likely to remain effeminate. And in those rare cases, as Duval notes, where the competition between male and female elements was absolutely undecided, a hermaphrodite could be formed.

All of this implies, as I have suggested, the persistent doubleness, the inherent twinship, of all individuals. But we should not conclude that the esoteric Neoplatonic speculations about androgyny in the Renaissance were in fact widespread; on the contrary, perceptions of gender doubleness were almost always closely linked to a belief in an internal power struggle between male and female principles. Proper individuation occurred as a result of the successful resolution of the friction between the competing elements, a resolution that was almost entirely bound up in medical manuals, as in theological tracts, with patriarchal ideology: "By how much the more the Masculine Atoms abound in a Female Infant," writes Nathaniel Highmore, a seventeenth-century English physician, "by so much the more the Fetus is stronger, healthier, and more Man-like, a Virago. If the Female Atoms abound much in a Male Infant, then is that issue more weak and effeminate."[18] One peculiar consequence of this view was that normal women had to submit to the weaker internal principle, to accept a certain debility, in order to achieve full female identity, an identity that itself entailed submission to a man; women were *by definition* the weaker sex. A further consequence is that women had momentarily to overcome their inherent defect, and hence their female nature, to produce the seed necessary for generation. Not surprisingly, this overcoming was thought to be difficult; accordingly, the medical texts prescribe extended foreplay as an integral part of sexual intercourse and, for cases where caresses and lascivious words fail, provide recipes for vaginal douches designed to "heat" women beyond their normal bodily temperature.[19]

But if the Galenic heritage brought with it the notion that human singleness was achieved out of an inherent doubleness, it also brought with it a very different notion: since Galen it had been believed that the male and female sexual organs were altogether comparable, indeed mirror images of each other. Though Fallopius published in the 1560s his celebrated description of the female genitalia, and belief in female testicles gave way in the later seventeenth century to the discovery of the ovaries, the specific functioning of the ovaries was not well understood until the nineteenth century.[20] In the sixteenth and seventeenth centuries, physicians and laymen of sharply divergent schools agreed that male and female sexual organs were fully homologous. "The spermatic vessels in women," writes the celebrated French surgeon, Ambroise Paré, "do nothing differ from those in men in substance, figure, composure, number, connexion, temper, original and use, but only in magnitude and distribution. . . . For their Testicles, they differ little from mens but in quantity [that is, size]. For they are lesser and in figure more hollow and flat, by reason of their defective heat which could not elevate or lift them up to their just magnitude" (Paré, *Works,* p. 126). The womb seems unique to women, but in fact it is "given by nature in stead of the *Scrotum,* as the neck there of, and the annexed parts in stead of the yard; so that if any more exactly consider the parts of generation in women and men, he shall find that they differ not much in number, but only in situation and use."

Centuries earlier, Galen had invited his readers to engage in the topographical analysis implicit in Paré's description of the genitals: "Turn outward the woman's, turn inward, so to speak, and fold double the man's, and you find them the same in both in every respect."[21] If you imagine the male genitals inverted, you will find that the penis has become the cervix and the vagina, and the scrotum has been transformed into the womb with the testicles on either side. Conversely, Galen suggests, think of the "uterus turned outward and projecting": "Would not the testes (ovaries) then necessarily be inside it? Would it not contain them like a scrotum? Would not the neck (the cervix), hitherto concealed inside the perineum but now pendent, be made into the male member? . . . In fact," he concludes, "you could not find a single male part left over that had not simply changed its position: for the parts that are inside in woman are outside in man."

To be sure, this exact homology implies a difference that derives from the female's being colder, and hence less perfect, than the male. This defect keeps the female genitals from being born, as it were, a fate Galen images in an astonishing metaphor:

You can see something like this in the eyes of the mole, which have vitreous and crystalline humors and the tunics that surround these . . . and they have these just as much as animals do that make use of their eyes. The mole's eyes, however, do not open, nor do they project but are left there imperfect and remain like the eyes of other animals when these are still in the uterus.[22]

This double analogy gives a vertiginous twist to the topographical argument: not only are the female genitals an inverted version of the male genitals, but they are also like the perfectly formed but functionally useless eyes of the mole, which are in turn like the blind eyes of creatures that have not yet emerged from the womb. By invoking birth the metaphor implicitly acknowledges the functional utility it is intended to deny, and this paradox, far from embarrassing Galen, enables him to sustain a double vision of the female body, at once defective and perfectly suited to its function, a vision that endured for centuries. For Paré and most other Renaissance physicians, the delicate balance of sexual identity and difference expresses simultaneously the providential order of generation and the defectiveness of women, their failure to reach nature's goal: a penis. "For that which man hath apparent without, that women have hid within, both by the singular providence of Nature, as also by the defect of heat in women, which could not drive and thrust forth those parts as in men."[23]

One consequence of this belief in differential homology is a fascination with the possibility of sex change—almost always from female to male, that is, from defective to perfect. Paré recounts several such cases, including that of a fifteen-year-old peasant girl named Marie who one day was "rather robustly" chasing her swine, which were going into a wheat field. As Marie in midpursuit leaped over a ditch, "at the very moment the genitalia and male rod came to be developed."[24] After consulting with physicians and the bishop, Marie changed her name to Germain and went on to serve in the king's retinue. On his way to Italy, Montaigne stopped to see Germain for himself—he had not married, Montaigne was told, but he had "a big, very thick beard." The prodigy was not at home, however. In the town, Montaigne noted in his journal, "there is still a song commonly in the girls' mouths, in which they warn one another not to stretch their legs too wide for fear of becoming males, like Marie Germain."[25]

Here again the prodigious is of interest because it reveals the natural. After all, such a spectacular change merely repeats or represents the normal development of males through the healthy operation of bodily heat. As with the two-seed theory, the implication of this developmental account is that men grow out of or pass through women, though now the formulation is reversed: where the two-seed theory imagines an individual identity emerging from the struggle between conflicting principles, the topographical account imagines gender as the result of the selective forcing out through heat of the original internal organ—like the reversal of a rubber glove—so that where there was once only one sex, there are now two.

Duval's work reflects this fascination with sex change, but it also registers and uneasily accommodates the anatomical discoveries that were beginning to cast serious doubts on the whole notion of homology. There cannot truly be a sexual metamorphosis, argues Duval, for despite the great resemblance between the male and female sexual organs, the latter cannot simply be converted into the former or vice versa. If you actually try to envisage such a transformation, you discover that it cannot be represented. "If you imagine the vulva completely turned inside out . . . you will have to envisage a large-mouthed bottle hanging from the woman, a bottle whose mouth rather than base would be attached to the body and which would bear no resemblance to what you had set out to imagine" (*On Hermaphrodites*, 375).

Like others of his generation, Duval is balanced uneasily between acceptance of the ancient concept of homology and a recognition that it does not quite work. This recognition does not lead him to give up a concept upon which a great deal depends, but it does shape his account of Marin le Marcis so that it illustrates not an instance of sexual metamorphosis but an embodied transvestism that momentarily confounds sexual categories only to give way in the end to the clarification of gender and hence to proper, communally sanctioned, identity.[26] Transvestism *represents* a structural identity between man and woman—identity revealed in the dramatic disclosure of the penis concealed behind the labia—but it does not *present* this identity as a reality. On the contrary, in some ways the case serves to marginalize, to render prodigious, the old wisdom. There has been no transformation from woman into man—Marie was always in some sense Marin, whose true gender was concealed by his anomalous genital structure—but the myth of such mobility is preserved in the very form of the account that denies its anatomical possibility.

The fascination with all that seems to unsettle sexual differentiation—hermaphroditism, gender metamorphosis, women who conceal the inward form of men and men who conceal the inward form of women—never decisively overturns in the Renaissance discourse of sexuality the proper generative order that depends upon a distinction between the sexes. To be sure, Duval writes, "many women have been transformed into men." But, he continues, it is more accurate to say that "the male genitals, formerly hidden, have been discovered in many who were once thought to be women; whereupon they changed their names, clothing, and vocations" (372). Even the much rarer cases of authentic hermaphroditism are not permitted to remain unresolved ambiguities; judges order that such people determine by which sex they are more aroused and on this basis choose—once and for all—their gender (302). Thereafter any violation will be severely punished, indeed treated as a capital crime.

Despite this insistence on a determinate sexual identity, Duval and others cling to a notion of deep structural homology between male and female genitals, because without it the traditional psychology and physiology of sex would be thrown into confusion. Hence even when the belief that the woman was a defective male was abandoned by most physicians and the form of the female anatomy was attributed to function rather than inadequate heat, the notion of an alignment between the sexes proved surprisingly durable. It was supported by the drawings of the anatomists who found what they had expected to find: that the uterus was analogous to the scrotum and the vagina to the penis. And if by the early seventeenth century Duval, for example, recognized that this analogy was by no means perfect, he could easily shift the grounds of comparison to the clitoris, "a particle in the shape of a small penis" ("une particule representant la forme d'un petit membre viril" [63]).[27] By the close of the century, the immensely popular *Aristotle's Master-piece* informed its readers that "to say that Woman has true Seed, is false and erroneous"; what Galen and Hippocrates had taken to be testicles are in reality ovaries.[28] But this does not mean, the manual argues, that there is a "vast difference between the Members of the two Sexes" (93); the clitoris is like a penis "in Situation, Substance, Composition and Erection, growing sometimes out of the Body two inches" (99). In some lascivious women, the clitoris swells to the size of a male organ and can be used to abuse women and girls—hence the suspicion that almost led to Marin le Marcis's execution.[29]

Like all of nature's gifts, this feminine penis could be abused, but its proper function was to help provide the "delectable pleasure" necessary to enable the woman to "yield forth" her seed. At least in the Galenic thought that dominated sixteenth- and seventeenth-century medicine, female ejaculation was at the center of the homology between the sexes, for as Paré declared, "generation or conception cannot follow without the concourse of two seeds, well and perfectly wrought in the very same moment of time" (887). Everything in the process of conception hinges on sperm, which is the sole generative principle in a world without eggs, and sperm cannot be produced by either sex without intense sexual delight.

There is an elaborate medical literature on the purpose of erotic pleasure—as that which enables men to overcome their natural revulsion at the defectiveness of women; that which enables

women to overcome their natural reluctance to endure the pain
and put their lives at risk in childbearing; that which compensates
for the Fall of Man. Sexual pleasure may be thought to link us to
the beasts, writes Duval, but in fact in its specifically human form it
is one of the marks of God's special favor. The Sovereign Creator
was not content that his best beloved creatures mate as the other
animals do, with the male mounting the female's back or, in the
case of elephants, camels, and other heavy beasts, with the male
and female turning their backs on one another (an ancient notion I
find difficult to envisage). For human coition God ordained a different practice: men and women look into each other's faces—"the
beautiful lines and features" of the human face—so that they may
be aroused to a more fervent desire to generate images of themselves and hence to make those beloved faces live again in their
offspring. And as they look upon one another and make love,
drawn into the genital "labyrinth of desire" that God created specially for them and obeying the "tacit commandments" engraved as
a benediction in their very bodies, men and women avenge themselves upon their enemy death. For to leave behind one's own
image—"drawn to the life in one's child" ("vif & naivement
representé en son successeur")—is not to die.[30]

Following an ancient medical tradition, Duval offers, simultaneously and bound together, two apparently contradictory accounts of the origin of gender: in one a determinate sexual identity emerges when a double nature becomes single, that is, when
either male or female seed, co-present in every person, establishes
dominance; in the other a determinate sexual identity emerges
when a single nature becomes double, that is, when the unitary
genital structure (identified as male in its perfect form) divides
into two distinct forms, internal and external. Why two accounts?
If there were only one authentic structure—outward and visible
in the man, inverted and hidden in the woman—gender difference would be reduced to a mere illusion, a trick performed with
mirrors, and generation would be difficult to imagine. If there
were two interlaced structures—from which gender emerged only
by domination and submission—differentiation would also be
threatened, since we would always discover two persons where
we thought to find one. Identity is at once made possible and
dissolved by the slippage between these conflicting theories: to

this extent, though gender for the Renaissance has everything to do with determinate boundaries (for the period—as the case of Marin indicates—was intolerant of ambiguity), it has equally to do with the friction between boundaries.

The link between these two accounts is heat: through heat the struggle between the male and female seed is determined, and again through heat the genital structure of the male emerges from its hidden place, and again through heat ejaculation and orgasm are produced. This caloric model of sexuality is not exclusively genital; breast milk, for example, is also generated by the heating of the blood, and blood itself is produced by the heating of food. Sexual warmth does not differ essentially from other warmth; it is only a particularly vehement instance of the principle of all animate life and therefore can be generated to some degree by food, wine, and the power of imagination.[31]

Duval is unusually idealizing, but the essential elements of his account of coition are widely shared: seed is produced and emitted by the concoction, or cooking, of blood; this cooking is accomplished through erotic friction between men and women. Hence the recurrent images in the medical literature of what a seventeenth-century English gynecologist calls "the *Fervour* of a very *Libidinous Tickling*."[32] For as Thomas Vicary puts it in *The Englishman's Treasure; or, the True Anatomy of Man's Body* (1586), "by the labour and chafing of the testicles or stones, [the best and purest] blood is turned into another kind, and is made sparme,"[33] and by a still further chafing this "sparme" is released into the heated womb. Hence, too, Duval's account of the way in which his rubbing in the course of the medical examination caused Marin le Marcis's hidden penis to yield forth its seed and produce proof of his sexual identity. And that chafing was an official, public repetition and confirmation of the erotic friction, in bed with Jeane le Febvre, that originated Marin's transformation from Marie.

Marin le Marcis is an object of public interest, concern, and scrutiny because of this transformation. His socially articulated individuality—his emergence from the anonymous mass of men and women into the light of representation—is for the Renaissance a moment of prodigious instability on the way to integration into the normal structures of gender and reproduction.[34] Those structures are not, however, the secure, ontologically grounded *bases* for identity; on the contrary, they are themselves necessarily built up out of sexual confusion, friction, and transformation. "It is when the normal is secure that playful aberration is benign," writes C. L. Barber; Marin's case suggests that the palace of the normal is constructed on the shifting sands of the aberrant.

iii

If we seem to have swerved far from the world of Shakespearean theater, let us recall once again some of the features of the story of Marin le Marcis: a love that cannot at first declare itself and that encounters, when it finally does so, life-threatening obstacles; a dizzying confusion of identity centered on cross-dressing; an intense experience of desire—the biological imperative—that seeks to satisfy itself in a sanctified union; the intervention of authority initially to block this union but eventually to free the hero from the threat of death and remove the obstacle to marriage; the wildly unconventional drive toward conventionality. This is, of course, the plot outline of a prototypical Shakespearean comedy, and I want to propose briefly that the resemblance is more than fortuitous.

I hasten to disclaim any suggestion that Shakespeare took a lively interest in the medical discourse about sex, or that he favored one theory of generation over another, or—most unlikely of all— that he had read Paré, let alone heard of Marin le Marcis and Jacques Duval. But the state of Shakespeare's knowledge of medical science is not the important issue here. The relation I wish to establish between medical and theatrical practice is not one of cause and effect or source and literary realization. We are dealing rather with a shared code, a set of interlocking tropes and similitudes that function not only as the objects but as the conditions of representation. Shakespearean comedy constantly appeals to the body and in particular to sexuality as the heart of its theatrical magic; "great creating nature"—the principle by which the world is and must be peopled—is the comic playwright's tutelary spirit. But there is no unmediated access to the body, no direct appropriation of sexuality; rather sexuality is itself a network of historically contingent figures that constitute the culture's categorical understanding of erotic experience. These figures function as modes of translation between distinct social discourses, channels through which the shared commotion of sexual excitement circulates.[35]

How does a play come to possess sexual energy? What happens when a body is translated from "reality" to the stage or when a male actor is translated into the character of a woman? What does it mean for a Renaissance comedy, that most artificial of forms, to invoke nature or for nature, in the reified form of medical discourse, to assume the artificial form of a Renaissance comedy? By focusing on the precise shape of certain cultural figures for the body—here the body as natural transvestite and as a generator of heat through friction—we can venture an answer to these questions. We can grasp the meaning of the natural swerving that resolves the plot complications of *Twelfth Night*. We can begin to understand why all memorable representation of individuality in Shakespeare—from the gross monumental fat of Falstaff to Richard III's hunchback, from Macduff's untimely birth to Viola's uncanny twinship—is marked by the prodigious. And we can comprehend why Shakespeare repeatedly calls attention to the playing of all the women's parts—Kate, Portia, Viola, Juliet, Cleopatra, all of them—by boys.

Accounts of Shakespeare's plays constantly appeal, most often at the climactic point in the argument, to natural forces that underlie both social customs and literary models and give the characters their special power. These critical invocations of nature are not themselves a misreading—on the contrary, the plays actively solicit them—but the mistake is to imagine that the natural forces invoked are timeless and free-floating. Between Shakespeare's culture and our own there has been at least a partial shift in male gender perception from a search for the hidden penis in women to a search for the hidden womb in men, and with this shift the "natural forces" invoked in the representation of individuals have themselves changed. Moreover, a transformation of the way we understand the relation between sexual pleasure and generation has intensified this change. A culture that imagines—or, better still, knows as an indisputable biological fact—that women need not experience any pleasure at all to conceive will offer different representational resources than a culture that knows, as a widely accepted physical truth, that women have occulted, inward penises that for the survival of mankind must be brought, through

...eat of erotic friction, to the point of ejaculation. More specifically, a conception of gender that is teleologically male and insists
upon a verifiable sign that confirms nature's final cause finds its
supreme literary expression in a transvestite theater; by contrast, a
conception of gender that is symbolically female insists upon a
genetic rather than a teleological account of identity, interests itself
in the inward material matrix of individuality, and finds its supreme literary expression in the novel.[36]

The medical texts that we have been examining suggest that the
generative power of nature centers on fruitful, pleasurable chafing,
and I want to propose that this notion—which functions less as a
technical explanation than as a virtually irresistible assumption on
which to build technical explanations—resonates in the fashioning
of Shakespearean characters, particularly in comedy. The theatrical
representation of individuality is in effect modeled on what the
culture thought occurred during sexual foreplay and intercourse:
erotic chafing is the central means by which characters in plays like
*The Taming of the Shrew, A Midsummer Night's Dream, Much Ado
about Nothing, As You Like It,* and *Twelfth Night* realize their identities and form loving unions.[37]

The enemies of the Elizabethan and Jacobean theater charged that
the playhouse was "Venus' Palace," a place of erotic arousal.[38] For all
its insistence upon the solemn ceremony of marriage, Shakespearean comedy curiously confirms the charge, not only by gesturing
forward to the pleasures of the marriage bed but also by the staging
of its own theatrical pleasures. "Men and women," wrote the great
anatomist William Harvey, "are never more brave, sprightly, blithe,
valiant, pleasant or beautiful than when about to celebrate the act."[39]
Shakespeare's enactment of the celebration confers on his comic
heroes and heroines something of the special beauty of sexual
arousal.

More than any of his contemporaries, Shakespeare discovered
how to use the erotic power that the theater could appropriate,
how to generate plots that would not block or ignore this power
but draw it out, develop it, return it with interest, as it were, to the
audience. And this Shakespearean discovery, perfected over a six-
or seven-year period in the comedies from *Taming* to *Twelfth Night,*
entailed above all the representation of the emergence of identity
through the experience of erotic heat. This Promethean heat,

which is, as we have seen, the crucial practical agent of sexuality in the Renaissance, would seem to be precisely what is excluded from theatrical presentation—it takes place internally, out of sight, in the privileged intimacy of the body. But sexual heat, we recall, is not different in kind from all other heat, including that produced by the imagination. Shakespeare realized that if sexual chafing could not be presented literally onstage, it could be represented figuratively: friction could be fictionalized, chafing chastened and hence made fit for the stage, by transforming it into the witty, erotically charged sparring that is the heart of the lovers' experience.

By means of this transformation Shakespeare invested his comedies with a powerful sexual commotion, a collective excitation, an imaginative heat that the plots promise will be realized offstage, in the marriage beds toward which they gesture: "We'll begin these rites, / As we do trust they'll end, in true delights" (*As You Like It* 5.4.197–98). But if this promised end, like Viola's suit of women's clothes, holds out to the audience a fantasy of resolution, a genital, generative literalizing of chafing, it does not simply collapse fiction into friction. On the contrary, the unrepresented consummations of unrepresented marriages call attention to the unmooring of desire, the generalizing of the libidinal, that is the special pleasure of Shakespearean fiction. For the representation of chafing is not restricted to Shakespeare's lovers; it is diffused throughout the comedies as a system of foreplay. This diffusion is one of the creative principles of comic confusion: hence, for example, Viola/Cesario's cheeky replies to Olivia arouse the latter's passion in a way Orsino's sighs and groans cannot.

Moreover, for Shakespeare friction is specifically associated with verbal wit; indeed at moments the plays seem to imply that erotic friction *originates* in the wantonness of language and thus that the body itself is a tissue of metaphors or, conversely, that language is perfectly embodied. Take for a single instance the following unremarkable exchange between Viola and Feste the clown:

Viola:	'Save thee, friend, and thy music! Dost thou live by thy tabor?
Clown:	No, sir, I live by the church.
Viola:	Art thou a churchman?
Clown:	No such matter, sir. I do live by the church; for I do live at my house, and my house doth stand by the church.

Viola:	So thou mayst say the king lies by a beggar, if a beggar dwells near him; or the church stands by thy tabor, if thy tabor stand by the church.
Clown:	You have said, sir. To see this age! A sentence is but a chev'ril glove to a good wit. How quickly the wrong side may be turn'd outward!
Viola:	Nay, that's certain. They that dally nicely with words may quickly make them wanton.
Clown:	I would therefore my sister had had no name, sir.
Viola:	Why, man?
Clown:	Why, sir, her name's a word, and to dally with that word might make my sister wanton.

(3.1.1–20)

The brief, almost schematic, enactment of verbal friction leads to a perception of the suppleness of language, and particularly its capacity to be inverted, as imaged by the chev'ril glove. It is as if the cause of Marie le Marcis's sexual arousal and transformation were now attributable to the ease—the simple change of one letter—with which Marie is turned into Marin. "Her name's a word, and to dally with that word might make my sister wanton."

Dallying with words is the principal Shakespearean representation of erotic heat. Hence his plots go out of their way to create not only obstacles in the lovers' path but occasions for friction between them: to select but a single example, when Rosalind escapes from the danger posed by her uncle and finds herself on her own in the woods with Orlando, she does not throw herself into her beloved's arms but rather initiates an occasion for playful tension between them: "I will speak to him like a saucy lackey, and under that habit play the knave with him" (*As You Like It* 3.2.95–97). Critics have often remarked that the scenes of chafing that follow—Rosalind's supposed "cure" for the madness of love—are a symbolic testing of the strength of Orlando's love, but that love is never really in doubt. The chafing functions rather as a symbolic enactment of the lovers' mutual desires and a witty experimental fashioning of Rosalind's identity. We should add that the unique qualities of that identity—those that give Rosalind her independence, her sharply etched individuality—will not, as Shakespeare conceives the play, endure: they are bound up with exile, disguise, and freedom from ordinary constraint, and they will vanish, along with the playful chafing, when the play is done. What begins as a physiological necessity is reimagined as an improvisational self-fashioning that longs for self-effacement and reabsorption in the community. This longing is the sign of a social system that marks out singularity, particularly in women, as prodigious, though the disciplining of singularity is most often represented in Shakespearean comedy as romantic choice, an act of free will, an expression of love.

Why should that fashioning be bound up with cross-dressing (Rosalind, you will recall, is pretending to be a boy named Ganymede)? In part, I suggest, because the transformation of gender identity figures the emergence of an individual out of a twinned sexual nature. That emergence, let us recall, begins in the womb, but it never results in the absolute exclusion of the other seed, and the presence of both genders remains evident through adolescence.[40]

Shakespeare's most ingenious representation of this twinned gender identity, which must have empowered the transvestite performances of his company's boy actors, is in *Twelfth Night*, with its fiction of male and female identical twins who are at the border of adulthood: "Not yet old enough for a man, nor young enough for a boy" (1.5.156–57). With a change of a few conventional signals, the exquisitely feminine Viola and the manly Sebastian are indistinguishable: hence, perhaps, the disquieting intensity of Antonio's passion for Sebastian and the ease with which the confused Olivia is "betroth'd both to a maid and man" (5.1.263). Near the play's opening, Orsino nicely captures the gender confusion in an unintentionally ironic description of his young page Cesario—actually Viola in disguise:

> thy small pipe
> Is as the maiden's organ, shrill and sound,
> And all is semblative a woman's part.
>
> (1.4.32–34)

At the play's close, Orsino has not yet seen Viola—whom he intends to marry—in woman's clothes; she remains in appearance Cesario and therefore still the mirror image of her brother:

> One face, one voice, one habit, and two persons,
> A natural perspective, that is and is not!
>
> (5.1.216–17)

To be sure, the play suggests that beneath her "masculine usurp'd attire" is a body in which the feminine elements are dominant, and the "true" mettle of her sex resolves the play's ambiguities by attaching Orsino's desire to an appropriate and "natural" object. Viola will in the end—that is, when the play is done—put off her assumed male role and become "Orsino's mistress, and his fancy's queen" (5.1.388). But this transformation is not enacted—it remains "high fantastical"—and the only authentic transformation that the Elizabethan audience could anticipate when the play was done was the metamorphosis of Viola back into a boy.

Though Shakespeare characteristically represents his women characters—Rosalind, Portia, Viola—as realizing their identities through cross-dressing, this whole conception of individuation seems to me bound up with Renaissance conceptions of the emergence of male identity. Viola in disguise is said to look like one whose "mother's milk were scarce out of him" (1.5.161–62); in effect a boy is still close to the state of a girl and passes into manhood only when he has put enough distance between himself and his mother's milk. If a crucial step in male individuation is separation from the female, this separation is enacted inversely in the rites of cross-dressing; characters like Rosalind and Viola pass through the state of being men in order to become women. Shakespearean women are in this sense the representation of Shakespearean men, the projected mirror images of masculine self-differentiation.[41]

Why should the comedies traffic in mirror images? Why don't they represent this male trajectory of identity through male characters dressing up as women? In part because women had less freedom of movement, real or imaginary, than men, and hence donning women's clothes would entail not the rolling on which the course of nature depends but rather a stilling of momentum. In part because a passage from male to female was coded ideologically as a descent from superior to inferior and hence as an unnatural act or a social disgrace. And in part because women were, as we have seen, already understood to be inverted mirror images of men in their very genital structure. One consequence of this conceptual scheme—"For that which man hath apparent without, that women have hid within"—is an apparent homoeroticism in all sexuality. Though by divine and human decree the consummation of desire could be licitly figured only in the love of a man and a woman, it did not follow that desire was inherently heterosexual. The delicious confusions of *Twelfth Night* depend upon the mobility of desire. And if poor Antonio is left out in the cold, Orsino does in a sense get his Cesario. I should add as a corollary to this set of exchanges and transformations that men love women precisely *as representations*, a love the original performances of these plays literalized in the person of the boy actor.

For the Renaissance theater there is a further dimension to transvestism, one that returns us for the last time to the case of Marin le Marcis. Within the imaginary women's bodies, there are other bodies—the bodies of the actors playing the parts of Shakespearean women. From the perspective of the medical discourse we have been exploring, this final transvestism serves to secure theatrically the dual account of gender: on the one hand, we have plays that insist upon the chafing between the two sexes and the double nature of individuals; on the other hand, we have a theater that reveals, in the presence of the man's (or boy's) body beneath the woman's clothes, a different sexual reality. The open secret of identity—that within differentiated individuals is a single structure, identifiably male—is presented literally in the all-male cast.[42] Presented but not represented, for the play—plots, characters, and the pleasure they confer—cannot continue without the fictive existence of two distinct genders and the friction between them.

Chapter Four

Shakespeare and the Exorcists

Between the spring of 1585 and the summer of 1586, a group of English Catholic priests led by the Jesuit William Weston, alias Father Edmunds, conducted a series of spectacular exorcisms, principally in the house of a recusant gentleman, Sir George Peckham of Denham, Buckinghamshire. The priests were outlaws—by an act of 1585 the mere presence in England of a Jesuit or seminary priest constituted high treason—and those who sheltered them were guilty of a felony, punishable by death. Yet the exorcisms, though clandestine, drew large crowds, almost certainly in the hundreds, and must have been common knowledge to hundreds more. In 1603, long after the arrest and punishment of those involved, Samuel Harsnett, then chaplain to the bishop of London, wrote a detailed account of the cases, based on sworn statements taken from four of the demoniacs and one of the priests. It has been recognized since the eighteenth century that Shakespeare was reading Harsnett's book, *A Declaration of Egregious Popish Impostures*, as he was writing *King Lear*.[1]

The relation between these two texts enables us to glimpse with unusual clarity and precision the institutional negotiation and exchange of social energy. The link between *King Lear* and *A Declaration of Egregious Popish Impostures* has been known for centuries, but the knowledge has remained almost entirely inert, locked in the conventional pieties of source study. From Harsnett, we are told, Shakespeare borrowed the names of the foul fiends by whom Edgar, in his disguise as the bedlam beggar Poor Tom, claims to be possessed. From Harsnett too the playwright derived some of the language of madness, several of the attributes of hell, and a number of colorful adjectives. These and other possible borrowings have been carefully cataloged, but the question of their significance has been not only unanswered but, until recently, unasked.[2] For a long time the prevailing model for the study of literary sources, a model in effect parceled out between the old historicism and the new criticism, blocked such a question. As a freestanding, self-sufficient, disinterested art work produced by a solitary genius, *King Lear* has only an accidental relation to its sources: they provide a glimpse of the "raw material" that the artist fashioned. Insofar as this "material" is taken seriously at all, it is as part of the work's "historical background," a phrase that reduces history to a decorative setting or a convenient, well-lighted pigeonhole. But once the differentiations on which this model is based begin to crumble, then source study is compelled to change its character: history cannot simply be set against literary texts as either stable antithesis or stable background, and the protective isolation of those texts gives way to a sense of their interaction with other texts and hence of the permeability of their boundaries. "When I play with my cat," writes Montaigne, "who knows if I am not a pastime to her more than she is to me?"[3] When Shakespeare borrows from Harsnett, who knows if Harsnett has not already, in a deep sense, borrowed from Shakespeare's theater what Shakespeare borrows back? Whose interests are served by the borrowing? And is there a larger cultural text produced by the exchange?

Such questions do not lead, for me at least, to the *O altitudo!* of radical indeterminacy. They lead rather to an exploration of the institutional strategies in which both *King Lear* and Harsnett's *Declaration* are embedded. These strategies, I suggest, are part of an intense and sustained struggle in late sixteenth- and early seventeenth-century England to redefine the central values of society. Such a redefinition entailed transforming the prevailing standards of judgment and action, rethinking the conceptual categories by which the ruling elites constructed their world and which they attempted to impose on the majority of the population. At the heart of this struggle, which eventuated in a murderous civil war, was the definition of the sacred, a definition that directly involved secular as well as religious institutions, since the legitimacy of the state rested explicitly on its claim to a measure of sacredness. What is the sacred? Who defines and polices its boundaries? How can society distinguish between legitimate and illegitimate claims to sacred authority? In early modern England rivalry among elites competing for the major share of authority was characteristically expressed not only in parliamentary factions but also in bitter struggles over religious doctrine and practice.

Harsnett's *Declaration* is a weapon in one such struggle, the attempt by the established and state-supported Church of England to eliminate competing religious authorities by wiping out pockets of rivalrous charisma. Charisma, in Edward Shils's phrase, is "awe-arousing centrality,"[4] the sense of breaking through the routine into the realm of the "extraordinary" to make direct contact with the ultimate, vital sources of legitimacy, authority, and sacredness. Exorcism was for centuries one of the supreme manifestations in Latin Christianity of this charisma: "In the healing of the possessed," Peter Brown writes, "the *praesentia* of the saints was held to be registered with unfailing accuracy, and their ideal power, their *potentia*, shown most fully and in the most reassuring manner."[5] Reassuring, that is, not only or even primarily to the demoniac but to the community of believers who bore witness to the ritual and, indeed, through their tears and prayers and thanksgiving, participated in it. For unlike the sorcerer who practiced his art most frequently in the dark corners of the land, in remote rural hamlets and isolated cottages, the charismatic healer depended upon an audience: the great exorcisms of the late Middle Ages and early Renaissance took place at the heart of cities, in churches packed with spectators.

"Great troupes did daily flock thither," writes the Dominican exorcist Sebastian Michaelis about a series of exorcisms he conducted in Aix-en-Provence in the early seventeenth century, and they were, he argues, deeply moved by what they witnessed. Thus, for example, from the body of the young nun Louise, the demon Verrine cried out "with great and ghastly exclamations" that heretics and sinners would be deprived of the vision of God "for ever, for ever, for ever, for ever, for ever." The spectators were so "affrighted" with these words "that there gushed from their eyes abundance of tears, when they called to remembrance their offences which they had committed."[6]

As voluminous contemporary accounts declare, then, exorcisms were moving testimonials to the power of the true faith. But by the late sixteenth century in Protestant England neither the *praesentia* nor the *potentia* of the exorcist was reassuring to religious authorities, and the Anglican church had no desire to treat the urban masses to a spectacle whose edifying value had been called into question. Moving testimonials extorted from the devil himself—praise of the Virgin, awe in the presence of the Eucharist, acknowledgment of the authority of the pope—now seemed both fraudulent and treasonous, and the danger was as great when it came not from a Catholic healer but from a stubbornly nonconforming Protestant. Although the latter did not celebrate the power of the Virgin—when someone tried to invoke Mary's name at a Protestant exorcism, the presiding exorcist sternly rebuked him, "for there is no other name under Heaven, whereby we may challenge Salvation, but th'only name of Jesus Christ"[7]—he exalted the power of fasting and prayer and made it clear that this power did not depend upon a state-sponsored ecclesiastical hierarchy. The authorities could easily close the cathedrals to such sedition, but even relatively small assemblies in obscure private houses far from the cities had come to represent a threat.

In the *Declaration* Harsnett specifically attacks exorcism as practiced by Jesuits, but he had earlier leveled the same charges at a Puritan exorcist. And he does so not, as we might expect, to claim a monopoly on the practice for the Anglican church but to expose exorcism itself as a fraud. On behalf of established religious and secular authority, Harsnett wishes to cap permanently the great rushing geysers of charisma released in rituals of exorcism. Spiritual *potentia* will henceforth be distributed with greater moderation and control through the whole of the Anglican hierarchy, at whose pinnacle sits the sole legitimate possessor of absolute charismatic authority, the monarch, Supreme Head of the Church in England.

The arguments that Harsnett marshals against exorcism have a rationalistic cast that may mislead us, for despite appearances we are not dealing with the proto–Enlightenment attempt to construct a rational faith. Harsnett denies the presence of the demonic in those whom Father Edmunds claimed to exorcise but finds it in the exorcists themselves: "And who was the devil, the broacher, herald, and persuader of these unutterable treasons, but *Weston* [alias

Edmunds] the Jesuit, the chief plotter, and . . . all the holy Covey of the twelve devilish comedians in their several turns: for there was neither devil, nor urchin, nor Elf, but themselves" (154–55). Hence, writes Harsnett, the "Dialogue between *Edmunds*, & the devil" was in reality a dialogue between "the devil *Edmunds*, and *Edmunds* the devil, for he played both parts himself" (86).

This strategy—the reinscription of evil onto the professed enemies of evil—is one of the characteristic operations of religious authority in the early modern period and has its secular analogues in more recent history when famous revolutionaries are paraded forth to be tried as counter-revolutionaries. The paradigmatic Renaissance instance is the case of the *benandanti*, analyzed brilliantly by the historian Carlo Ginzburg.[8] The *benandanti* were members of a northern Italian folk cult who believed that they went forth seasonally to battle with fennel stalks against their enemies, the witches. If the *benandanti* triumphed, their victory assured the peasants of good harvests; if they lost, the witches would be free to work their mischief. The Inquisition first became interested in the practice in the late sixteenth century; after conducting a series of lengthy inquiries, the Holy Office determined that the cult was demonic and in subsequent interrogations attempted, with some success, to persuade the witch-fighting *benandanti* that they were themselves witches.

Harsnett does not hope to persuade exorcists that they are devils; he wishes to expose their fraudulence and relies on the state to punish them. But he is not willing to abandon the demonic altogether, and it hovers in his work, half accusation, half metaphor, whenever he refers to Father Edmunds or the pope. Satan's function was too important for him to be cast off lightly by the early seventeenth-century clerical establishment. The same state church that sponsored the attacks on superstition in *A Declaration of Egregious Popish Impostures* continued to cooperate, if less enthusiastically than before, in the ferocious prosecutions of witches. These prosecutions, significantly, were handled by the secular judicial apparatus—witchcraft was a criminal offense like aggravated assault or murder—and hence reinforced rather than rivaled the bureaucratic control of authority. The eruption of the demonic into the human world was not denied altogether, but the problem would be processed through the proper secular channels. In cases of witchcraft, the devil was defeated in the courts through the simple expedient of hanging his human agents, not, as in cases of possession, compelled by a spectacular spiritual counterforce to speak out and depart.

Witchcraft then was distinct from possession, and though Harsnett himself is skeptical about accusations of witchcraft, his principal purpose is to expose a nexus of chicanery and delusion in the practice of exorcism.[9] By doing so he hopes to drive the practice out of society's central zone, to deprive it of its prestige, and to discredit its apparent efficacy.[10] In late antiquity, as Peter Brown has demonstrated, exorcism was based on the model of the Roman judicial system: the exorcist conducted a formal *quaestio* in which the demon, under torture, was forced to confess the truth.[11] Now, after more than a millennium, this power would once again be vested solely in the state.

Harsnett's efforts, backed by his powerful superiors, did seriously restrict the practice of exorcism. Canon 72 of the new Church Canons of 1604 ruled that henceforth no minister, unless he had the special permission of his bishop, was to attempt "upon any pretense whatsoever, whether of possession or obsession, by fasting and prayer, to cast out any devil or devils, under pain of the imputation of imposture or cozenage and deposition from the ministry."[12] Since special permission was rarely, if ever, granted, in effect exorcism had been officially halted. But it proved easier to drive exorcism from the center to the periphery than to strip it entirely of its power. Exorcism had been a process of reintegration as well as a manifestation of authority; as the ethnographer Shirokogorov observed of the shamans of Siberia, exorcists could "master" harmful spirits and restore "psychic equilibrium" to whole communities as well as to individuals.[13] The pronouncements of English bishops could not suddenly banish from the land inner demons who stood, as Peter Brown puts it, "for the intangible emotional undertones of ambiguous situations and for the uncertain motives of refractory individuals."[14] The possessed gave voice to the rage, anxiety, and sexual frustration that built up easily in the authoritarian, patriarchal, impoverished, and plague-ridden world of early modern England. The Anglicans attempted to dismantle a corrupt and inadequate therapy without effecting a new and successful cure. In the absence of exorcism Harsnett could offer the possessed only the slender reed of Jacobean medicine; if the recently deciphered journal of the Buckinghamshire physician Richard Napier is at all representative, doctors in the period struggled to treat a significant number of cases of possession.[15]

But for Harsnett the problem does not really exist, for he argues that the great majority of cases of possession are either fraudulent or subtly called into existence by the ritual designed to treat them. Eliminate the cure and you eliminate the disease. He is forced to concede that at some distant time possession and exorcism were authentic, for Christ himself had driven a legion of unclean spirits out of a possessed man and into the Gadarene swine (Mark 5:1–19); but the age of miracles has passed, and corporeal possession by demons is no longer possible. The spirit abroad is "the spirit of illusion" (*Discovery*, p. A3). Whether they profess to be Catholics or Calvinists does not matter; all modern exorcists practice the same time-honored trade: "the feat of juggling and deluding the people by counterfeit miracles" (*Discovery*, p. A2). Exorcists sometimes contend, Harsnett acknowledges, that the casting out of devils is not a miracle but a wonder—"*mirandum & non miraculum*"—but "both terms spring from one root of wonder or marvel: an effect which a thing strangely done doth procure in the minds of the beholders, as being above the reach of nature and reason" (*Discovery*, p. A4[r–v]).

The significance of exorcism, then, lies not in any intrinsic quality of the ritual or in the character of the marks of possession but in the impression made upon the minds of the spectators. In *The Discovery of Witchcraft* (1584), a remarkable book that greatly influenced Harsnett, Reginald Scot detailed some of the means used to shape this impression: the cunning manipulation of popular superstitions; the exploitation of grief, fear, and credulity; the skillful handling of illusionistic devices developed for the stage; the blending of spectacle and commentary; the deliberate arousal of anxiety coupled with the promise to allay it. Puritan exorcists throw themselves into histrionic paroxysms of prayer; Catholic exorcists deploy holy water, smoldering brimstone, and sacred relics. They seem utterly absorbed in the plight of the wretches who writhe in spectacular contortions, vomit pins, display uncanny strength, foam at the mouth, cry out in weird voices. But all of this apparent absorption in the supernatural crisis is an illusion; there is nothing real out there on the bed, in the chair, on the pulpit. The only serious action is transpiring in the minds of the audience.

Hence the exorcists take care, notes Harsnett, to practice their craft only when there is "a great assembly gathered together," and the ritual is then explicitly presented to this assembly with a formal prologue: "The company met, the *Exorcists* do tell them, *what a work of God they have in hand*, and after a long discourse, *how Sathan doth afflict the parties*, and *what strange things they shall see:* the said parties are brought forth, as it were a Bear to the stake, and being either bound in a chair, or otherwise held fast, they fall to their fits, and play their pranks point by point exactly, according as they have been instructed" (*Discovery*, p. 62).

What seems spontaneous is in fact carefully scripted, from the shaping of audience expectations to the rehearsal of the performers. Harsnett grants that to those who suspect no fraud the effect is extraordinarily powerful: "They are cast thereby into a wonderful astonishment" (*Discovery*, p. 70). Aroused by wonder to a heightened state of both attention and suggestibility, the beholders are led to see significance in the smallest gestures of the possessed and to apply that significance to their own lives. But the whole moving process is a dangerous fraud that should be exposed and punished in the courts.

To substantiate these charges the English church needed, in the language of spy stories, to "turn" one of the participants in the spectacle of possession and exorcism. In the mid-1590s the authorities were alerted to the activities of a charismatic Puritan healer named John Darrel. Through fasting and prayer he had helped to exorcise one Thomas Darling, popularly known as the Boy of Burton, and had then gone on to a still greater success in a case of mass possession, known as the Seven in Lancashire. Alarmed by this success, the authorities in 1598 found what they were looking for: William Sommers, aged twenty-one, an unstable musician's apprentice in Nottingham who was being exorcized by Darrel in a series of spectacular spiritual encounters. Under great pressure Sommers confessed to imposture and exposed—or claimed to expose—Darrel's secret methods: "As I did use any of the said gestures," testified Sommers, recalling his first manifestation in Nottingham of the symptoms of possession,

Oh would M. Darrell say, to the standers by: see you not how he doth thus, and thus? These things signify that such and such sins do reign in this town. They also that were present having heard M. Darrell, would as I tossed with my hands, and tumbled up and down upon my bed presently collect and say: oh, he doth so for this sin, and so for that sin, whereby it came to pass, that I could do nothing in any of my fits, either that night or the day after, either stir my head, or any part of my body: look merrily, or sadly, sit or lie, speak or be silent, open or shut mine eyes, but some would still make an interpretation of it: as to be done by the Devil in me, to declare such sins in Nottingham, as they themselves imagined. (*Discovery*, p. 117)

Darrel denied ever offering an interpretation of Sommers's gestures, but he confirmed the nature of the performance:

This evening, he acted many sins by signs & gestures, most lively representing & shadowing, them out unto us: as namely brawling, quarreling, fighting, swearing, robbing by the highways, picking and cutting of purses, burglary, whoredom, pride in men and women, hypocrisy, sluggishness in hearing of the word, drunkenness, gluttony, also dancing with the toys thereunto belonging, the manner of Antic dancers, the games of dicing and carding, the abuse of the Viol, with other instruments. At the end of sundry of these, he laughed exceedingly, diverse times clapping his hands on his thighs for joy: percase to shadow out the delight, that both himself, and sinners take in their sins. And at the end of some of them, as killing and stealing, he showed how he brought them to the Gallows, making a sign thereof. (*Discovery*, pp. 118–19)

According to Harsnett, on the Sunday following this display one of Darrel's colleagues delivered from the pulpit an "authentical reading" of the "dumb show," and this reading was in turn followed by a popular ballad: a campaign, in short, to extend the exorcist's influence beyond the immediate circle of beholders to both the elite and the masses. Harsnett, in response, participates in a massive counter-campaign to destroy this influence. Hounding or imprisoning Darrel was not enough, for persecution could easily heighten his popular appeal, and even were he conveniently to disappear, he would be succeeded by others. The exorcist had to be attacked where he had his power: in the minds of beholders or potential beholders.

Accounts of exorcism in the late sixteenth and early seventeenth centuries make it clear that the spectacle of the symptoms of demonic possession had a profoundly disturbing effect on those who witnessed them. The spectacle was evidently more than that of physical or psychic anguish; after all, the men and women of this period would have been accustomed and perhaps hardened to the sight of abject misery. Quite apart from the spectacle of public maimings and executions, an Elizabethan who survived to adolescence must have already been an aficionado of human wretchedness.

Demonic possession was something more: it was utterly strange—a fearful visitation of the perverted spiritual presences of the other world—and at the same time uncannily intimate, for if the demons were exotic tormenters with weird names, the victims were neighbors enduring their trials in altogether familiar surroundings. Hence the testimony taken from those who witnessed the sufferings combines the homely and the bizarre: an evil spirit that appeared in Suffolk became "a thick dark substance about a foot high, like to a sugar loaf, white on the top";[16] young Mary Glover's voice sounded to one witness like "the hissing of a violent *Squib*," to another like a *"Hen* that hath the *squack*," to a third like "the loathsome noise that a *Cat* maketh forcing to cast her gorge";[17] William Sommers's "entrails shot up & down like a weavers shuttle."[18] Sommers's cries seemed unutterably strange—he shrieked "with 3 several voices so hideously, and so terribly," a surgeon reports, "as they were not like any human creature"—but each of the witnesses seems to have tried immediately to place the extraordinary events in the context of the familiar. William Aldred, a preacher, reports that he stood in a crowd of about one hundred fifty persons and watched Sommers having his fits. What he noticed was Darrel praying and preaching; "then the whole congregation breaking their hitherto continued silence cried out all at once as it were with one voice unto the Lord, to relieve the distressed person: and within a quarter of an hour, or thereabouts it pleased God to hear their prayers." Joan Pie, the wife of Nottingham baker Robert Pie, also saw the fits; what she noticed was that suddenly Sommers "was plucked round upon a heap, as though his body had lain like a great brown loaf." Richard Mee, butcher, remarked that Sommers suddenly screeched "like a swine when he is in sticking."[19]

The domestication of the demonic (a zany Elizabethan version of *What Do People Do All Day?*) only serves to intensify for most of the witnesses the wonder of the supernatural visitation. Harsnett's task is to demolish this experience of wonder; he seeks to shine the sharp, clear light of ridicule on the exorcist's mysteries and thus to expose them as shabby tricks. Among the demoniac's most frightening symptoms was a running lump—variously described as resembling a kitten, a mouse, a halfpenny white loaf, a goose egg, a French walnut, and a hazelnut—that could be seen under the coverlet, moving across his body as he lay in a trance. One of the bystanders, apparently less awestruck than the rest, impulsively pounced on the lump and found that he had seized Sommers's hand. In his confession Sommers confirmed that he achieved his effect by no more complicated means than moving his fingers and toes under the coverlet. It seems impossible for this miserable expedient to produce so much as a frisson, but a skeptical witness, quoted by Harsnett, tried it out at home: "And it fell out to be so agreeable with that which the boy did, as my wife being in bed with me, was on the sudden in great fear, that *Somers* spirit had followed me" (*Discovery*, p. 240).

Held up to the light, the devil's coin is a pathetic counterfeit, fit only to frighten women and boys. Yet Harsnett is not content simply to publish Sommers's confession of fraud, in part, perhaps, because there was reason to believe that the confession was forced, in part because even if Sommers were proven to be a mere actor, other demoniacs clearly believed in all sincerity that they were possessed by devils. Moreover, the polemic had to be conducted with an odd blend of rhetorical violence and doctrinal caution. "If neither possession, nor witchcraft (contrary to that hath been so long generally & confidently affirmed)," wrote Darrel in his own defense, "why should we think that there are Devils? If no Devils, no God."[20]

No one in the Anglican church was prepared to deny the existence of Satan, any more than they were prepared to deny the existence of God. What role did Satan play then in the fraudulent dramas in which his name figured so prominently? In the case of Catholic exorcists, Harsnett is prepared to locate the demonic in the very figures who profess themselves to be the agents of God:

Dissemblers, jugglers, impostors, players with God, his son, his angels, his saints: devisers of new devils, feigned tormentors of spirits, usurpers of the key of the bottomless pit, whippers, scourgers, batfoulers of fiends, Pandars, Ganimedeans, enhancers of lust, deflowerers of virgins, defilers of houses, uncivil, unmanly, unnatural venereans, offerers of their own mass to supposed devils, depravers of their own relics, applying them to unspeakable, detestable, monstrous deformities: prostituters of all the rites, ornaments, and ceremonies of their Church to impure villainies: profaners of all parts of the service, worship, and honour of God: violators of tombs, sacrilegious, blasphemers of God, the blessed Trinity, and the virgin *Mary*, in the person of a counterfeit devil: seducers of subjects, plotters, conspirators, contrivers of bloody & detestable treasons, against their anointed Sovereign: it would pose all hell to sample them with such another dozen. (*Declaration*, pp. 160–61)

In short, they were Jesuits. But Darrel was a Protestant and, by all accounts, a man of austere and upright life. If he could not be portrayed as the devil incarnate, where was the devil to be found? One answer, proposed by Harsnett's allies John Deacon and John Walker, was that Satan could produce the *illusion* of demonic possession. "The *Devil* (being always desirous to work among the dear children of *God* the greatest *disturbance* that may be, and finding withal some such lewd disposed *person* as is naturally inclined to all manner of *knaveries*) he taketh the opportunity of so fit a *subject*, and worketh so cunningly upon the *corruption* of *that lewd persons nature*, as the *party* himself is easily brought to believe, and to bear others also in hand, that he is (in deed and in truth) *essentially possessed of Satan*."[21]

The problem with this argument is that it undermines the clarity and force of the confession of fraudulence the authorities had worked so hard to obtain. That confession was intended to establish a fixed, stable opposition between counterfeit—the false claim of demonic agency—and reality: the unblinking, disenchanted grasp of the mechanics of illusion mongering. Now after all the devil is discovered hovering behind the demoniac's performance. And if the Prince of Darkness is actually present, then the alleged evidence of fraudulence need not trouble the exorcist. For as Satan in possessing someone has sought to hide himself under the cover of human agency, so when detected he may wish to convince observers that the signs of possession are counterfeits. "Sathan in his subtlety," argued Darrel, "hath done in the boy some sleight and trifling things, at divers times, of purpose to deceive the beholders, and to bear them in hand, that he did never greater things in him: thereby to induce them to think, that he was a counterfeit" (*Discovery*, p. 231).[22]

If Satan can counterfeit counterfeiting, there can be no definitive confession, and the prospect opens of an infinite regress of disclosure and uncertainty. "How shall I know that this is thou *William Somers?*" asked Darrel, after the boy confessed to fraud. At first Sommers had been possessed only in body; now, said the exorcist, he is "also possessed in soul" (*Discovery*, p. 186). As Harsnett perceives, this "circular folly" at the heart of the practice of exorcism prevents a decisive judicial falsification. What Harsnett needs is not further evidence of fraud in particular cases—for such evidence can always be subverted by the same strategy of demonic doubt—but a counter-strategy to disclose fraudulence *always and everywhere:* in every gesture of the demoniac, in every word and deed of the exorcist. To demystify exorcism definitively, Harsnett must demonstrate not only why the ritual was so empty but why it was so effective, why beholders could be induced to believe that they were witnessing the ultimate confrontation between good and evil, why a few miserable shifts could produce the experience of horror and wonder. He must identify not merely the specific institutional motives behind exorcism—the treasonous designs of the Catholic church or the seditious mischief of self-styled Protestant saints—but the source of the extraordinary power in exorcism itself, a power that seems to transcend the specific and contradictory ideological designs of its practitioners. He needs an explanatory model, at once metaphor and analytical tool, by which all beholders will see fraud where once they saw God. Harsnett finds that explanatory model in *theater*.[23]

Exorcisms, Harsnett argues, are stage plays, most often tragicomedies, that cunningly conceal their theatrical inauthenticity and hence deprive the spectators of the rational disenchantment that frames the experience of a play. The audience in a theater knows that its misrecognition of reality is temporary, deliberate, and playful; the exorcist seeks to make the misrecognition permanent and invisible. Harsnett is determined to make the spectators see the theater around them, to make them understand that what seems spontaneous is rehearsed, what seems involuntary carefully crafted, what seems unpredictable scripted.

Not all of the participants themselves may fully realize that they are in a stage play. The account in *A Declaration of Egregious Popish Impostures* presents the exorcists, Father Edmunds and his cohorts, as self-conscious professionals and the demoniacs (mostly impressionable young servingwomen and unstable, down-at-heels young gentlemen) as amateurs subtly drawn into the demonic stage business. Those selected to play the possessed in effect learn their roles without realizing at first that they are roles.

The priests begin by talking conspicuously about successful exorcisms abroad and describing in lurid detail the precise symptoms of the possessed. They then await occasions on which to improvise: a servingman "being pinched with penury, & hunger, did lie but a night, or two, abroad in the fields, and being a melancholic person, was scared with lightning, and thunder, that happened in the night, & lo, an evident sign, that the man was possessed" (24); a dissolute young gentleman "had a spice of the *Hysterica passio*" or, as it is popularly called, "the Mother" (25),[24] and that too is a sign of possession. An inflamed toe, a pain in the side, a fright taken from the sudden leaping of a cat, a fall in the kitchen, an intense depression following the loss of a beloved child—all are occasions for the priests to step forward and detect the awful presence of the demonic, whereupon the young "scholars," as Harsnett wryly terms the naive performers, "*frame* themselves jump and fit unto the Priests humors, to mop, mow, jest, rail, rave, roar, commend & discommend, and as the priests would have them, upon fitting occasions (according to the difference of times, places, and comers in) in all things to play the devils accordingly" (38).

To glimpse the designing clerical playwright behind the performance is to transform terrifying supernatural events into a human strategy. One may then glimpse the specific material and symbolic interests served by this particular strategy, above all by its clever disguising of the fact that it is a strategy.

The most obvious means by which the authorities of the English church and state could make manifest the theatricality of exorcism was the command performance: the ability to mime the symptoms at will would, it was argued, decisively prove the possession a counterfeit. Hence we find the performance test frequently applied in investigations of alleged supernatural visitations. In the 1590s, for example, Ann Kerke was accused of bewitching a child to death and casting the child's sister into a fit that closely resembled that of a demoniac: "her mouth being drawn aside like a purse, her teeth gnashing together, her mouth foaming, and her eyes staring."[25]

The judge, Lord Anderson, ordered the sister to "show how she was tormented: she said she could not shew it, but when the fit was on her" (100). The reply was taken to be strong corroboration of the authenticity of the charge, and Anne Kerke was hanged.

A similar, if subtler, use of the performance test occurs in the early 1620s. Thomas Perry, known as the Boy of Bilson, would fall into fits upon hearing the opening verse from the gospel of John; other verses from Scriptures did not have the same effect. Three Catholic priests were called in to exorcise the evil spirit that possessed him. During the boy's fit—watched by a large crowd—one of the priests commanded the devil "to show by the sheet before him, how he would use one dying out of the Roman Catholic Church? who very unwillingly, yet at length obeyed, tossing, plucking, haling, and biting the sheet, that it did make many to weep and cry forth."[26] A similar but still fiercer demonstration was evoked in response to the names Luther, Calvin, and Fox. Then, predictably, the priest commanded the devil "to show what power he had on a good Catholic that died out of mortal sin? he thrust down his arms, trembled, holding down his head, and did no more" (51).[27] The Catholics triumphantly published an account of the case, *A Faithful Relation*.

English officials, understandably annoyed by such propaganda, remanded Perry to the custody of the bishop of Coventry and Lichfield. To test if the boy was authentically possessed or "an execrable wretch, who playest the devils part," the Bishop read aloud the verse that set off the symptoms; the boy fell into fits. When the boy recovered, the bishop told him that he would read the same verse in Greek; once again the boy fell into fits. But in fact the Bishop had not read the correct verse, and the boy had been tricked into performance. Since the Devil was "so ancient a scholar as of almost 6000 years standing" (59), he should have known Greek. The possession was proved to be a counterfeit, and the boy, it is said, confessed that he had been instructed by an old man who promised that he would no longer have to go to school.

The Protestants now produced their own account of the case, *The Boy of Bilson; or, A True Discovery of the Late Notorious Impostures of Certain Romish Priests in Their Pretended Exorcism.* "Although these and the like pranks have been often hissed of[f] the Stage, for stale and gross forgeries," the author declares, since the Catholics have ventured to publish their version, it is necessary to set the record straight. A reader of the Catholic account should understand "that he hath seen a *Comedy*, wherein the Actors, which present themselves, are these, A crafty *old man*, teaching the feats and pranks of counterfeiting a person *Demoniacal* and possessed of the *Devil*; the next, a most docible, subtle, and expert young *Boy*, far more dextrous in the Practique part, than his Master was in the Theory; after him appear three Romish *Priests*, the Authors of seducement, conjuring their only imaginary *Devils*, which they brought with them; and lastly, a *Chorus* of credulous people easily seduced, not so much by the subtlety of those *Priests*, as by their own sottishness" (9).

Performance kills belief; or rather acknowledging theatricality kills the credibility of the supernatural. Hence in the case of William Sommers the authorities not only took the demoniac's confession of fraud but also insisted that he perform his simulated convulsions before the mayor and three aldermen of Nottingham. If he could act his symptoms, then the possession would be decisively falsified. Darrel countered that "if he can act them all in such manner and form as is deposed, then he is, either still possessed, or more than a man: for no humans power can do the like."[28] But the officials denied that the original performances themselves, stripped of the awe that the spectators brought to them, were particularly impressive. Sommers's possession, Harsnett had said, was a "dumb show" that depended upon an interpretive supplement, a commentary designed at once to intensify and control the response of the audience by explicating both the significance and the relevance of each gesture. Now the state would in effect seize control of the commentary and thereby alter the spectators' perceptions. Sommers's audience would no longer see a demoniac; they would see someone playing a demoniac. Demonic possession would become theater.

After the civic officials had satisfied themselves that Sommers's possession was a theatrical imposture, an ecclesiastical commission was convened to view a repeat performance. In a bizarre twist, however, Sommers unexpectedly withdrew his confession before the startled commissioners, and he signaled this withdrawal by falling into spectacular fits before the moment appointed for the performance. The commissioners, unprepared to view these convulsions as a deliberate or self-conscious exhibition, declared that they were evidently of supernatural origin. But in less than two weeks, before the mayor and two justices, the wretched Sommers, under renewed state pressure, reaffirmed his confession of fraud, and a few days later he once again "proved" his claim by simulating fits, this time before the assize judge. The next step might have been to ask a court of law to determine whether Sommers's expressly simulated fits were identical to those he underwent when he was not confessing imposture. But the authorities evidently regarded this step, which Darrel himself demanded,[29] as too risky; instead, without calling Sommers to appear, they first obtained a conviction of the exorcist on charges of imposture and then launched a national campaign to persuade the public that possession and exorcism were illicit forms of theater.

Sommers's oscillation between the poles of authenticity and illusion are for Harsnett an emblem of the maddening doubleness implicit in the theatricality of exorcism: its power to impose itself on beholders and its half-terrifying, half-comic emptiness. Exorcists could, of course, react by demonizing the theater: Puritans like Darrel argued at length that the playhouse was Satan's temple, while the Jesuit exorcists operating clandestinely in England implied that theatrical representations of the devil in mystery plays were not mere imitations of reality but lively images based on a deep bond of resemblance. When in the 1580s a devil possessing Sara Williams refused to tell his name, the exorcist, according to the Catholic *Book of Miracles*, "caused to be drawn upon a piece of paper, the picture of a vice in a play, and the same to be burned with hallowed brimstone, whereat the devil cried out as being grievously tormented."[30] Harsnett remarks in response that "it was a pretty part in the old Church-plays, when the nimble Vice would skip up nimbly like Jacke an Apes into the devils neck, and ride the devil a course, and belabour him with his wooden dagger, til he made him roar, whereat the people would laugh to see the devil so vice-haunted" (114–15). Sara's devils, he concludes contemptuously, "be surely some of those old vice-haunted cashiered wooden-beaten devils, that were wont to frequent the stages . . . who are so scared with the *Idea* of a vice, & a dagger, as they durst never since look a paper-vice in the face" (115). For Harsnett the attempt to demonize the theater merely exposes the theatricality of the demonic; once we acknowledge this theatricality, he suggests, we can correctly perceive the actual genre of the performance: not tragedy but farce.

The theatricality of exorcism, to which the *Declaration* insistently calls attention, has been noted repeatedly by modern ethnographers who do not share Harsnett's reforming zeal or his sense of outrage.[31] In an illuminating study of possession among the Ethiopians of Gondar, Michel Leiris notes that the healer carefully instructs the *zâr*, or spirit, who has seized on someone how to behave: the types of cries appropriate to the occasion, the expected violent contortions, the "decorum," as Harsnett would put it, of the trance state.[32] The treatment is in effect an initiation into the performance of the symptoms, which are then cured precisely because they conform to the stereotype of the healing process. One must not conclude, writes Leiris, that there are no "real"—that is, sincerely experienced—cases of possession, for many of the patients (principally young women and slaves) seem genuinely ill, but at the same time no cases are exempt from artifice (27–28). Between authentic possession, spontaneous and involuntary, and inauthentic possession, simulated to provide a show or to extract some material or moral benefit, there are so many subtle shadings that it is impossible to draw a firm boundary (94–95). Possession in Gondar *is* theater, but theater that cannot confess its own theatrical nature, for this is not "theater played" (*théâtre joué*) but "theater lived" (*théâtre vécu*), lived not only by the spirit-haunted actor but by the audience. Those who witness a possession may at any moment be themselves possessed, and even if they are untouched by the *zâr*, they remain participants rather than passive spectators. For the theatrical performance is not shielded from them by an impermeable membrane; possession is extraordinary but not marginal, a heightened but not separate state. In possession, writes Leiris, the collective life itself takes the form of theater (96).

Precisely those qualities that fascinate and charm the ethnographer disgust the embattled clergyman: where Leiris can write of "authentic" possession in the unspoken assurance that none of his readers actually believe in the existence of "zârs," Harsnett, granted no such assurance and culturally threatened by the alternative vision of reality, struggles to prove that possession is by definition inauthentic; where the former sees a complex ritual integrated into the social process, the latter sees "a *Stygian* comedy to make silly people afraid" (69); where the former sees the theatrical expression of collective life, the latter sees the theatrical promotion of specific and malevolent institutional interests. And where Leiris's central point is that possession is a theater that does not confess its own theatricality, Harsnett's concern is to enforce precisely such a confession: the last 112 pages of *A Declaration of Egregious Popish Impostures* reprint the "several Examinations, and confessions of the parties pretended to be possessed, and dispossessed by *Weston* the Jesuit, and his adherents: set down word for word as they were taken upon oath before her Majesty's Commissioners for causes Ecclesiastical" (172). These transcripts prove, according to Harsnett, that the solemn ceremony of exorcism is a "play of sacred miracles," a "wonderful pageant" (2), a "devil Theater" (106).

The confession of theatricality, for Harsnett, demolishes exorcism. Theater is not the disinterested expression of the popular spirit but the indelible mark of falsity, tawdriness, and rhetorical manipulation. And these sinister qualities are rendered diabolical by the very concealment of theatricality that so appeals to Leiris. The spectators do not know that they are responding to a powerful, if sleazy, tragicomedy; their tears and joy, their transports of "commiseration and compassion" (74), are rendered up not to a troupe of acknowledged players but to seditious Puritans or to the supremely dangerous Catholic church. For Harsnett the theatrical seduction is not merely a Jesuitical strategy; it is the essence of the church itself: Catholicism is a "Mimic superstition" (20).[33]

Harsnett's response is to try to drive the Catholic church into the theater, just as during the Reformation Catholic clerical garments—the copes and albs and amices and stoles that were the glories of medieval textile crafts—were sold to the players. An actor in a history play taking the part of an English bishop could conceivably have worn the actual robes of the character he was representing. Far more than thrift is involved here. The transmigration of a single ecclesiastical cloak from the vestry to the wardrobe may stand as an emblem of the more complex and elusive institutional exchanges that are my subject: a sacred sign, designed to be displayed before a crowd of men and women, is emptied, made negotiable, traded from one institution to another. Such exchanges are rarely so tangible; they are not usually registered in inventories, not often sealed with a cash payment. Nonetheless they occur constantly, for through institutional negotiation and exchange differentiated expressive systems, distinct cultural discourses, are fashioned.

What happens when the piece of cloth is passed from the church to the playhouse? A consecrated object is reclassified, assigned a cash value, transferred from a sacred to a profane setting, deemed suitable for the stage. The theater company is willing to pay for the object not because it contributes to naturalistic representation but because it still bears a symbolic value, however attenuated. On the bare Elizabethan stage costumes were particularly important—companies were willing to pay more for a good costume than for a good play—and that importance in turn reflected the culture's fetishistic obsession with clothes as a mark of status and degree. And if for the theater the acquisition of clerical garments was a significant appropriation of symbolic power, why would the church part with that power? Because for the Anglican polemicists, as for a long tradition of moralists in the West, the theater signifies the unscrupulous manipulation for profit of popular faith; the cynical use of setting and props to generate unthinking consent; the external and trivialized staging of what should be deeply inward; the tawdry triumph of spectacle over reason; the evacuation of the divine presence from religious mystery, leaving only vivid but empty ceremonies; the transformation of faith into bad faith.[34] Hence selling Catholic vestments to the players was a form of symbolic aggression: a vivid, wry reminder that Catholicism, as Harsnett puts it, is "the Pope's playhouse."[35]

This blend of appropriation and aggression is similarly at work in the transfer of possession and exorcism from sacred to profane representation. *A Declaration of Egregious Popish Impostures* takes pains to identify exorcism not merely with "the theatrical"—a category that scarcely exists for Harsnett—but with the actual theater; at issue is not so much a metaphorical concept as a functioning institution. For if Harsnett can drive exorcism into the theater—if he can show that the stately houses in which the rituals were performed were playhouses, that the sacred garments were what he calls a "lousy holy wardrobe" (78), that the terrifying writhings were simulations, that the uncanny signs and wonders were contemptible stage tricks, that the devils were the "cashiered wooden-beaten" Vices from medieval drama (115), and that the exorcists were "vagabond players, that coast from Town to Town" (149)—then the ceremony and everything for which it stands will, as far as he is concerned, be emptied out. And with this emptying out Harsnett will have driven exorcism from the center to the periphery—in the case of London quite literally to the periphery, where increasingly stringent urban regulation had already driven the public playhouses.

In this symbolically charged zone of pollution, disease, and licentious entertainment Harsnett seeks to situate the practice of exorcism.[36] What had once occurred in solemn glory at the very center of the city would now be staged alongside the culture's other vulgar spectacles and illusions. Indeed the sense of the theater's tawdriness, marginality, and emptiness—the sense that everything the players touch is rendered hollow—underlies Harsnett's analysis not only of exorcism but of the entire Catholic church. Demonic possession is a particularly attractive cornerstone for such an analysis, not only because of its histrionic intensity but because the theater itself is by its nature bound up with possession. Harsnett did not have to believe that the cult of Dionysus out of which the Greek drama evolved was a cult of possession; even the ordinary and familiar theater of his own time depended upon the apparent transformation of the actor into the voice, the actions, and the face of another.

ii

With his characteristic opportunism and artistic self-consciousness, Shakespeare in his first known play, *The Comedy of Errors* (1590), was already toying with the connection between theater, illusion, and spurious possession. Antipholus of Syracuse, accosted by his twin's mistress, imagines that he is encountering the devil: "Sathan, avoid. I charge thee tempt me not" (4.3.48). The Ephesian Antipholus's wife, Adriana, dismayed by the apparently mad behavior of her husband, imagines that the devil has possessed him, and she dutifully calls in an exorcist: "Good Doctor Pinch, you are a conjurer, / Establish him in his true sense again." Pinch begins the solemn ritual:

> I charge thee, Sathan, hous'd within this man,
> To yield possession to my holy prayers,
> And to thy state of darkness hie thee straight:
> I conjure thee by all the saints in heaven!
>
> (4.4.54–57)

But he is interrupted with a box on the ears from the outraged husband: "Peace, doting wizard, peace! I am not mad." For the exorcist, such denials only confirm the presence of an evil spirit: "the fiend is strong within him" (4.4.107). At the scene's end, Antipholus is dragged away to be "bound and laid in some dark room."

The false presumption of demonic possession in *The Comedy of Errors* is not the result of deception; it is an instance of what Shakespeare's source calls a "suppose"—an attempt to make sense of a series of bizarre actions gleefully generated by the comedy's screwball coincidences. Exorcism is the straw people clutch at when the world seems to have gone mad. In *Twelfth Night*, written some ten years later, Shakespeare's view of exorcism, though still comic, has darkened. Possession now is not a mistaken "suppose" but a fraud, a malicious practical joke played on Malvolio. "Pray God he be not bewitch'd!" (3.4.101) Maria piously exclaims at the sight of the cross-gartered, leering gull, and when he is out of earshot, Fabian laughs: "If this were play'd upon a stage now, I could condemn it as an improbable fiction" (3.4.127–28).[37] The theatrical self-consciousness is intensified when Feste the clown is brought in to conduct a mock exorcism: "I would I were the first that ever dissembled in such a gown" (4.2.5–6), he remarks sententiously as he disguises himself as Sir Topas the curate. If the jibe had a specific reference for the play's original audience, it would be to the Puritan Darrel, who had only recently been convicted of dissembling in the exorcism of Sommers. Now, the scene would suggest, the tables are being turned on the self-righteous fanatic. "Good Sir Topas," pleads Malvolio, "do not think I am mad; they have laid me here in hideous darkness." "Fie, thou dishonest Sathan!" Feste replies; "I call thee by the most modest terms, for I am one of those gentle ones that will use the devil himself with courtesy" (4.2.29–33).

By 1600, then, Shakespeare had clearly marked out possession and exorcism as frauds, so much so that in *All's Well That Ends Well* a few years later he could casually use the term *exorcist* as a synonym for illusion monger: "Is there no exorcist / Beguiles the truer office of mine eyes?" cries the King of France when Helena, whom he thought dead, appears before him; "Is't real that I see?" (5.3.304–6). When in 1603 Harsnett was whipping exorcism toward the theater, Shakespeare was already at the entrance to the Globe to welcome it.

Given Harsnett's frequent expressions of the "antitheatrical prejudice," this welcome may seem strange, but in fact nothing in *A
Declaration of Egregious Popish Impostures* necessarily implies hostility
to the theater as a professional institution. It was Darrel, not
Harsnett, who represented an implacable threat to the theater, for
where the Anglican polemicist saw the theatrical in the demonic, the
Puritan polemicist saw the demonic in the theatrical: "The Devil,"
wrote Stephen Gosson, "is the efficient cause of plays."[38] Harsnett's
work attacks a form of theater that pretends it is not entertainment
but sober reality; his polemic virtually depends upon the existence
of an officially designated commercial theater, marked off openly
from all other forms and ceremonies of public life precisely by virtue
of its freely acknowledged fictionality. Where there is no pretense to
truth, there can be no *imposture:* this argument permits so ontologically anxious a figure as Sir Philip Sidney to defend poetry—"Now
for the poet, he nothing affirms, and therefore never lieth."

In this spirit Puck playfully defends *A Midsummer Night's Dream:*

> If we shadows have offended,
> Think but this, and all is mended,
> That you have but slumb'red here
> While these visions did appear.
> And this weak and idle theme,
> No more yielding but a dream.
>
> (5.1.423–28)

With a similarly frank admission of illusion Shakespeare can
open the theater to Harsnett's polemic. Indeed, as if Harsnett's
momentum carried *him* into the theater along with the fraud he
hotly pursues, Shakespeare in *King Lear* stages not only exorcism,
but Harsnett *on* exorcism: "Five fiends have been in poor Tom at
once: of lust, as Obidicut; Hobbididence, prince of dumbness;
Mahu, of stealing; Modo, of murder; Flibbertigibbet, of mopping
and mowing, who since possesses chambermaids and waiting-
women" (4.1.58–63).[39]

Those in the audience who had read Harsnett's book or heard of
the notorious Buckinghamshire exorcisms would recognize in
Edgar's lines an odd joking allusion to the chambermaids, Sara and
Friswood Williams, and the waiting woman, Ann Smith, principal
actors in Father Edmunds's "devil Theater." The humor of the

anachronism here is akin to that of the Fool's earlier quip, "This prophecy Merlin shall make, for I live before his time" (3.2.95–96); both sallies of wit show a cheeky self-consciousness that dares deliberately to violate the historical setting to remind the audience of the play's conspicuous doubleness, its simultaneous distance and contemporaneity.

A Declaration of Egregious Popish Impostures supplies Shakespeare not only with an uncanny anachronism but also with the model for Edgar's histrionic disguise. For it is not the *authenticity* of the demonology that the playwright finds in Harsnett—the usual reason for authorial recourse to a specialized source (as, for example, to a military or legal handbook)—but rather the inauthenticity of a theatrical role. Shakespeare appropriates for Edgar a documented fraud, complete with an impressive collection of what the *Declaration* calls "uncouth non-significant names" (46) that have been made up to sound exotic and that carry with them a faint but ineradicable odor of spuriousness.

In Sidney's *Arcadia*, which provided the outline of the Gloucester subplot, the good son, having escaped his father's misguided attempt to kill him, becomes a soldier in another land and quickly distinguishes himself. Shakespeare insists not only on Edgar's perilous fall from his father's favor but upon his marginalization: Edgar becomes the possessed Poor Tom, the outcast with no possibility of working his way back toward the center. "My neighbors," writes John Bunyan in the 1660s, "were amazed at this my great conversion from prodigious profaneness to something like a moral life; and truly so well they might for this my conversion was as great as for a Tom of Bethlem to become a sober man."[40] Although Edgar is only a pretend Tom o' Bedlam and can return to the community when it is safe to do so, the force of Harsnett's argument makes mimed possession even more marginal and desperate than the real thing.

Indeed Edgar's desperation is bound up with the stress of "counterfeiting," a stress he has already noted in the presence of the mad and ruined Lear and now, in the lines I have just quoted, feels more intensely in the presence of his blinded and ruined father. He is struggling with the urge to stop playing or, as he puts it, with the feeling that he "cannot daub it further" (4.1.52). Why he does not simply reveal himself to Gloucester at this point is unclear. "And yet I must" is all he says of his continued disguise, as he recites the catalog of devils and leads his despairing father off to Dover Cliff.[41]

The subsequent episode—Gloucester's suicide attempt—deepens the play's brooding upon spurious exorcism. "It is a good *decorum* in a Comedy," writes Harsnett, "to give us empty names for things, and to tell us of strange Monsters within, where there be none" (142); so too the "Miracle-minter" Father Edmunds and his fellow exorcists manipulate their impressionable gulls: "The priests do report often in their patients hearing the dreadful forms, similitudes, and shapes, that the devils use to depart in out of those possessed bodies . . . : and this they tell with so grave a countenance, pathetical terms, and accommodate action, as it leaves a very deep impression in the memory, and fancy of their actors" (142–43). Thus by the power of theatrical suggestion the anxious subjects on whom the priests work their charms come to believe that they too have witnessed the devil depart in grotesque form from their own bodies, whereupon the priests turn their eyes heavenward and give thanks to the Blessed Virgin. In much the same manner Edgar persuades Gloucester that he stands on a high cliff, and then, after his credulous father has flung himself forward, Edgar switches roles and pretends that he is a bystander who has seen a demon depart from the old man:

> As I stood here below, methought his eyes
> Were two full moons; he had a thousand noses,
> Horns welk'd and waved like the enridged sea.
> It was some fiend; therefore, thou happy father,
> Think that the clearest gods, who make them honors
> Of men's impossibilities, have preserved thee.
>
> (4.6.69–74)

Edgar tries to create in Gloucester an experience of awe and wonder so intense that it can shatter his suicidal despair and restore his faith in the benevolence of the gods: "Thy life's a miracle" (4.6.55), he tells his father.[42] For Shakespeare as for Harsnett this miracle minting is the product of specifically histrionic manipulations; the scene at Dover is a disenchanted analysis of both religious and theatrical illusions. Walking about on a perfectly flat stage, Edgar does to Gloucester what the theater usually does to the audience: he persuades his father to discount the evidence of his senses—"Methinks the ground is even"—and to accept a palpable fiction: "Horrible steep" (4.6.3). But the audience at a play never absolutely accepts such fictions: we enjoy being brazenly lied to, we welcome for the sake of pleasure what we know to be untrue, but we withhold from the theater the simple assent we grant to everyday reality. And we enact this withholding when, depending on the staging, either we refuse to believe that Gloucester is on a cliff above Dover Beach or we realize that what we thought was a cliff (in the convention of theatrical representation) is in reality flat ground.

Hence in the midst of the apparent convergence of exorcism and theater, we return to the difference that enables *King Lear* to borrow comfortably from Harsnett: the theater elicits from us complicity rather than belief. Demonic possession is responsibly marked out for the audience as a theatrical fraud, designed to gull the unsuspecting: monsters such as the fiend with the thousand noses are illusions most easily imposed on the old, the blind, and the despairing; evil comes not from the mysterious otherworld of demons but from this world, the world of court and family intrigue. In *King Lear* there are no ghosts, as there are in *Richard III*, *Julius Caesar*, or *Hamlet*; no witches, as in *Macbeth*; no mysterious music of departing daemons, as in *Antony and Cleopatra*.

King Lear is haunted by a sense of rituals and beliefs that are no longer efficacious, that have been *emptied out*. The characters appeal again and again to the pagan gods, but the gods remain utterly silent.[43] Nothing answers to human questions but human voices; nothing breeds about the heart but human desires; nothing inspires awe or terror but human suffering and human depravity. For all the invocation of the gods in *King Lear*, it is clear that there are no devils.

Edgar is no more possessed than the sanest of us, and we can see for ourselves that there was no demon standing by Gloucester's side. Likewise Lear's madness has no supernatural origin; it is linked, as in Harsnett, to *hysterica passio*, exposure to the elements, and extreme anguish, and its cure comes at the hands not of an exorcist but of a doctor. His prescription involves neither religious rituals (as in Catholicism) nor fasting and prayer (as in Puritanism) but tranquilized sleep:

> Our foster-nurse of nature is repose,
> The which he lacks; that to provoke in him
> Are many simples operative, whose power
> Will close the eye of anguish.
>
> $(4.4.12-15)^{44}$

King Lear's relation to Harsnett's book is one of reiteration then, a reiteration that signals a deeper and unexpressed institutional exchange. The official church dismantles and cedes to the players the powerful mechanisms of an unwanted and dangerous charisma; in return the players confirm the charge that those mechanisms are theatrical and hence illusory. The material structure of Elizabethan and Jacobean public theaters heightened this confirmation; unlike medieval drama, which was more fully integrated into society, Shakespeare's drama took place in carefully demarcated playgrounds. *King Lear* offers a double corroboration of Harsnett's arguments. Within the play, Edgar's possession is clearly designated as a fiction, and the play itself is bounded by the institutional signs of fictionality: the wooden walls of the play space, payment for admission, known actors playing the parts, applause, the dances that followed the performance.

The theatrical confirmation of the official position is neither superficial nor unstable. And yet, I want now to suggest, Harsnett's arguments are alienated from themselves when they make their appearance on the Shakespearean stage. This alienation may be set in the context of a more general observation: the closer Shakespeare seems to a source, the more faithfully he reproduces it on stage, the more devastating and decisive his transformation of it. Let us take, for a small initial instance, Shakespeare's borrowing from Harsnett of the unusual adjective *corky*—that is, sapless, dry, withered. The word appears in the *Declaration* in the course of a sardonic explanation of why, despite the canonist Mengus's rule that only old women are to be exorcised, Father Edmunds and his crew have a particular fondness for tying in a chair and exorcising young women. Along with more graphic sexual innuendos, Harsnett observes that the theatrical role of a demoniac requires "certain actions, motions, distortions, dislocations, writhings, tumblings, and turbulent passions . . . not to be performed but by suppleness of sinews. . . . It would (I fear me) pose all the cunning Exorcists, that are this day to be found, to teach an old corky woman to writhe, tumble, curvet, and fetch her morris gambols" (23).

Now Shakespeare's eye was caught by the word "corky," and he reproduces it in a reference to old Gloucester. But what had been a flourish of Harsnett's typically bullying comic style becomes part of the horror of an almost unendurable scene, a scene of torture that begins when Cornwall orders his servant to take the captive Gloucester and "Bind fast his corky arms" (3.7.29). The note of bullying humor is still present in the word, but it is present in the character of the torturer.

This one-word instance of repetition as transvaluation may suggest in the smallest compass what happens to Harsnett's work in the course of *Lear*. The *Declaration*'s arguments are loyally reiterated, but in a curiously divided form. The voice of skepticism is assimilated to Cornwall, to Goneril, and above all to Edmund, whose "naturalism" is exposed as the argument of the younger and illegitimate son bent on displacing his legitimate older brother and eventually on destroying his father. The fraudulent possession and exorcism are given to the legitimate Edgar, who is forced to such shifts by the nightmarish persecution directed against him. Edgar adopts the role of Poor Tom not out of a corrupt will to deceive but out of a commendable desire to survive. Modo, Mahu, and the rest are fakes, exactly as Harsnett said they were, but Edgar's impostures are the venial sins of a will to endure. And even "venial sins" is too strong: the clever inventions enable a decent and unjustly persecuted man to live. Similarly, there is no grotesque monster standing on the cliff with Gloucester—there is not even a cliff—but only Edgar, himself hunted down like an animal, trying desperately to save his father from suicidal despair.

All of this has an odd and unsettling resemblance to the situation of the Jesuits in England, if viewed from an unofficial perspective.[45] The resemblance does not necessarily resolve itself into an allegory in which Catholicism is revealed to be the persecuted legitimate elder brother forced to defend himself by means of theatrical illusions against the cold persecution of his skeptical bastard brother Protestantism. But the possibility of such a radical undermining of the orthodox position exists, and not merely in the cool light of our own historical distance. In 1610 a company of traveling players in

Yorkshire included *King Lear* and *Pericles* in a repertoire that included a "St. Christopher Play" whose performance came to the
attention of the Star Chamber. The plays were performed in the
manor house of a recusant couple, Sir John and Lady Julyan Yorke,
and the players themselves and their organizer, Sir Richard Cholm-
eley, were denounced for recusancy by their Puritan neighbor, Sir
Posthumus Hoby.[46] It is difficult to resist the conclusion that someone in Stuart Yorkshire believed that *King Lear*, despite its apparent
staging of a fraudulent possession, was not hostile, was strangely
sympathetic even, to the situation of persecuted Catholics. At the
very least, we may suggest, the current of sympathy is enough to
undermine the intended effect of Harsnett's *Declaration:* an intensified adherence to the central system of official values. In Shakespeare, the realization that demonic possession is a theatrical imposture leads not to a clarification—the clear-eyed satisfaction of the
man who refuses to be gulled—but to a deeper uncertainty, a loss of
moorings, in the face of evil.

"Let them anatomize Regan," Lear raves, "see what breeds
about her heart. Is there any cause in nature that make these hard
hearts?" (3.6.76–78). We know that there is no cause *beyond* nature;
the voices of evil in the play—"Thou, Nature, art my goddess";
"What need one?"; "Bind fast his corky arms"—do not well up
from characters who are possessed. I have no wish to live in a
culture where men believe in devils; I fully grasp that the torturers
of this world are all too human. Yet Lear's anguished question
insists on the pain this understanding brings, a pain that reaches
beyond the king. Is it a relief to understand that the evil was not
visited upon the characters by demonic agents but released from
the structure of the family and the state by Lear himself?

Edgar's pretended demonic possession, by ironic contrast, is
homiletic; the devil compels him to acts of self-punishment, the
desperate masochism of the very poor, but not to acts of viciousness.
Like the demoniacs who in Harsnett's contemptuous account praise
the Mass and the Catholic church, Poor Tom gives a highly moral
performance: "Take heed o' th' foul fiend. Obey thy parents, keep
thy word's justice, swear not, commit not with man's sworn spouse,
set not thy sweet heart on proud array. Tom's a-cold" (3.4.80–83). Is
it a relief to know that Edgar only mimes this little sermon?

All attempts by the characters to explain or relieve their sufferings through the invocation of transcendent forces are baffled. Gloucester's belief in the influence of "these late eclipses in the sun and moon" (1.2.103) is dismissed decisively, even if the spokesman for the dismissal is the villainous Edmund. Lear appeals almost constantly to the gods:

> O Heavens!
> If you do love old men, if your sweet sway
> Allow obedience, if you yourselves are old,
> Make it your cause; send down, and take my part.
> (2.4.189–92)

But his appeals are left unanswered. The storm in the play seems to several characters to be of more than natural intensity, and Lear above all tries desperately to make it *mean* something (as a symbol of his daughters' ingratitude, a punishment for evil, a sign from the gods of the impending universal judgment), but the thunder refuses to speak. When Albany calls Goneril a "devil" and a "fiend" (4.2.59, 66), we know that he is not identifying her as a supernatural being—it is impossible, in this play, to witness the eruption of the denizens of hell into the human world—just as we know that Albany's prayer for "visible spirits" to be sent down by the heavens "to tame these vild offenses" (4.2.46–47) will be unanswered.

In *King Lear*, as Harsnett says of the Catholic church, "neither God, Angel, nor devil can be gotten to speak" (169). For Harsnett this silence betokens a liberation from lies; we have learned, as the last sentence of his tract puts it, "to loathe these despicable Impostures and return unto the truth" (*Declaration*, p. 171). But for Shakespeare the silence leads to the desolation of the play's close:

> Lend me a looking-glass,
> If that her breath will mist or stain the stone,
> Why then she lives.
> (5.3.262–64)

The lines voice a hope that has repeatedly tantalized the audience: a hope that Cordelia will not die, that the play will build toward a revelation powerful enough to justify Lear's atrocious suffering, that we are in the midst of what the Italians called a *tragedia di fin lieto*, that is, a play in which the villains absorb the tragic punishment while the good are wondrously restored.[47] Lear appeals, in effect, to the conventions of this genre. The close of a tragicomedy frequently requires the audience to will imaginatively a miraculous turn of events, often against the evidence of its senses (as when the audience persuades itself that the two actors playing Viola and Sebastian in *Twelfth Night* really *do* look identical, in spite of the ocular proof to the contrary, or when at the close of *The Winter's Tale* the audience accepts the fiction that Hermione is an unbreathing statue in order to experience the wonder of her resurrection). But the close of *King Lear* allows an appeal to such conventions only to reverse them with bitter irony: to believe Cordelia dead, the audience, insofar as it can actually see what is occurring onstage, must work against the evidence of its own senses. After all, the actor's breath would have misted the stone, and the feather held to Cordelia's mouth must have stirred. But we remain convinced that Cordelia is, as Lear first says, "dead as earth."

In the wake of Lear's first attempt to see some sign of life in Cordelia, Kent asks, "Is this the promis'd end?" Edgar echoes the question: "Or image of that horror?" And Albany says, "Fall, and cease!" By itself Kent's question has an oddly literary quality, as if he were remarking on the end of the play, either wondering what kind of ending this is or implicitly objecting to the disastrous turn of events. Edgar's response suggests that the "end" is the end of the world, the Last Judgment, here experienced not as a "promise"—the punishment of the wicked, the reward of the good—but as a "horror." But like Kent, Edgar is not certain about what he is seeing: his question suggests that he may be witnessing not the end itself but a possible "image" of it, while Albany's enigmatic "Fall, and cease!" empties even that image of significance. The theatrical means that might have produced a "counterfeit miracle" out of this moment are abjured; there will be no imposture, no histrionic revelation of the supernatural.

Lear repeats this miserable emptying out of the redemptive hope in his next lines:

> This feather stirs, she lives! If it be so,
> It is a chance which does redeem all sorrows
> That ever I have felt.
>
> (5.3.266–68)

Deeply moved by the sight of the mad king, a nameless gentleman had earlier remarked,

> Thou hast one daughter
> Who redeems nature from the general curse
> Which twain have brought her to.
>
> (4.6.205–7)

Now in Lear's words this vision of universal redemption through Cordelia is glimpsed again, intensified by the king's conscious investment in it.

What would it mean to "redeem" Lear's sorrows? To buy them back from the chaos and brute meaninglessness they now seem to signify? To reward the king with a gift so great that it outweighs the sum of misery in his entire long life? To reinterpret his pain as the necessary preparation—the price to be paid—for a consummate bliss? In the theater such reinterpretation would be represented by a spectacular turn in the plot—a surprise unmasking, a sudden reversal of fortunes, a resurrection—and this dramatic redemption, however secularized, would almost invariably recall the consummation devoutly wished by centuries of Christian believers. This consummation had in fact been represented again and again in medieval Resurrection plays, which offered the spectators ocular proof that Christ had risen.[48] Despite the pre–Christian setting of Shakespeare's play, Lear's craving for just such proof—"This feather stirs, she lives!"—would seem to evoke precisely this theatrical and religious tradition, but only to reveal itself, in C. L. Barber's acute phrase, as "post–Christian."[49] *If it be so:* Lear's sorrows are not redeemed; nothing can turn them into joy, but the forlorn hope of an impossible redemption persists, drained of its institutional and doctrinal significance, empty and vain, cut off even from a theatrical realization, but like the dream of exorcism, ineradicable.

The close of *King Lear* in effect acknowledges that it can never satisfy this dream, but the acknowledgment must not obscure the play's having generated the craving for such satisfaction. That is, Shakespeare does not simply inherit and make use of an anthropological given; rather, at the moment when the official religious and secular institutions are, for their own reasons, abjuring the ritual they themselves once fostered, Shakespeare's theater moves to ap-

propriate it. Onstage the ritual is effectively contained in the ways
we have examined, but Shakespeare intensifies as a theatrical experience the need for exorcism, and his demystification of the practice
is not identical in its interests to Harsnett's.

Harsnett's polemic is directed toward a bracing anger against the
lying agents of the Catholic church and a loyal adherence to the true
established Church of England. He writes as a representative of that
true church, and this institutional identity is reinforced by the secular institutional imprimatur on the confessions that are appended to
the *Declaration*. The joint religious and secular apparatus works to
strip away imposture and discover the hidden reality that is,
Harsnett says, the theater. Shakespeare's play dutifully reiterates
this discovery: when Lear thinks he has found in Poor Tom "the
thing itself," "unaccommodated man," he has in fact found a man
playing a theatrical role. But if false religion is theater, and if the
difference between true and false religion is the presence of theater,
what happens when this difference is enacted in the theater?

What happens, as we have already begun to see, is that the
official position is *emptied out*, even as it is loyally confirmed. This
"emptying out" resembles Brecht's "alienation effect" and, even
more, Althusser and Macheray's "internal distantiation." But the
most fruitful terms for describing the felt difference between Shakespeare's art and the religious ideology to which it gives voice are to
be found, I think, in the theological system to which Harsnett
adhered. What is the status of the Law, asks Hooker, after the
coming of Christ? Clearly the Savior effected the "evacuation of the
Law of Moses." But did that abolition mean "that the very name of
Altar, of Priest, of Sacrifice itself, should be banished out of the
world"? No, replies Hooker; even after evacuation, "the words
which were do continue: the only difference is, that whereas before
they had a literal, they now have a metaphorical use, and are as so
many notes of remembrance unto us, that what they did signify in
the letter is accomplished in the truth."[50] Both exorcism and
Harsnett's own attack on exorcism undergo a comparable process
of evacuation and transformed reiteration in *King Lear*. Whereas
before they had a literal, they now have a literary use and are as so
many notes of remembrance unto us, that what they did signify in
the letter is accomplished—with a drastic swerve from the sacred to
the secular—in the theater.

Edgar's possession is a theatrical performance exactly in Harsnett's terms, but there is no saving institution, purged of theater, against which it may be set, nor is there a demonic institution that the performance may be shown to serve. On the contrary, Edgar mimes in response to a free-floating, contagious evil more terrible than anything Harsnett would allow. For Harsnett the wicked are corrupt individuals in the service of a corrupt church; in *King Lear* neither individuals nor institutions can adequately contain the released and enacted wickedness; the force of evil in the play is larger than any local habitation or name. In this sense, Shakespeare's tragedy reconstitutes as theater the demonic principle demystified by Harsnett. Edgar's fraudulent, histrionic performance is a response to this principle: evacuated rituals, drained of their original meaning, are preferable to no rituals at all.

Shakespeare does not counsel, in effect, that for the dream of a cure one accept the fraudulent institution as true—that is the argument of the Grand Inquisitor. He writes for the greater glory and profit of the theater, a fraudulent institution that never pretends to be anything but fraudulent, an institution that calls forth what is not, that signifies absence, that transforms the literal into the metaphorical, that evacuates everything it represents. By doing so the theater makes for itself the hollow round space within which it survives. The force of *King Lear* is to make us love the theater, to seek out its satisfactions, to serve its interests, to confer on it a place of its own, to grant it life by permitting it to reproduce itself over generations. Shakespeare's theater has outlived the institutions to which it paid homage, has lived to pay homage to other, competing, institutions that in turn it seems to represent and empty out. This complex, limited institutional independence, this marginal and impure autonomy, arises not out of an inherent, formal self-reflexiveness but out of the ideological matrix in which Shakespeare's theater is created and re-created.

Further institutional strategies lie beyond a love for the theater. In a move that Ben Jonson rather than Shakespeare seems to have anticipated, the theater itself comes to be emptied out in the interests of reading. In the argument made famous by Charles Lamb and Coleridge, and reiterated by Bradley, theatricality must be discarded to achieve absorption, and Shakespeare's imagination yields forth its sublime power not to a spectator but to one who, like Keats, sits down to reread *King Lear*. Where institutions like the King's Men had been thought to generate their texts, now texts like *King Lear* appear to generate their institutions. The commercial contingency of the theater gives way to the philosophical necessity of literature.

Why has our culture embraced *King Lear*'s massive display of mimed suffering and fraudulent exorcism? Because the judicial torture and expulsion of evil have for centuries been bound up with the display of power at the center of society. Because we no longer believe in the magical ceremonies through which devils were once made to speak and were driven out of the bodies of the possessed. Because the play recuperates and intensifies our need for these ceremonies, even though we do not believe in them, and performs them, carefully marked out for us as frauds, for our continued consumption. Because with our full complicity Shakespeare's company and scores of companies that followed have catered profitably to our desire for spectacular impostures.

And also, perhaps, because the Harsnetts of the world would free us from the oppression of false belief only to reclaim us more firmly for the official state church, and the "solution"—confirmed by the rechristening, as it were, of the devil as the pope—is hateful. Hence we embrace an alternative that seems to confirm the official line, and thereby to take its place in the central system of values, yet at the same time works to unsettle all official lines.[51] Shakespeare's theater empties out the center that it represents and in its cruelty—Edmund, Goneril, Regan, Cornwall, Gloucester, Cordelia, Lear: all dead as earth—paradoxically creates in us the intimation of a fullness that we can savor only in the conviction of its irremediable loss:

> we that are young
> Shall never see so much, nor live so long.

Chapter Five

(E✦3)

Martial Law in the Land
of Cockaigne

I want to begin this chapter with a sermon that Hugh Latimer, the great Protestant divine martyred during the reign of Mary Tudor, delivered before the Lady Catharine Bertie, duchess of Suffolk, in 1552. In the course of expounding his text, the Lord's Prayer, Latimer tells of something that happened many years before in Cambridge. He had gone with Thomas Bilney—the man who converted Latimer and who was himself martyred in the later years of Henry VIII's rule—to the town prison to urge the condemned to acknowledge their faults and to bear patiently their punishments. Among the prisoners was a pregnant woman who had been convicted of murdering one of her children. The woman claimed that the child had been sick for a year and had died of natural causes. Her husband being away, she alone witnessed the death. She went, she said, to her neighbors and friends to seek their help to prepare the child for burial, but it was harvest time and no one was at home. Therefore alone, "in an heaviness and trouble of spirit," she made the necessary preparations and buried the dead. But when her husband returned home, he—who "loved her not; and therefore . . . sought means to make her out of the way"—accused her of murdering the child.[1] The accusation was believed by the Cambridge jury, and the woman was sentenced to be executed, the execution being delayed only until such time as she delivered her baby.

When Latimer spoke with her in prison, the woman steadfastly maintained her innocence, and after "earnest inquisition" he came to believe her story. Immediately thereafter it chanced that he was called to Windsor to preach before Henry VIII. After the sermon the king graciously strolled with the minister in a gallery. Latimer knelt, told the woman's story, begged the king for a royal pardon on her behalf, and received it. He returned to Cambridge, pardon in hand, but he kept it hidden, exhorting the woman to confess the truth. She held fast to her professions of innocence.

In due time the woman had her baby, and Latimer consented to be its godfather. The moment had thus come for the woman's execution, and she was in an agony of apprehension. But she was fearful, Latimer found, not because she was about to die but because she would die without being "churched"—that is, without the Catholic rite of purification based on the Jewish rituals traditionally held after childbirth (or menstruation) to cleanse the woman of the stain associated with any blood or discharge. "For she thought," writes Latimer, "that she should have been damned, if she should suffer without purification."

Latimer and Bilney then set about to disabuse her of this doctrinal error. They explained that the law of purification "was made unto the Jews, and not unto us; and that women lying in child-bed be not unclean before God." Significantly, Latimer opposed not the ritual of purification but only the belief that such a ritual cleanses women of sin, for women, he argues, "be as well in the favour of God before they be purified as after." Purification is not a theological but rather "a civil and politic law, made for natural honesty sake; signifying, that a woman before the time of her purification, that is to say, as long as she is a green woman, is not meet to do such acts as other women, nor to have company with her husband: for it is against natural honesty, and against the commonwealth." Only when the poor prisoner accepted this doctrinal point and agreed that she could go to her death unchurched and still receive salvation did Latimer produce the royal pardon and let her go.

I want to suggest that this little story reveals characteristic Renaissance beliefs and practices, and I propose to begin by noting some aspects of the gender relations it sketches.

First, we encounter the story as an allegorically charged but "real-life" tale about a woman, a tale that Latimer relates in a sermon originally delivered before another woman. As such, perhaps it subtly suggests, in the presence of a social superior, Latimer's moral superiority and power and so reestablishes male dominance in a moment of apparent inferiority.[2]

Second, the story could perhaps have been told about a male prisoner in the grip of a comparable "superstition"—let us imagine, for example, that he feared damnation if he did not have auricular confession and absolution prior to execution—but the prisoner's being female manifestly enhances its special symbolic charge. The woman's body after childbirth is polluted in "nature" and in the commonwealth but not in the eyes of God: hence she can exemplify directly and in the flesh the crucial theological distinction between, on the one hand, the domain of law and nature and, on the other, the order of grace and salvation. The distinction applies to all of humanity, but the male body passes through no fully comparable moments of pollution.[3]

Third, the particular suitability of the woman's body for this theological allegory rests on an implied Pauline syllogism, conveniently reinforced by Latimer's saving of the woman: the woman is to the man as the man is to God. And this syllogism intersects with other implied analogical relations: the woman is to the man as the simple peasant is to the gentleman and as the prisoner is to the free man.

Fourth, Latimer functions as part of a highly educated, male, professional elite that takes power over the woman away from her husband and lodges it in the punishing and pardoning apparatus of the state. The husband, as Latimer tells the story, had thought he could use that apparatus as an extension of his own power, but instead a gap is disclosed between patriarchal authority in the marital relation and patriarchal authority in the society at large.[4]

Fifth, the male professional elite, whether constituted as a body of jurists, theologians, or physicians, attempts to regulate the female body: to identify its periods of untouchability or pollution, to cleanse it of its stains, to distinguish between "superstitious" practices and those conducive to public health. What we are witnessing is an instance of transcoding and naturalization: Latimer attempts to transfer the practice of purification from the religious to the civil sphere.[5] He goes out of his way to distinguish an appeal to "natural honesty"—that is, the demands of cleanliness, decorum, and health—from "superstition": thus he denies that before purification a woman sheds a malign influence on the objects about her and denounces those who "think they may not fetch fire nor any thing in that house where there is a green woman." Such folk beliefs are for Latimer part of the orbit of Catholicism and pose a threat to the commonwealth far greater than any posed by a "green woman." The religious rituals to ward off defilement are themselves defiling and must be cleansed by driving them out of the precinct of the sacred and into the realm of the secular.

Rituals of purification thus transcoded from the religious to the civil sphere serve to shape certain late sixteenth- and early seventeenth-century representations, in particular theatrical representations, of women. Thus, for example, Hermione in Shakespeare's *Winter's Tale* complains bitterly that her husband has denied her "The child-bed privilege . . . which 'longs / To women of all fashion" (3.2.103–4) and has brutally hurried her into "th' open air, before" she has "got strength of limit." Leontes has denied his wife the "child-bed privilege" because he believes that her adulterous body is defiled beyond redemption; she is, he is convinced, permanently and irreparably stained. Her sullying, as he perceives it, of the "purity and whiteness" of his sheets threatens to defile him as well, and he imagines that he can save himself only by denouncing and destroying her. The secularized ritual is disrupted by a primal male nausea at the thought of the female body, the nausea most fully articulated in *King Lear:*

> But to the girdle do the gods inherit,
> Beneath is all the fiends': there's hell, there's darkness,
> There is the sulphurous pit, burning, scalding,
> Stench, consumption. Fie, fie, fie! pah, pah!
> Give me an ounce of civet; good apothecary,
> Sweeten my imagination.
>
> (4.6.126–31)[6]

In *The Winter's Tale* this nausea appears to be awakened in some obscure way by Hermione's pregnancy, as if what it revealed was beyond the power of any ritual to cleanse. The play suggests that Leontes is horribly staining himself, and its last act movingly depicts a ceremony conducted by a woman, Paulina, to cleanse the king. *The Winter's Tale* then at once symbolically rehearses and reverses the ritual pattern that we glimpse in Latimer: the tainting of the female, her exclusion from the social contacts that normally govern her sex, and her ultimate reintegration into a renewed community.

We could go on to look at other instances of the "green woman" and the tainted man in Renaissance drama, but for an understanding of the circulation of social energy the representational content of Latimer's story is less resonant than its strategic practice. Latimer and Bilney choose to leave the poor prisoner hanging, as it were, until she has accepted the doctrinal point: "So we travailed with this woman till we brought her to a good trade; and at the length showed her the king's pardon and let her go." A student of Shakespeare will immediately think of *Measure for Measure* where in the interest of moral reformation, Duke Vincentio, disguised as a holy friar, forces Claudio to believe that he is about to be executed—indeed forces virtually all of the major characters to face dreaded punishments—before he pardons everyone.

The resemblance between the tales arises not because Latimer's sermon is one of Shakespeare's sources but because Latimer is practicing techniques of arousing and manipulating anxiety, and these techniques are crucial elements in the representational technology of the Elizabethan and Jacobean theater.[7]

English dramatists developed extraordinary mastery of these techniques; indeed one of the defining characteristics of the dramaturgy of Marlowe and Shakespeare, as opposed to that of their medieval predecessors, is the startling increase in the level of represented and aroused anxiety. There is, to be sure, fear and trembling in the mysteries and moralities of the fifteenth and early sixteenth centuries, but a dread bound up with the fate of particular situated individuals is largely absent, and the audience shares its grief and joy in a collective experience that serves either to ward off or to absorb private emotions. Marlowe's *Faustus*, by contrast, though it appears conventional enough in its plot and overarching religious ideology, seems like a startling departure from everything that has preceded it precisely because the dramatist has heightened and individuated anxiety to an unprecedented degree and because he has contrived to implicate his audience as individuals in that anxiety.

Not all theatrical spectacles in the late sixteenth century are equally marked by the staging of anxiety: both civic pageantry and the masque are characterized by its relative absence. But in the public theater the manipulation of anxiety plays an important part and is brought to a kind of perfection in Shakespeare. This is obviously and overwhelmingly the case in the tragedies: *Othello,* for example, remorselessly heightens audience anxiety, an anxiety focused on the audience's inability to intervene and stop the murderous chain of lies and misunderstandings. But it is equally the case, in a different register, in the comedies. The pleasures of love, courtship, music, dance, and poetry in these plays are continually seasoned by fear, grief, and the threat of shame and death. The comedy of *The Comedy of Errors,* for example, floats buoyantly on a sea of epistemological and ontological confusion that is represented as having potentially fatal consequences. The audience's anxiety at these consequences, and for that matter at its own confusion, is different from that in a tragedy but is nonetheless an important element in the aesthetic experience. We could argue that anxiety in the comedies is an emotion experienced only by the characters and not by the audience, that comic pleasure lies in contemplating the anxiety of others. But this Hobbesian account does not do justice to the currents of sympathy in the plays and overlooks Shakespeare's efforts to make us identify powerfully with the dilemmas that his characters face. A sardonic detachment, such as one feels in response to a play like Ben Jonson's *Every Man in His Humour,* is not called forth by *The Merchant of Venice* or *Twelfth Night,* plays in which the audience's pleasure clearly depends upon a sympathetic engagement with the characters' situation and hence the acceptance of a measure of anxiety.[8]

It is worth stressing, however, that the audience accepts theatrical anxiety for the sake of pleasure, since this pleasure enables us to make an important distinction between the manipulation of anxiety in the theater and the comparable practice in Latimer.[9] The dramatist may have a palpable ideological purpose, generating anxiety, for example, to persuade women to submit to their husbands, or to warn men against paranoid suspicions of women, or to persuade subjects to obey even corrupt authority rather than risk rebellion. But in the public theater such purposes are subordinated to the overriding need to give pleasure. Anxiety takes its place alongside other means—erotic arousal, the excitement of spectacle, the joys of exquisite language, the satisfaction of curiosity about other peoples and places, and so forth—that the players employ to attract and satisfy their customers. The whole point of anxiety in the theater is to make it give such delight that the audience will pay for it again and again.[10] And this delight seems bound up with the marking out of theatrical anxiety as represented anxiety—not wholly real, either in the characters onstage or in the audience.[11]

Latimer, by contrast, insists that the anxiety in which he traffics is real. He does not, as far as we can tell, withhold the prisoner's pardon to heighten her subsequent pleasure; his purpose rather is to use her anxiety as a tool to transform her attitude toward what he regards as superstition.[12] Why should anxiety be used for this purpose? The answer perhaps seemed too obvious for Latimer to articulate: anxiety, in the form of threats of humiliation and beating, had long been used as an educative tool. To be sure, the threat of hanging goes well beyond what Shakespeare's Duke Vincentio in *Measure for Measure* calls "the threat'ning twigs of birch" (1.3.24), but Latimer presumably believes that at moments of crisis, moments beyond hope itself, men and women have to face the truth; their defenses are down, and they are forced to confront their salvation or perdition.[13] Latimer may also believe that we are all in effect under a death sentence from which we can be redeemed only by a mysterious and gratuitous act of pardon from God. The situation of the Cambridge prisoner is that of all mankind: hence the appropriateness of the story in a sermon on the Lord's Prayer. If he risked presumptuously casting himself or Henry VIII in the role of God, he could have appealed in good conscience to his certainty that he was God's humble servant. And if he seemed cruel, he could have told himself that he too would prefer death to doctrinal error. "Be of good comfort, Master Ridley, and play the man," Latimer was to say as the flames rose around his feet. "We shall this day light such a candle, by God's grace, in England, as I trust shall never be put out."

Latimer's last words, as the martyrologist Foxe reports them, move us beyond anxiety to the still point of absolute faith, but very few sixteenth-century Englishmen succeeded in reaching that point. (I doubt that many sixteenth-century Englishmen *wanted* to reach that point.) Those who governed the church had to be content that the faithful remain in a condition of what we may call salutary anxiety, and those who governed the state actively cultivated that condition. For the ruling elite believed that a measure of insecurity and

fear was a necessary, healthy element in the shaping of proper loyal-
ties, and Elizabethan and Jacobean institutions deliberately evoked
this insecurity. Hence the church's constant insistence upon the fear
and trembling, the sickness unto death, that every Christian should
experience; hence too the public and increasingly spectacular character of the punishments inflicted by the state.

At his accession to the English throne, in response to a murky
conspiracy known as the Bye Plot, James I staged a particularly
elaborate display of the techniques of salutary anxiety. Two of the
alleged conspirators—the priests Watson and Clarke—were tortured horribly, "to the great discontent of the people," writes one
observer, "who now think that matters were not so heinous as
were made show of."[14] As usual, the dismembered bodies were
stuck on the city gates. A week later another conspirator, George
Brooke, was executed, and then after several more days, the sheriff
led to the scaffold Lords Grey and Cobham and Sir Gervase Markham, who had also been condemned to die. Markham, who had
hoped for a reprieve, looked stunned with horror. After a delay,
the sheriff told him that since he seemed ill prepared to face death,
he would be granted a two-hour reprieve; similar delays were
granted to Grey and Cobham. The prisoners were then assembled
together on the scaffold, "looking strange one upon the other,"
wrote Dudley Carleton, who witnessed the scene, "like men be-
headed, and met again in the other world." At this point the sheriff
made a short speech, asking the condemned if the judgments
against them were just. When the wretches assented, he proclaimed that the merciful king had granted them their lives.[15]

The florid theatricality of the occasion was not lost on Carleton;
the three men, he observed, were "together on the stage as use is at
the end of the play." And in his letter granting the reprieve, James
himself seems to confirm Carleton's perception. The king suggests
that his clemency is in part a response to the "hearty and general . . . applause" given him on his entry into England, applause
in which "all the kin, friends, and allies" of the condemned participated.[16] The cheering had stopped after the first three executions,
for if some anxiety is salutary, it may also go too far and evoke not
obedience but a sullen withdrawal into discontented silence or
even an outburst of rash rebellion. These scenarios are at most only
partially and superficially in the control of the authorities; if at such

times the prince seems to manipulate the anxieties of others, he inevitably discloses his own half-buried fears.[17] The executioner held up Brooke's severed head and cried, "God save the king!" But the cry "was not seconded," Carleton notes, "by the voice of any one man but the sheriff." The spectators to the display of royal clemency, on the other hand, once again found their voices, for their anxiety had been turned into gratitude: "There was then no need to beg a *plaudite* of the audience," remarks Carleton, "for it was given with such hues and cries, that it went down from the castle into the town, and there began afresh."[18] So too the audience may have cheered the flurry of pardons in the last act of *Measure for Measure*.

But why should Renaissance England have been institutionally committed to the arousal of anxiety? After all, there was plenty of anxiety without the need of such histrionic methods; like other European countries of the period, England had experienced a population growth that put a heavy strain on food supplies, and the struggle for survival was intensified by persistent inflation, unemployment, and epidemic disease. But perhaps precisely because this anxiety was pervasive and unavoidable, those in power wanted to incorporate it ideologically and manage it. Managed insecurity may have been reassuring both to the managers themselves and to those toward whom the techniques were addressed.

Public maimings and executions were designed to arouse fear and to set the stage for the royal pardons that would demonstrate that the prince's justice was tempered with mercy.[19] If there were only fear, the prince, it was said, would be deemed a tyrant; if there were only mercy, it was said that the people would altogether cease to be obedient. Similarly, religious anxiety was welcomed, even cultivated, as the necessary precondition of the reassurance of salvation. William Tyndale suggested that St. Paul had written the Epistle to the Romans precisely to generate a suffering that could then be joyously relieved: "For except thou have born the cross of adversity and temptation, and hast felt thyself brought unto the very brim of desperation, yea, and unto hell-gates, thou canst never meddle with the sentence of predestination without thine own harm."[20]

What would be the harm? Why shouldn't the order of things be simply revealed without the prior generation of anxiety? Because, answers Tyndale, unless one is "under the cross and suffering of tribulation," it is impossible to contemplate that order "without secret wrath and grudging inwardly against God"; that is, "it shall not be possible for thee to think that God is righteous and just." Salutary anxiety, then, blocks the anger and resentment that would well up against what must, if contemplated in a secure state, seem an unjust order. And the great virtue of the technique is that it blocks *secret* wrath and *inward* grudging—that is, it does not merely suppress the expression of undesirable responses but represses those responses at their source, so that potential anger gives way to obedience, loyalty, and admiration.

Renaissance England had a subtle conception of the relation between anxiety and the fashioning of the individual subject, and its governing institutions developed discursive and behavioral strategies to implement this conception by arousing anxiety and then transforming it through pardon into gratitude, obedience, and love. These strategies were implicated from their inception in the management of spectacles and the fashioning of texts; that is, they are already implicated in cultural practices that are essential to the making and staging of plays. There was no need in this case for special modifications to adapt the techniques of salutary anxiety to the theater. Indeed the theater is a virtual machine for deploying these techniques in a variety of registers, from the comic anxiety that gives way to the clarification and release of marriage to the tragic anxiety that is at once heightened and ordered by the final solemnity of death. It is not surprising that the disguised duke of *Measure For Measure*, who fuses the strategies of statecraft and religion, has also seemed to many critics an emblem of the playwright.

This perception seems to me fundamentally correct, but it is complicated by what happens to the techniques of salutary anxiety when they are transferred to the stage. Even as it is evoked with extraordinary technical skill, salutary anxiety is emptied out in the service of theatrical pleasure. This emptying out through representation enables Shakespeare at once to identify the playwright with the mastery of salutary anxiety and to subject that mastery to complex ironic scrutiny. If Shakespeare in *Measure for Measure* seems to represent the protagonist's task as inflicting anxiety for ideological purposes, he also clearly calls that task into question. In a scene that particularly recalls Latimer's story, the disguised duke pays a

pastoral visit to "the afflicted spirits" in the town prison. "Do me
the common right," he asks the provost,

> To let me see them, and to make me know
> The nature of their crimes, that I may minister
> To them accordingly.

> (2.3.5–8)

"Repent you," he asks the pregnant Juliet, who has been impris-
oned for fornication, "of the sin you carry?" The question, collaps-
ing the sin and its fruit into one another, is a harsh one, but the
prisoner replies serenely: "I do; and bear the shame most patiently." Sensing an unwelcome doctrinal slippage in the shift from
sin to shame, Duke Vincentio proposes to teach the unfortunate
Juliet

> how you shall arraign your conscience,
> And try your penitence, if it be sound,
> Or hollowly put on.

"I'll gladly learn," Juliet replies, and the remainder of the short
scene provides a revealing glimpse of the duke's methods and
interests:

Duke: Love you the man that wrong'd you?

Juliet: Yes, as I love the woman that wrong'd him.

Duke: So then it seems your most offenseful act
Was mutually committed?

Juliet: Mutually.

Duke: Then was your sin of heavier kind than his.

Juliet: I do confess it, and repent it, father.

Duke: 'Tis meet so, daughter, but lest you do repent
As that the sin hath brought you to this shame,
Which sorrow is always toward ourselves, not heaven,
Showing we would not spare heaven as we love it
But as we stand in fear—

Juliet: I do repent me as it is an evil,
And take the shame with joy.

Duke: There rest.
Your partner, as I hear, must die to-morrow,
And I am going with instruction to him.
Grace go with you, *Benedicite!*

Juliet: Must die to-morrow? O injurious love,
                That respites me a life whose very comfort
                Is still a dying horror!

Provost: 'Tis pity of him.

                                                    (2.3.24–42)

The duke's questioning of the prisoner is based upon the medieval distinction between *attrition* and *contrition*. As one fourteenth-century theologian puts it, "When the will of a man clinging to sin is overcome by fear and by consideration of the punishment owed for sin, and on account of this recoils from sin, he is said to be 'attrite'; but when not only from fear of punishment, but also from love of eternal life he totally recoils from sin by fully detesting it, he is called 'contrite.' "[21] Juliet interrupts and in effect silences the duke's attempt to draw this doctrinal distinction:

        I do repent me as it is an evil,
        And take the shame with joy.

These words may express a perfect contrition, but they may also signal a quiet rejection of the whole system for which the duke speaks. "I do repent me as it is an evil"—but is it an evil? The provost had remarked of Claudio that he was "a young man / More fit to do another such offense / Than die for this" (2.3.13–15). "And take the shame with joy": earlier Juliet referred to her unborn child as "the shame." If she is still doing so, then her words affirm not repentance but love for her child. In either case, Juliet's words here and throughout the exchange are remarkable for their tranquillity. Each of Duke Vincentio's questions would seem to be an attempt to awaken an instructive anxiety, but the attempt appears to fail.

In response to Juliet's words the duke can only reply, "There rest." But as if this "rest" contradicts his own interest in arousing rather than allaying anxiety, he immediately continues by casually informing Juliet that the man she loves will be executed the next day. Her response provides ample evidence of anxiety, but that anxiety does not appear to serve an orthodox ideological purpose:

            O injurious love,
        That respites me a life whose very comfort
        Is still a dying horror!

Again the words are ambiguous (and emendations have been proposed), but Juliet appears either to be calling into question the divine love about which the duke has just been lecturing her or the human love whose fruit—the baby she carries in her womb—has presumably afforded her a "respite" from the execution to which her conviction for fornication would have doomed her. In either case, the anxiety she is expressing simply brushes aside the theological categories the duke had taken it upon himself to instill in her.

None of the duke's other attempts to awaken anxiety and to shape it into what he regards as a proper attitude has the desired effect. When Claudio voices what sounds like an admirable acceptance of his situation—"I have hope to live, and am prepar'd to die"—Duke Vincentio replies, "Be absolute for death: either death or life / Shall thereby be the sweeter" (3.1.4–6). Here the duke would appear to be molding Claudio's emotions into philosophical detachment, but the strategy fails since Claudio almost immediately abandons his detachment and frantically sues for life. We may say that the duke has succeeded in raising Claudio's anxiety level, but the moral purpose for which he set out to do so seems to have collapsed.

The duke had embarked on his course because Vienna seemed insufficiently anxious in the presence of authority:

> Now, as fond fathers,
> Having bound up the threat'ning twigs of birch,
> Only to stick it in their children's sight
> For terror, not to use, in time the rod
> Becomes more mock'd than fear'd; so our decrees,
> Dead to infliction, to themselves are dead,
> And liberty plucks justice by the nose;
> The baby beats the nurse, and quite athwart
> Goes all decorum.
>
> (1.3.23–31)

But at the close of the play, society at large seems singularly unaffected by the renewed exercise in anxiety. The magnificent emblems of indifference are the drunken Barnadine and the irrepressible Lucio: if they are any indication, the duke's strategy has not changed the structure of feeling or behavior in Vienna in the slightest degree. All that it has done is to offer the spectators pleasure in the spectacle. But that pleasure is precisely Shakespeare's professional purpose, and his ironic reflections on salutary anxiety do not at all diminish his commitment to it as a powerful theatrical technique.

ii

When near the close of his career Shakespeare reflected upon his own art with still greater intensity and self-consciousness than in *Measure for Measure,* he once again conceived of the playwright as a princely creator of anxiety. But where in *Measure for Measure* disguise is the principal emblem of this art, in *The Tempest* the emblem is the far more potent and disturbing power of magic. Prospero's chief magical activity throughout *The Tempest* is to harrow the other characters with fear and wonder and then to reveal that their anxiety is his to create and allay. The spectacular storm in the play's first scene gives way to Miranda's empathic agitation: "O! I have suffered/With those that I saw suffer. . . . O, the cry did knock/ Against my very heart." "The direful spectacle of the wrack," replies Prospero,

> which touch'd
> The very virtue of compassion in thee,
> I have with such provision in mine art
> So safely ordered that there is no soul—
> No, not so much perdition as an hair
> Betid to any creature in the vessel
> Which thou heardst cry, which thou saw'st sink.
>
> (1.2.26–32)

Miranda has been treated to an intense experience of suffering and to a still more intense demonstration of her father's power, the power at once to cause such suffering and to cancel it. Later in the play the threat of "perdition"—both loss and damnation—will be concentrated against Prospero's enemies, but it is important to recall that at the start the management of anxiety through the "provision" of art is practiced upon Prospero's beloved daughter. Her suffering is the prelude to the revelation of her identity, as if Prospero believes that this revelation can be meaningful only in the wake of the amazement and pity he artfully arouses. He is setting out to fashion her identity, just as he is setting out to refashion the inner lives of his enemies, and he employs comparable disciplinary techniques.

With his daughter, Prospero's techniques are mediated and soft-ened: she suffers at the sight of the sufferings of unknown wretches. With his enemies the techniques are harsher and more direct—the spectacle they are compelled to watch is not the wreck of others but of their own lives. In one of the play's most elaborate scenes, Prospero stands above the stage, invisible to those below him, and conjures up a banquet for Alonso, Antonio, Sebastian, and their party; when they move toward the table, Ariel appears like a Harpy and, with a clap of his wings and a burst of thunder and lightning, makes the table disappear. Ariel then solemnly recalls their crimes against Prospero and sentences the guilty in the name of the powers of Destiny and Fate:

> Thee of thy son, Alonso,
> They have bereft; and do pronounce by me
> Ling'ring perdition (worse than any death
> Can be at once).
>
> (3.3.75–78)

Prospero is delighted at Ariel's performance:

> My high charms work,
> And these, mine enemies, are all knit up
> In their distractions. They now are in my pow'r.
>
> (3.3.88–90)

To compel others to be "all knit up / In their distractions," to cause a paralyzing anxiety, is the dream of power, a dream perfected over bitter years of exile.[22] But as we have already seen, the artful manipu-lation of anxiety is not only the manifestation of aggression; it is also a strategy for shaping the inner lives of others and for fashioning their behavior. Hence we find Prospero employing the strategy not only upon those he hates but upon his daughter and upon the man whom he has chosen to be his daughter's husband. Ferdinand and Miranda fall in love instantly—"It goes on, I see, / As my soul prompts it" (1.2.420–21), remarks Prospero—but what is missing from their love is precisely the salutary anxiety that Prospero under-takes to impose: "this swift business / I must uneasy make, lest too light winning / Make the prize light" (1.2.451–53). To Miranda's horror, he accuses Ferdinand of treason and employs his magic charms once again to cause a kind of paralysis: "My spirits," exclaims Ferdinand, "as in a dream, are all bound up" (1.2.487). The rituals of humiliation and suffering through which Prospero makes Ferdinand and Miranda pass evidently have their desired effect: at the end of the play the couple displayed to the amazed bystanders are revealed to be not only in a state of love but in a state of symbolic war. The lovers, you will recall, are discovered playing chess, and Miranda accuses Ferdinand of cheating. The deepest happiness is represented in this play as a state of playful tension.

Perhaps the supreme representation of this tension in *The Tempest* is to be found not in Prospero's enemies or in his daughter and son-in-law but in himself. The entire action of the play rests on the premise that value lies in controlled uneasiness, and hence that a direct reappropriation of the usurped dukedom and a direct punishment of the usurpers has less moral and political value than an elaborate inward restaging of loss, misery, and anxiety. Prospero directs this restaging not only against the others but also—even principally—against himself. That is, he arranges for the reenactment in a variety of registers and through different symbolic agents of the originary usurpation, and in the play's most memorable yet perplexing moment, the princely artist puts himself through the paralyzing uneasiness with which he has afflicted others. The moment to which I refer is that of the interrupted wedding masque. In the midst of the climactic demonstration of Prospero's magical powers, the celebration of the paradisal "green land" where spring comes at the very end of harvest, Prospero suddenly starts, breaks off the masque, and declares that he had "forgot that foul conspiracy / Of the beast Caliban and his confederates / Against my life" (4.1.139–41).

In recalling the conspiracy, Prospero clearly exhibits signs of extreme distress: Ferdinand is struck by the "passion / That works him strongly," and Miranda says that "never till this day" has she seen him "touch'd with anger, so distemper'd" (4.1.143–45). Noticing that Ferdinand looks "in a mov'd sort," as if he were "dismay'd," Prospero tells him to "be cheerful" and informs him that "Our revels now are ended." The famous speech that follows has the effect of drastically evacuating the masque's majestic vision of plenitude. "Let me live here ever," the delighted Ferdinand had exclaimed, enchanted by the promise of an aristocrat's equivalent of the Land of Cockaigne:

> Honor, riches, marriage-blessing,
> Long continuance, and increasing,
> Hourly joys be still upon you!
>
> (4.1.106–8)

But Prospero now explains that the beneficent goddesses "Are melted into air, into thin air" (4.1.150). What had seemed solid is "baseless"; what had seemed enduring ("the great globe itself")

> shall dissolve,
> And like this insubstantial pageant faded
> Leave not a rack behind.
>
> (4.1.154–56)

Prospero offers this sublime vision of emptiness to make Ferdinand feel "cheerful"—secure in the consciousness that life is a dream. It is difficult to believe in the effectiveness of these professed attempts at reassurance: like Duke Vincentio's religious consolations in *Measure for Measure*, they seem suited more to heighten anxiety than to allay it. The ascetic security Prospero articulates has evidently not stilled his own "beating mind":

> Sir, I am vex'd;
> Bear with my weakness, my old brain is troubled.
> Be not disturb'd with my infirmity.
>
> (4.1.158–60)

Since Prospero's art has in effect created the conspiracy as well as the defense against the conspiracy, and since the profession of infirmity comes at the moment of his greatest strength, we may conclude that we are witnessing the practice of salutary anxiety operating at the center of the play's world, in the consciousness of Prospero himself, magician, artist, and prince. This does not mean that Prospero's anxiety about the conspiracy, about his enemies and servants and daughter, about his own inward state is not genuinely felt, nor does it mean that he is in absolute, untroubled control either of the characters whom he has brought onto the island or of himself. Rapt in his own magical vision of bounteousness, he has forgotten a serious threat to his life: "The minute of their plot / Is almost come" (4.1.141–42). But it is important to take seriously his deep complicity in his present tribulations, for only by actively willing them can he undo the tribulations that he unwillingly and unwittingly brought about years before. At that time, absorbed in his occult studies, he had been unaware of the dangers around him; now as the condition of a return to his dukedom, he himself brings those dangers to the center of his retreat. This center, whether we regard it as emblematic of the dominant religious, aesthetic, or political institution, is not the still point in a turbulent world but the point at which the anxieties that shape the character of others are screwed up to their highest pitch. Precisely from that point—and as a further exemplification of the salutary nature of anxiety—reconciliation and pardon can issue forth. This pardon is not a release from the power in which Prospero holds everyone around him but, as with Latimer and James I, its ultimate expression.[23]

Shakespeare goes beyond Latimer and James, however, in envisaging a case in which anxiety does not appear to have its full redeeming effect, a case in which the object of attention refuses to be fashioned inwardly, refuses even to acknowledge guilt, and yet is pardoned. The generosity of the pardon in this instance is inseparable from a demonstration of supreme force. "For you, most wicked sir," Prospero says to his brother Antonio,

> whom to call brother
> Would even infect my mouth, I do forgive
> Thy rankest fault—all of them; and require
> My dukedom of thee, which perforce, I know
> Thou must restore.
>
> (5.1.130–34)

Antonio's silence at this point suggests that he remains unrepentant, but it also expresses eloquently the paralysis that is the hallmark of extreme anxiety. It has been argued convincingly that the truculence of the villains at the close of the play marks the limit of Prospero's power—as Prospero's failure to educate Caliban has already shown, the strategy of salutary anxiety cannot remake the inner life of everyone—yet at the very moment the limit is marked, the play suggests that it is relatively inconsequential. It would no doubt be preferable to receive the appropriate signs of inward gratitude from everyone, but Prospero will have to content himself in the case of Antonio with the full restoration of his dukedom.[24]

iii

What I have been describing here is the theatrical appropriation and staging of a sixteenth- and seventeenth-century social practice. But the strategy of salutary anxiety is not simply reflected in a secondhand way by the work of art, because the practice itself is already implicated in the artistic traditions and institutions out of which this particular representation, *The Tempest*, has emerged. Latimer may have been indifferent or hostile to the drama and to literature in general, but his tale of the Cambridge prisoner seems shaped by literary conventions, earlier tales of wronged innocence and royal pardons. And if the practice he exemplifies helps to empower theatrical representations, fictive representations have themselves helped to empower his practice.[25] So too Dudley Carleton, watching men about to go to their deaths, thinks of the last act of a play, and when a pardon is granted, the spectators applaud. This complex circulation between the social dimension of an aesthetic strategy and the aesthetic dimension of a social strategy is difficult to grasp because the strategy in question has an extraordinarily long and tangled history, one whose aesthetic roots go back at least as far as Aristotle's *Poetics*. But we may find a more manageable, though still complex, model in the relation between *The Tempest* and one of its presumed sources, William Strachey's account of the tempest that struck an English fleet bound for the fledgling colony at Jamestown.[26]

Strachey's account, with its bravura description of a violent storm at sea and its tale of Englishmen providentially cast ashore on an uninhabited island rumored to be devil haunted, is likely, along with other New World materials, to have helped shape *The Tempest*. The play was performed long before Strachey's narrative was printed in Purchas's *Pilgrims* as "A true reportory of the wrack, and redemption of Sir Thomas Gates Knight," but scholars presume that Shakespeare read a manuscript version of the work, which takes the form of a confidential letter written to a certain "noble lady."[27] My interest is not the particular verbal echoes, which have been painstakingly researched since Malone in 1808 first called attention to them, but the significance of the relation between the two texts, or rather between the institutions that the texts serve. For it is important to grasp that we are dealing not with the reflections of isolated individuals musing on current events but with expressions whose context is corporate and institutional.

William Strachey was a shareholder and secretary of the Virginia Company's colony at Jamestown; his letter on the events of 1609–10 was unpublished until 1625, not for want of interest but because the Virginia Company was engaged in a vigorous propaganda and financial campaign on behalf of the colony, and the company's leaders found Strachey's report too disturbing to allow it into print. Shakespeare too was a shareholder in a joint-stock company, the King's Men, as well as its principal playwright and sometime actor; *The Tempest* also remained unpublished for years, again presumably not for want of interest but because the theater company resisted losing control of its playbook. Neither joint-stock company was a direct agent of the crown: despite the legal fiction that they were retainers of the monarch, the King's Men could not have survived through royal patronage alone, and they were not in the same position of either dependence or privilege as other household servants; the crown had deliberately withdrawn from the direction of the Virginia Company. Royal protection and support, of course, remained essential in both cases, but the crown would not assume responsibility, nor could either company count on royal financial support in times of need. Committed for their survival to attracting investment capital and turning a profit, both companies depended on their ability to market stories that would excite, interest, and attract supporters. Both Strachey and Shakespeare were involved in unusually direct and intricate ways in every aspect of their companies' operations: Strachey as shareholder, adventurer, and eventually secretary; Shakespeare as shareholder, actor, and playwright. Because of these multiple positions, both men probably identified intensely with the interests of their respective companies.

I want to propose that the relation between the play and its alleged source is a relation between joint-stock companies.[28] I do not mean that there was a direct, contractual connection.[29] As we have already seen with Latimer, the transfer of cultural practices and powers depends not upon contracts but upon networks of resemblance. In the case of Strachey and Shakespeare, there *are*, in point of fact, certain intriguing institutional affiliations: as Charles Mills Gayley observed many years ago, a remarkable number of social and professional connections link Shakespeare and the stockholders and directors of the Virginia Company; moreover, Strachey in 1605 wrote a prefatory sonnet commending Jonson's *Sejanus* and in 1606 is listed as a shareholder in an acting company known as the Children of the Queen's Revels, the company that had taken over the Blackfriars Theater from Richard Burbage.[30] Still, I should emphasize that these affiliations do not amount to a direct transfer of properties; we are dealing with a system of mimetic rather than contractual exchange. The conjunction of Strachey's unpublished letter and Shakespeare's play signals an institutional circulation of culturally significant narratives. And as we shall see, this circulation has as its central concern the public management of anxiety.

Strachey tells the story of a state of emergency and a crisis of authority. The "unmerciful tempest" that almost sank Sir Thomas Gates's ship, the *Sea Venture,* provoked an immediate collapse of the distinction between those who labor and those who rule, a distinction, we should recall, that is at the economic and ideological center of Elizabethan and Jacobean society: "Then men might be seen to labour, I may well say, for life, and the better sort, even our Governour, and Admiral themselves, not refusing their turn. . . . And it is most true, such as in all their life times had never done hours work before (their minds now helping their bodies) were able twice forty eight hours together to toil with the best" (in Purchas, 19:9–11). "The best"—the violence of the storm has turned Strachey's own language upside down: now it is the common seamen, ordinarily despised and feared by their social superiors, who are, as the Romans called their aristocrats, the *optimi viri,* the best of men.[31] Indeed the storm had quite literally a leveling force: while the governor was "both by his speech and authority heartening every man unto his labour," a great wave "struck him from the place where he sat, and groveled him, and all us about him on our faces, beating together with our breaths all thoughts from our bosoms, else then that we were now sinking" (10).

Even after the ship had run aground in the Bermudas and the one hundred fifty men, women, and children on board had been saved, the crisis of authority was not resolved; indeed it only intensified then, not because of a leveling excess of anxiety but because of its almost complete absence in the colonists. The alarm of the rulers makes itself felt in quirks of Strachey's style. He reports, for example, that many palmettos were cut down for their edible tops, but the report has a strange nervous tone, as the plants are comically turned into wealthy victims of a popular uprising: "Many an ancient Burgher was therefore heaved at, and fell not for his place, but for his head: for our common people, whose bellies never had ears, made it no breach of Charity in their hot bloods and tall stomachs to murder thousands of them" (19).

The strain registered here in the tone stands for concerns that are partially suppressed in the published text, concerns that are voiced in a private letter written in December 1610 by Richard Martin, secretary of the Virginia Company in London, to Strachey, who was by then in Jamestown. Martin asks Strachey for a full confidential report on "the nature & quality of the soil, & how it is like to serve you without help from hence, the manners of the people, how the Barbarians are content with your being there, but especially how our own people do brook their obedience, how they endure labor, whether willingly or upon constraint, how they live in the exercise of Religion, whether out of conscience or for fashion, And generally what ease you have in the government there, & what hope of success."[32]

Here the deepest fears lie not with the human or natural resources of the New World but with the discipline of the English colonists and common seamen. And the principal questions—whether obedience is willing or forced, whether religious observance is sincere or feigned—suggest an interest in inner states, as if the shareholders in the Virginia Company believed that only with a set of powerful inward restraints could the colonists be kept from rebelling at the first sign of the slippage or relaxation of authority. The company had an official institutional interest in shaping and controlling the minds of its own people. But the Bermuda shipwreck revealed the difficulty of this task as well as its importance: set apart from the institutional and military safeguards established at Jamestown, Bermuda was an experimental space, a testing ground where the extent to which disciplinary anxiety had been internalized by the ordinary venturers could be measured.

The results were not encouraging. As Strachey and others remark, Bermuda was an extraordinarily pleasant surprise: the climate was healthful, the water was pure, there were no native inhabitants to contend with, and, equally important, there was no shortage of food. Tortoises—"such a kind of meat, as a man can neither absolutely call Fish nor Flesh" (24)[33]—were found in great number, and the skies were dark with great flocks of birds:

Our men found a pretty way to take them, which was by standing on the Rocks or Sands by the Sea side, and hollowing, laughing, and making the strangest out-cry that possibly they could: with the noise whereof the Birds would come flocking to that place, and settle upon the very arms and head of him that so cried, and still creep nearer and nearer, answering the noise themselves: by which our men would weigh them with their hands, and which weighed heaviest they took for the best and let the others alone. (Purchas, 19:22–23)

Even to us, living for the most part in the confident expectation of full bellies, this sounds extraordinary enough; to seventeenth-century voyagers, whose ordinary condition was extreme want and who had dragged themselves from the violent sea onto an unknown shore with the likely prospect of starvation and death, such extravagant abundance must have seemed the fantastic realization of old folk dreams of a land where the houses were roofed with pies and the pigs ran about with little knives conveniently stuck in their precooked sides. In this Land of Cockaigne setting, far removed not only from England but from the hardships of Jamestown, the authority of Sir Thomas Gates and his lieutenants was anything but secure. For the perception that Bermuda was a providential deliverance contained within it a subversive corollary: why leave? why press on to a hungry garrison situated in a pestiferous swamp and in grave tension with the surrounding Algonquian tribesmen?[34]

According to Strachey, Gates was initially concerned less about his own immediate authority than about the possible consequences of his absence in Virginia. The *Sea Venture* had come to grief in the tempest, but Gates thought (correctly, as it happened) that the other two vessels might have reached their destination, and this thought brought not only consolation but anxiety, which focused, in characteristic Renaissance fashion, on the ambitions of the younger generation. Fearful about "what innovation and tumult might happily [haply] arise, among the younger and ambitious spirits of the new companies to arrive in Virginia" (26) in his absence, Gates wished to construct new ships as quickly as possible to continue on to Jamestown, but the sailors and the colonists alike began to grumble at this plan. In Virginia, they reasoned, "nothing but wretchedness and labour must be expected, with many wants and a churlish entreaty"; in Bermuda, all things "at ease and pleasure might be enjoyed" (29) without hardship or threatening. There is, at least as Strachey reports it, virtually no internalization of the ideology of colonialism; the voyagers appear to think of themselves as forced to endure a temporary exile from home. As long as "they were (for the time) to lose the fruition both of their friends and Country, as good, and better it were for them, to repose and seat them where they should have the least outward wants the while" (29). And to this dangerous appeal—the appeal, in Strachey's words, of "liberty, and fulness of sensuality" (35)—was added a still more dangerous force: religious dissent.

Arguments against leaving Bermuda began to be voiced not only among the "idle, untoward, and wretched number of the many" (29) but among the educated few. One of these, Stephen Hopkins, "alleged substantial arguments, both civil and divine (the Scripture falsely quoted) that it was no breach of honesty, conscience, nor Religion, to decline from the obedience of the Governour, or refuse to go any further, led by his authority (except it so pleased themselves) since the authority ceased when the wrack was committed, and with it, they were all then freed from the government of any man" (30–31). Hopkins evidently accepted the governor's authority as a contractual obligation that continued only so long as the enterprise remained on course. Once there was a swerve from the official itinerary, that authority, not granted a general or universal character, lapsed, and the obedience of the subject gave way to the will and pleasure of each man.[35] We cannot know, of course, if Hopkins said anything so radical, but this is how his "substantial arguments, both civil and divine," sounded to those in command. In Strachey's account, at least, the shipwreck had led to a profound questioning of authority that seems to anticipate the challenge posed by mid-seventeenth-century radicals like Winstanley. What are the boundaries of authority? What is the basis of its claim to be obeyed? How much loyalty does an individual owe to a corporation?

When the seditious words were reported to Gates, the governor convened a martial court and sentenced Hopkins to death, but the condemned man was so tearfully repentant that he received a pardon. This moving scene—the saving public display of anxiety—evidently did not settle the question of authority, however, for

shortly after, yet another mutiny arose, this time led by a gentleman named Henry Paine. When Paine was warned that he risked
execution for "insolency," he replied, Strachey reports, "with a
settled and bitter violence, and in such unreverent terms, as I
should offend the modest ear too much to express it in his own
phrase; but its contents were, how that the Governour had no
authority of that quality, to justify upon any one (how mean soever
in the colony) an action of that nature, and therefore let the Governour (said he) kiss, &c." (34). When these words, "with the omitted additions," were reported, the governor, "who had now the
eyes of the whole Colony fixed upon him," condemned Paine "to
be instantly hanged; and the ladder being ready, after he had made
many confessions, he earnestly desired, being a Gentleman, that
he might be shot to death, and towards the evening he had his
desire, the Sun and his life setting together" (34). "He had his
desire"—Strachey's sarcasm is also perhaps the representation of
what those in authority regarded as an intolerable nonchalance, a
refusal to perform those rituals of tearful repentance that apparently saved Hopkins's life. In effect Paine is killed to set an example, condemned to die for cursing authority, for a linguistic crime,
for violating discursive decorum, for inadequate anxiety in the presence of power.

In his narrative, Strachey represents the norms Paine has challenged by means of his "&c."—the noble lady to whom he is writing, like Mr. Kurtz's intended, must be sheltered from the awful
truth, here from the precise terms of the fatal irreverent challenge
to authority. The suppression of the offending word enacts in miniature the reimposition of salutary anxiety by a governor "so solici-
tous and careful, whose both example . . . and authority, could lay
shame, and command upon our people" (28). The governor is full
of care—therefore resistant to the lure of the island—and he man-
ages, even in the midst of a paradisal plenty, to impose this care
upon others. When the governor himself writes to a fellow officer
explaining why all of the colonists must be compelled to leave the
island, he invokes not England's imperial destiny or Christianity's
advancement but the Virginia Company's investment: "The mean-
est in the whole Fleet stood the Company in no less than twenty
pounds, for his own personal Transportation, and things necessary
to accompany him" (36). On the strength of this compelling mo-

tive, new ships were built, and in an impressive feat of navigation, the whole company finally reached Jamestown.

Upon their arrival Gates and his people found the garrison in desperate condition—starving, confused, terrorized by hostile and treacherous Indians, and utterly demoralized. In Gates's view, the problem was almost entirely one of discipline, and he addressed it by imposing a set of "orders and instructions" upon the colony that transformed the "government" of Jamestown "into an absolute command." The orders were published in 1612 by Strachey as the *Laws Divine, Moral, and Martial,* an exceptionally draconian code by which whipping, mutilation, and the death penalty might be imposed for a wide range of offenses, including blasphemy, insubordination, even simple criticism of the Virginia Company and its officers. These orders, the first martial law code in America, suspended the traditional legal sanctions that governed the lives of Englishmen, customary codes based on mutual constraints and obligations, and instituted in their stead the grim and self-consciously innovative logic of a state of emergency. The company's claim upon the colonists had become total. The group that had been shipwrecked in Bermuda passed from dreams of absolute freedom to the imposition of absolute control.

Such then were the narrative materials that passed from Strachey to Shakespeare, from the Virginia Company to the King's Men: a violent tempest, a providential shipwreck on a strange island, a crisis in authority provoked by both danger and excess, a fear of lower-class disorder and upper-class ambition, a triumphant affirmation of absolute control linked to the manipulation of anxiety and to a departure from the island. But the swerve away from these materials in *The Tempest* is as apparent as their presence: the island is not in America but in the Mediterranean; it is not uninhabited—Ariel and Caliban (and, for that matter, Sycorax) were present before the arrival of Prospero and Miranda; none of the figures are in any sense colonists; the departure is for home rather than a colony and entails not an unequivocal heightening of authority but a partial diminution, signaled in Prospero's abjuration of magic.

> I'll break my staff,
> Bury it certain fadoms in the earth,
> And deeper than did ever plummet sound
> I'll drown my book.
>   (5.1.54–57)[36]

If the direction of Strachey's narrative is toward the promulgation of the martial law codes, the direction of *The Tempest* is toward forgiveness. And if that forgiveness is itself the manifestation of supreme power, the emblem of that power remains marriage rather than punishment.

The changes I have sketched are signs of the process whereby the Bermuda narrative is made negotiable, turned into a currency that may be transferred from one institutional context to another. The changes do not constitute a coherent critique of the colonial discourse, but they function as an unmooring of its elements so as to confer upon them the currency's liquidity. Detached from their context in Strachey's letter, these elements may be transformed and recombined with materials drawn from other writers about the New World who differ sharply from Strachey in their interests and motives—Montaigne, Sylvester Jourdain, James Rosier, Robert Eden, Peter Martyr—and then integrated in a dramatic text that draws on a wide range of discourse, including pastoral and epic poetry, the lore of magic and witchcraft, literary romance, and a remarkable number of Shakespeare's own earlier plays.

The ideological effects of the transfer to *The Tempest* are ambiguous. On the one hand, the play seems to act out a fantasy of mind control, to celebrate absolute patriarchal rule, to push to an extreme the dream of order, epic achievement, and ideological justification implicit in Strachey's text. The lower-class resistance Strachey chronicles becomes in Shakespeare the drunken rebellion of Stephano and Trinculo, the butler and jester who, suddenly finding themselves freed from their masters, are drawn to a poor man's fantasy of mastery: "the King and all our company else being drown'd, we will inherit here" (2.2.174–75). Similarly, the upper-class resistance of Henry Paine is transformed into the murderous treachery of Sebastian, in whom the shipwreck arouses dreams of an escape from subordination to his older brother, the king of Naples, just as Antonio had escaped subordination to his older brother Prospero:

Sebastian: I remember
             You did supplant your brother Prospero.

  Antonio: True.
             And look how well my garments sit upon me,
             Much feater than before. My brother's servants
             Were then my fellows, now they are my men.
                                                        (2.1.270–74)

By invoking fratricidal rivalry here Shakespeare is not only linking the Strachey materials to his own long-standing theatrical preoc-
cupations but also supplementing the contractual authority of a governor like Sir Thomas Gates with the familial and hence culturally
sanctified authority of the eldest son. To rise up against such a
figure, as Claudius had against old Hamlet or Edmund against Edgar, is an assault not only on a political structure but on the moral
and natural order of things: it is an act that has, as Claudius says,
"the primal eldest curse upon't." The assault is magically thwarted
by Ariel, the indispensable agent of Prospero's "art"; hence that art,
potentially a force of disorder, spiritual violence, and darkness, is
confirmed as the agent of legitimacy. Through his mastery of the
occult, Prospero withholds food from his enemies, spies upon them,
listens to their secret conversations, monitors their movements,
blocks their actions, keeps track of their dealings with the island's
native inhabitant, torments and disciplines his servants, defeats conspiracies against his life. A crisis of authority—deposition from
power, exile, impotence—gives way through the power of his art to
a full restoration. From this perspective Prospero's magic is the romance equivalent of martial law.

Yet *The Tempest* seems to raise troubling questions about this
authority. The great storm with which the play opens has some of
the leveling force of the storm that struck the *Sea Venture*. To be
sure, unlike Strachey's gentlemen, Shakespeare's nobles refuse
the boatswain's exasperated demand that they share the labor,
"Work you then," but their snarling refusal—"Hang, cur! hang,
you whoreson, insolent noisemaker!" (1.1.42–44)—far from securing their class superiority, represents them as morally beneath the
level of the common seamen.[37] Likewise, Shakespeare's king,
Alonso, is not "groveled" by a wave, but—perhaps worse—he is
peremptorily ordered below by the harried boatswain: "What
cares these roarers for the name of king? To cabin! silence! trouble
us not" (1.1.16–18). And if we learn eventually that these roarers
are in fact produced *by* a king—in his name and through his
command of a magical language—this knowledge does not altogether cancel our perception of the storm's indifference to the
ruler's authority and the idle aristocrat's pride of place.

The perception would perhaps be overwhelmed by the display of
Prospero's power were it not for the questions that are raised about

this very power. A Renaissance audience might have found the locus of these questions in the ambiguous status of magic, an ambiguity deliberately heightened by the careful parallels drawn between Prospero and the witch Sycorax and by the attribution to Prospero of claims made by Ovid's witch Medea. But for a modern audience, at least, the questions center on the figure of Caliban, whose claim to the legitimate possession of the island—"This island's mine by Sycorax my mother" (1.2.331)—is never really answered, or rather is answered by Prospero only with hatred, torture, and enslavement.[38] Though he treats Caliban as less than human, Prospero finally expresses, in a famously enigmatic phrase, a sense of connection with his servant-monster, standing anxious and powerless before him: "this thing of darkness I / Acknowledge mine" (5.1.275–76). He may intend these words only as a declaration of ownership, but it is difficult not to hear in them some deeper recognition of affinity, some half-conscious acknowledgment of guilt. At the play's end the princely magician appears anxious and powerless before the audience to beg for indulgence and freedom.

As the epilogue is spoken, Prospero's magical power and princely authority—figured in the linked abilities to raise winds and to pardon offenders—pass, in a startling display of the circulation of social energy, from the performer onstage to the crowd of spectators. In the play's closing moments the marginal, vulnerable actor, more than half-visible beneath the borrowed robes of an assumed dignity, seems to acknowledge that the imaginary forces with which he has played reside ultimately not in himself or in the playwright but in the multitude. The audience is the source of his anxiety, and it holds his release quite literally in its hands: without the crowd's applause his "ending is despair" (Epilogue, 15). This admission of dependence includes a glance at the multitude's own vulnerability:

> As you from crimes would pardon'd be,
> Let your indulgence set me free.
>
> (Epilogue, 19–20)

But it nonetheless implicates the prince as well as the player in the experience of anxiety and the need for pardon.

Furthermore, even if we may argue that such disturbing or even subversive reflections are contained within the thematic structure of the play, a structure that seems to support the kind of authority served by Strachey, we must acknowledge that the propagandists for colonization found little to admire in the theater. That is, the most disturbing effects of the play may have been located not in what may be perceived in the text by a subtle interpreter—implied criticisms of colonialism or subversive doubts about its structures of authority—but in the phenomenon of theatrical representation itself. In 1593 Sir Thomas Smith reminded each captain in Virginia that his task was "to lay the foundation of a good and . . . an eternal colony for your posterity, not a May game or stage play."[39] Festive, evanescent, given over to images of excess, stage plays function here as the symbolic opposite to the lasting colony. So too in a sermon preached in London in 1610 to a group of colonists about to set out for Virginia, William Crashaw declared that the enemies of the godly colony were the devil, the pope, and the players—the latter angry "because we resolve to suffer no Idle persons in Virginia."[40] Similarly, at the end of the martial law text, Strachey records an exceptionally long prayer that he claims was "duly said Morning and Evening upon the Court of Guard, either by the Captain of the watch himself, or by some one of his principal officers." If Strachey is right, twice a day the colonists would have heard, among other uplifting sentiments, the following: "Whereas we have by undertaking this plantation undergone the reproofs of the base world, insomuch as many of our own brethren laugh us to scorn, O Lord we pray thee fortify us against this temptation: let *Sanballat*, & *Tobias*, Papists & players, & such other *Ammonites* & *Horonites* the scum & dregs of the earth, let them mock such as help to build up the walls of Jerusalem, and they that be filthy, let them be filthy still."[41] Even if the content of a play seemed acceptable, the mode of entertainment itself was the enemy of the colonial plantation.

iv

What then is the relation between the theater and the surrounding institutions? Shakespeare's play offers us a model of unresolved and unresolvable doubleness: the island in *The Tempest* seems to be an image of the place of pure fantasy, set apart from surrounding discourses; and it seems to be an image of the place of power, the place in which all individual discourses are organized by the half-invisible ruler. By extension art is a well-demarcated, marginal, private sphere, the realm of insight, pleasure, and isolation; and art is a capacious, central, public sphere, the realm of proper political order made possible through mind control, coercion, discipline, anxiety, and pardon. The aesthetic space—or, more accurately, the commercial space of the theatrical joint-stock company—is constituted by the simultaneous appropriation of and swerving from the discourse of power.

And this doubleness in effect produces two different accounts of the nature of mimetic economy. In one account, aesthetic representation is unlike all other exchanges because it takes nothing; art is pure plenitude. Everywhere else there is scarcity: wretches cling to "an acre of barren ground, long heath, brown furze, any thing" (1.1.66–67), and one person's gain is another's loss. In works of art, by contrast, things can be imitated, staged, reproduced without any loss or expense; indeed what is borrowed seems enhanced by the borrowing, for nothing is used up, nothing fades. The magic of art resides in the freedom of the imagination and hence in liberation from the constraints of the body. What is produced elsewhere only by intense labor is produced in art by a magical command whose power Shakespeare figures in Ariel's response to Prospero's call:

> All hail, great master, grave sir, hail! I come
> To answer thy best pleasure; be't to fly,
> To swim, to dive into the fire, to ride
> On the curl'd clouds. To thy strong bidding, task
> Ariel, and all his quality.
>
> (1.2.189–93)

This account of art as pure plenitude is perhaps most perfectly imaged in Prospero's wedding masque, with its goddesses and nymphs and dancing reapers, its majestic vision of

> Barns and garners never empty;
> Vines with clust'ring bunches growing,
> Plants with goodly burthen bowing.
>
> (4.1.111–13)

But the prayer at the end of the martial law code reminds us that there is another version of mimetic economy, one in which aesthetic exchanges, like all other exchanges, always involve loss, even if it is cunningly hidden; in which aesthetic value, like all other value, actively depends upon want, craving, and absence; in which art itself—fantasy ridden and empty—is the very soul of scarcity. This version too finds its expression in *The Tempest* in the high cost Prospero has paid for his absorption in his secret studies, in Ariel's grumblings about his "pains" and "toil," and in the sudden vanishing—"to a strange, hollow, and confused noise"—of the masque that had figured forth plenitude and in Prospero's richly anxious meditation on the "baseless fabric" of his own glorious vision.

It is this doubleness that Shakespeare's joint-stock company bequeathed to its cultural heirs. And the principal beneficiary in the end was not the theater but a different institution, the institution of literature. Shakespeare served posthumously as a principal shareholder in this institution as well—not as a man of the theater but as the author of the book. During Shakespeare's lifetime, the King's Men showed no interest in and may have actually resisted the publication of a one-volume collection of their famous playwright's work; the circulation of such a book was not in the interests of their company. But other collective enterprises, including the educational system in which this study is implicated, have focused more on the text than on the playhouse.

For if Shakespeare himself imagined Prospero's island as the great Globe Theater, succeeding generations found that island more compactly and portably figured in the bound volume. The passage from the stage to the book signals a larger shift from the joint-stock company, with its primary interest in protecting the common property, to the modern corporation, with its primary interest in the expansion and profitable exploitation of a network of relations. Unlike the Globe, which is tied to a particular place and time and community, unlike even the traveling theater company, with its constraints of personnel and stage properties and playing space, the book is supremely portable. It may be readily detached from its immediate geographical and cultural origins, its original producers and consumers, and endlessly reproduced, circulated, exchanged, exported to other times and places.[42]

The plays, of course, continue to live in the theater, but Shakespeare's achievement and the cult of artistic genius erected around the achievement have become increasingly identified with his collected works. Those works have been widely acknowledged as the central literary achievement of English culture. As such they served—and continue to serve—as a fetish of Western civilization, a fetish Caliban curiously anticipates when he counsels Stephano and Trinculo to cut Prospero's throat:[43]

> Remember
> First to possess his books; for without them
> He's but a sot, as I am; nor hath not
> One spirit to command: they all do hate him
> As rootedly as I. Burn but his books.
>
> (3.2.91–95)

I want to close with a story that provides an oddly ironic perspective on Caliban's desire and exemplifies the continued doubleness of Shakespeare in our culture: at once the embodiment of civilized recreation, freed from the anxiety of rule, and the instrument of empire. The story is told by H. M. Stanley—the journalist and African explorer of "Doctor Livingstone, I presume?" fame—in his account of his journeyings through what he calls "the dark continent." In May 1877 he was at a place called Mowa in central Africa. I will let him tell the story in his own words:

On the third day of our stay at Mowa, feeling quite comfortable amongst the people, on account of their friendly bearing, I began to write down in my note-book the terms for articles in order to improve my already copious vocabulary of native words. I had proceeded only a few minutes when I observed a strange commotion amongst the people who had been flocking about me, and presently they ran away. In a short time we heard war-cries ringing loudly and shrilly over the table-land. Two hours afterwards, a long line of warriors, armed with muskets, were seen descending the table-land and advancing towards our camp. There may have been between five hundred and six hundred of them. We, on the other hand, had made but few preparations except such as would justify us replying to them in the event of the actual commencement of hostilities. But I had made many firm friends amongst them, and I firmly believed that I would be able to avert an open rupture.

When they had assembled at about a hundred yards in front of our camp, Safeni [the chief of another tribe with whom Stanley had become friendly] and I walked up towards them, and sat down midway. Some half-dozen of the Mowa people came near, and the shauri began.

"What is the matter, my friends?" I asked. "Why do you come with guns in your hands in such numbers, as though you were coming to fight? Fight! Fight us, your friends! Tut! this is some great mistake, surely."

"Mundelé," replied one of them, . . . "our people saw you yesterday make marks on some tara-tara" (paper). "This is very bad. Our country will waste, our goats will die, our bananas will rot, and our women will dry up. What have we done to you, that you should wish to kill us? We have sold you food, and we have brought you wine, each day. Your people are allowed to wander where they please, without trouble. Why is the Mundelé so wicked? We have gathered together to fight you if you do not burn that tara-tara now before our eyes. If you burn it we go away, and shall be friends as heretofore."

I told them to rest there, and left Safeni in their hands as a pledge that I should return. My tent was not fifty yards from the spot, but while going towards it my brain was busy in devising some plan to foil this superstitious madness. My note-book contained a vast number of valuable notes; plans of falls, creeks, villages, sketches of localities, ethnological and philological details, sufficient to fill two octavo volumes—everything was of general interest to the public. I could not sacrifice it to the childish caprice of savages. As I was rummaging my book box, I came across a volume of Shakespeare (Chandos edition), much worn and well thumbed, and which was of the same size as my field-book; its cover was similar also, and it might be passed for the note-book provided that no one remembered its appearance too well. I took it to them.

"Is this the tara-tara, friends, that you wish burnt?"

"Yes, yes, that is it!"

"Well, take it, and burn it or keep it."

"M-m. No, no, no. We will not touch it. It is fetish. You must burn it."

"I! Well, let it be so. I will do anything to please my good friends of Mowa."

We walked to the nearest fire. I breathed a regretful farewell to my genial companion, which during many weary hours of night had assisted to relieve my mind when oppressed by almost intolerable woes, and then gravely consigned the innocent Shakespeare to the flames, heaping the brush-fuel over it with ceremonious care.

"Ah-h-h," breathed the poor deluded natives, sighing their relief. "The Mundelé is good—is very good. He loves his Mowa friends. There is no trouble now, Mundelé. The Mowa people are not bad." And something approaching to a cheer was shouted among them, which terminated the episode of the Burning of Shakespeare.[44]

Stanley's precious notebook, with its sketches and ethnographic and philologic details, survived then and proved invaluable in charting and organizing the Belgian Congo, perhaps the most vicious of all of Europe's African colonies. As Stanley had claimed, everything was indeed of general interest to the public. After Stanley's death, the notebooks passed into the possession of heirs and then for many years were presumed lost. But they were rediscovered at the time of the Congo independence celebrations and have recently been edited. Their publication revealed something odd: while the notebook entry for his stay at Mowa records that the natives were angry at his writing—"They say I made strong medicine to kill their country"— Stanley makes no mention of the burning of Shakespeare.[45] Perhaps, to heighten that general interest with which he was so concerned, he made up the story. He could have achieved his narrative effect with only two books: Shakespeare and the Bible. And had he professed to burn the latter to save his notebook, his readers would no doubt have been scandalized.

For our purposes, it doesn't matter very much if the story "really" happened. What matters is the role Shakespeare plays in it, a role at once central and expendable—and, in some obscure way, not just expendable but exchangeable for what really matters: the writing that more directly serves power. For if at moments we can convince ourselves that Shakespeare *is* the discourse of power, we should remind ourselves that there are usually other discourses—here the notes and vocabulary and maps—that are instrumentally far more important. Yet if we try then to convince ourselves that Shakespeare is marginal and untainted by power, we have Stanley's story to remind us that without Shakespeare we wouldn't have the notes. Of course, this is just an accident—the accident of the books' resemblance—but then why was Stanley carrying the book in the first place?

For Stanley, Shakespeare's theater had become a book, and the book in turn had become a genial companion, a talisman of civility, a source not of salutary anxiety but of comfort in adversity. The anxiety in his account—and it is not salutary—is among the natives, and it is relieved only when, as Caliban had hoped, the book is destroyed. But the destruction of one book only saves another, more practical, more deadly. And when he returned to London or New York, Stanley could always buy another copy (Chandos edition) of his genial companion.

Notes

1. The Circulation of Social Energy

1. The classic formulation is by W. K. Wimsatt, Jr.: "In each poem there is something (an individual intuition—or a concept) which can never be expressed in other terms" ("The Structure of the 'Concrete Universal' in Literature," in *Criticism: The Foundations of Modern Literary Judgment*, ed. Mark Schorer, Josephine Miles, and Gordon McKenzie, rev. ed. [New York: Harcourt, Brace, and World, 1958], p. 403).

2. To be sure, a wide range of literary studies have implicitly, and on occasion explicitly, addressed the collective experience of theater: E. K. Chambers's encyclopedic studies of the theatrical institutions in the Middle Ages and the Renaissance, Glynne Wickham's volumes on early English stages, Robert Weimann's analysis of Shakespeare and the popular tradition, C. L. Barber's discussion of Shakespeare and folk rituals, a large number of books and articles on the rhetorical materials with which Shakespeare worked, and so forth. The present study is an attempt to supplement these volumes by exploring the poetics of Renaissance culture.

3. We may posit (and feel) the presence of a powerful and highly individuated creative intelligence, but that creativity does not lead us back to a moment of pure sublime invention, nor does it secure a formal textual autonomy.

4. Novels may have been read aloud to members of the household, but the differentiation of the domestic group is alien to the organization of the theatrical audience.

5. George Puttenham, *The Arte of English Poesie*, in *Elizabethan Critical Essays*, ed. G. Gregory Smith, 2 vols. (London: Oxford University Press, 1904) 2:148. See, likewise, Sir Philip Sidney, *An Apologie for Poetrie*, in Smith, 1:201. The term derives ultimately from Aristotle's *Rhetoric* (33.2.2), as interpreted especially by Quintilian (*Institutio* 8.3.89) and Scaliger (*Poetices* 3.27).

6. And back before the late sixteenth and early seventeenth centuries

as well, since the transactions that enable the creation of Shakespeare's plays are possible only because of prior transactions. Theoretically, at least, the chain has no end, though any inquiry has practical limits and, moreover, certain moments seem more important than others.

7. Jurgis Baltrušaitis, *Le Miroir: Essai sur une légende scientifique: Révélations, science fiction, et fallacies* (Paris: Elmayan, 1978).

8. These items are from the inventory of the Lord Admiral's Men in *Henslowe's Diary*, ed. R. A. Foakes and R. T. Rickert (Cambridge: Cambridge University Press, 1961), app. 2, pp. 320–25.

9. For the terms of "An Acte to Restraine Abuses of Players," see E. K. Chambers, *The Elizabethan Stage*, 4 vols. (Oxford: Clarendon, 1923), 4:338–9. It is not clear how strictly this regulation was enforced.

10. These maneuvers were not always successful. In 1639 it is reported that "Thursday last the players of the Fortune were fined 1000£ for setting up an altar, a bason, and two candlesticks, and bowing down before it upon the stage, and although they allege that it was an old play revived, and an altar to the heathen gods, yet it was apparent that this play was revived on purpose in contempt of the ceremonies of the Church" (quoted in Gerald Eades Bentley, *The Jacobean and Caroline Stage*, 7 vols. [Oxford: Clarendon, 1941–68], 1:277). Bentley expresses some reservations about the accuracy of this account.

11. Stephen Greenblatt, "The Cultivation of Anxiety: King Lear and His Heirs," *Raritan* 2 (1982): 92–124. I should add that the members of joint-stock companies in the early modern period customarily referred to each other in familial terms.

12. "Dynamic circulation" is Michel Foucault's phrase (*L'Usage des plaisirs*, vol. 2 of *Histoire de la sexualité* [Paris: Gallimard, 1984], pp. 52–53).

13. Glynne Wickham, who has argued that the Elizabethan regulations were somewhat more methodical than I have allowed, emphasizes the players' creative flexibility in response: "It is this freedom from rigidly doctrinaire approaches to play writing and play production, coupled with the will to adapt and improvise creatively within the limits of existing opportunities, which ultimately explains the triumph of Elizabethan drama over the censorship and the triumph of Jacobean and Caroline actors in bringing this drama successfully to birth despite the determined efforts of the clergy, town-councillors and Chambers of Commerce to suppress it" (*Early English Stages, 1300–1660*, vol. 2, part 2: 1576–1660 [London: Routledge and Kegan Paul, 1972], p. 208). But we might add—as Wickham himself recognizes—that some of the most severe regulations, such as those suppressing the great mystery cycles and prohibiting unlicensed playing troupes, very much helped the major Elizabethan and Jacobean companies.

14. For reflections on this distinction between retrospective and prospective necessity, see Pierre Bourdieu, *Outline of a Theory of Practice*, trans. Richard Nice (Cambridge: Cambridge University Press, 1977). I have found Bourdieu's book extremely suggestive.

15. In this regard, we may invoke what Bourdieu calls "a restricted definition of economic interest" that is the historical product of capitalism:

The constitution of relatively autonomous areas of practice is accompanied by a process through which symbolic interests (often described as "spiritual" or "cultural") come to be set up in opposition to strictly economic interests as defined in the field of economic transactions by the fundamental tautology "business is business"; strictly "cultural" or "aesthetic" interest, disinterested interest, is the paradoxical product of the ideological labour in which writers and artists, those most directly interested, have played an important part and in the course of which symbolic interests become autonomous by being opposed to material interests, i.e., by being symbolically nullified as interests. (p. 177)

2. Invisible Bullets

1. John Bakeless, *The Tragicall History of Christopher Marlowe*, 2 vols. (Cambridge, Mass.: Harvard University Press, 1942), 1:111. *Juggler* is a richly complex word, including in its range of associations con man, cheap entertainer, magician, trickster, storyteller, conjurer, actor, and dramatist.

2. On Harriot, see especially *Thomas Harriot, Renaissance Scientist*, ed. John W. Shirley (Oxford: Clarendon Press, 1974); Muriel Rukeyser, *The Traces of Thomas Harriot* (New York: Random House, 1970); and Jean Jacquot, "Thomas Harriot's Reputation for Impiety," *Notes and Records of the Royal Society* 9 (1952): 164–87. Harriot himself appears to have paid close attention to his reputation; see David B. Quinn and John W. Shirley, "A Contemporary List of Hariot References," *Renaissance Quarterly* 22 (1969): 9–26.

3. John Aubrey, *Brief Lives*, 2 vols., ed. Andrew Clark (Oxford: Clarendon Press, 1898), 1:286.

4. For the investigation of Ralegh, see *Willobie His Avisa* (1594), ed. G. B. Harrison (London: John Lane, 1926), app. 3, pp. 255–71; for Oliver's story, see Ernest A. Strathmann, *Sir Walter Ralegh: A Study in Elizabethan Skepticism* (New York: Columbia University Press, 1951), p. 50.

5. There are, to be sure, some evangelical professions of having been *saved* from atheism. On treason see Lacey Baldwin Smith, "English Treason Trials and Confessions in the Sixteenth Century," *Journal of the History of Ideas* 15 (1954): 471–98.

6. See, for example, the story William Strachey borrows from Henri Estienne's commentary on Herodotus: "Pope Leo the 10. answered Cardinall Bembo that alleadged some parte of the Ghospell vnto him: 'Lord Cardinall, what a wealth this fable of Iesus Christ hath gotten vs?' " (William Strachey, *The Historie of Travell into Virginia Britania* [1612], ed. Louis B. Wright and Virginia Freund, Hakluyt Society 2d ser., no. 103 [London, 1953], p. 101).

7. Jacquot, "Thomas Harriot's Reputation for Impiety," p. 167. In another official record, Popham is reported to have said ominously, "You know what men say of *Hereiat*" (John W. Shirley, "Sir Walter Ralegh and

Thomas Harriot," in *Thomas Harriot, Renaissance Scientist,* p. 27). The logic
(if that is the word for it) would seem to be this: since God clearly supports
the established order of things and punishes offenders with eternal torments, a criminal must be someone who has been foolishly persuaded that
God does not exist. The alternative theory posits wickedness, a corruption
of the will so severe as to lead people against their own better knowledge
into the ways of crime. The two arguments are often conflated, since
atheism is the heart of the greatest wickedness, as well as the greatest
folly.

8. Northrop Frye, *On Shakespeare* (New Haven: Yale University Press,
1986), p. 10 (see also p. 60: "Shakespeare's social vision is a deeply conservative one"); Franco Moretti, "'A Huge Eclipse': Tragic Form and the
Deconsecration of Sovereignty," in *The Power of Forms in the English Renaissance,* ed. Stephen Greenblatt (Norman, Okla.: Pilgrim Books, 1982), p. 31.
On the histories as occasioning an interrogation of ideology, see Jonathan
Dollimore and Alan Sinfield, "History and Ideology: The Instance of *Henry
V,*" in John Drakakis, *Alternative Shakespeares* (London: Methuen, 1985),
pp. 205–27.

9. Here is how Richard Baines construes Marlowe's version of this
argument: "He affirmeth . . . That the first beginning of Religioun was
only to keep men in awe. That it was an easy matter for Moyses being
brought vp in all the artes of the Egiptians to abuse the Jewes being a rude
& grosse people" (C. F. Tucker Brooke, *The Life of Marlowe* [London: Methuen, 1930], app. 9, p. 98). For other versions, see Strathmann, *Sir Walter
Ralegh,* pp. 70–72, 87.

10. "To come to those who have become princes through their own
merits and not by fortune, I regard as the greatest, Moses, Cyrus, Romulus, Theseus, and their like. And although one should not speak of Moses,
he having merely carried out what was ordered him by God, still he
deserves admiration, if only for that grace which made him worthy to
speak with God. But regarding Cyrus and others who have acquired or
founded kingdoms, they will all be found worthy of admiration; and if
their particular actions and methods are examined they will not appear
very different from those of Moses, although he had so great a Master [che
ebbe si gran precettore]" (Niccolò Machiavelli, *The Prince,* trans. Luigi
Ricci, revised E. R. P. Vincent [New York: Random House, 1950], p. 20).
Christian Detmold translated the *Discourses,* in the same volume.

The delicate ironies here are intensified in the remarks on ecclesiastical
principalities:

They are acquired either by ability or by fortune; but are maintained without either,
for they are sustained by ancient religious customs, which are so powerful and of
such quality, that they keep their princes in power in whatever manner they pro-
ceed and live. These princes alone have states without defending them, have subjects without governing them, and their states, not being defended are not taken
from them; their subjects not being governed do not resent it, and neither think nor
are capable of alienating themselves from them. Only those principalities, therefore,

are secure and happy. But as they are upheld by higher causes, which the human mind cannot attain to, I will abstain from speaking of them; for being exalted and maintained by God, it would be the work of a presumptuous and foolish man to discuss them. (*The Prince*, 41–42)

The sly wit of this passage depends not only on the subtle mockery but also on the possibility that the "ancient religious customs" are in fact politically efficacious.

11. Kyd, in Brooke, *Life of Marlowe*, app. 12, p. 107; Parsons, in Strathmann, *Sir Walter Ralegh*, p. 25.

12. Quoted in Jean Jacquot, "Ralegh's 'Hellish Verses' and the 'Tragicall Raigne of Selimus,' " *Modern Language Review* 48 (1953): 1.

13. This is the suggestion of Pierre Lefranc, *Sir Walter Ralegh, Ecrivain* (Quebec: Armand Colin, 1968), pp. 673–74; Lefranc gives a slightly different version of the verses (app. N, p. 673).

For a popular instance of Ralegh's reputation as a freethinker, see the poem circulated against him, with the refrain "Damnable friend of hell, / Mischievous Matchivell" (in Lefranc, p. 667). I should add that Ralegh was famous for a theatrical manner, so that it may have seemed all the more plausible to attach to his name verses from a play.

14. Thomas Harriot, *A briefe and true report of the new found land of Virginia: of the commodities there found and to be raysed, as well marchantable, as others for victuall, building and other necessarie vses for those that are and shalbe the planters there; and of the nature and manners of the naturall inhabitants* (London, 1588), in *The Roanoke Voyages, 1584–1590*, 2 vols., ed. David Beers Quinn, Hakluyt Society 2d ser. no. 104 (London, 1955), p. 375.

The illustrated edition of this account includes John White drawings of these priests and of the ceremonies over which they presided, along with a striking drawing of a dancing figure called "the conjurer." "They have commonly conjurers or jugglers," Harriot's annotation explains, "which use strange gestures, and often contrary to nature in their enchantments: For they be very familiar with devils, of whom they enquire what their enemies do, or other such things. . . . The Inhabitants give great credit unto their speech, which oftentimes they find to be true" (Thomas Harriot, *A Briefe and True Report*, facsimile of the 1590 Theodor De Bry edition [New York: Dover, 1972], p. 54). I will refer to this edition in my text as De Bry.

In the next generation, William Strachey would urge that when the colonists have the power, they should "performe the same acceptable service to god, that Iehu king of Israell did when he assembled all the priests of Baal, and slue them to the last man in their owne Temple" (*Historie of Travell*, p. 94).

The best introduction to the current scholarship on the Algonquians of southern New England is Bruce G. Trigger, ed., *Handbook of North American Indians*, vol. 15, *Northeast* (Washington, D.C.: Smithsonian, 1978).

15. Harriot goes on to note that the disciplinary force of religious fear is

supplemented by secular punishment: "although notwithstanding there is punishment ordained for malefactours, as stealers, whoremoonger, and other sortes of wicked doers; some punished with death, some with forfeitures, some with beating, according to the greatnes of the factes" (De Bry, p. 26).

16. See Karen Ordahl Kupperman, *Settling with the Indians: The Meeting of English and Indian Cultures in America, 1580–1640* (Totowa, N.J.: Rowman and Littlefield, 1975).

17. I should add that it quickly became a rhetorical trope to describe the mass of Europeans as little better than or indistinguishable from American savages.

18. *Discourses*, p. 148. The context of this observation is the continuing discussion of Numa's wisdom in feigning divine authority: "It is true that those were very religious times, and the people with whom Numa had to deal were very untutored and superstitious, which made it easy for him to carry out his designs, being able to impress upon them any new form. . . . I conclude that the religion introduced by Numa into Rome was one of the chief causes of the prosperity of that city" (147–48).

19. When in 1590 the Flemish publisher Theodor De Bry reprinted Harriot's *Briefe and True Report*, he made this belief explicit: along with engravings of John White's brilliant Virginia drawings, De Bry's edition includes five engravings of the ancient Picts, "to showe how that the Inhabitants of the great Bretannie haue bin in times past as sauuage as those of Virginia" (De Bry, p. 75).

20. In his notes to the John White engravings, Harriot also records his hopes for a widespread Algonquian conversion to Christianity: "Thes poore soules haue none other knowledge of god although I thinke them verye Desirous to know the truthe. For when as wee kneeled downe on our knees to make our prayers vnto god, they went abowt to imitate vs, and when they saw we moued our lipps, they also dyd the like. Wherfore that is verye like that they might easelye be brought to the knowledge of the gospel. God of his mercie grant them this grace" (De Bry, p. 71).

21. In Richard Hakluyt, *The Principal Navigations, Voyages, Traffiques, and Discoveries of the English Nation*, 12 vols. (Glasgow: James Maclehose and Sons, 1903–5), 10:54.

22. The situation is parodied in Shakespeare's *Tempest* when the drunken Caliban, rebelling against Prospero, sings:

> No more dams I'll make for fish,
>   Nor fetch in firing
>   At requiring,
> Nor scrape trenchering, nor wash dish.
>   (2.2.180–83)

23. For an alternative explanation of the principal sources of the Europeans' apparent apathy, see Karen Ordahl Kupperman, "Apathy and Death in Early Jamestown," *Journal of American History* 66 (1979): 24–40. Kupper-

man argues that there are significant parallels between the deaths of early colonists and the deaths of American prisoners in Korean prison camps.

24. On these catalogs, see Wayne Franklin, *Discoverers, Explorers, Settlers: The Diligent Writers of Early America* (Chicago: University of Chicago Press, 1979), pp. 69–122.

25. Quoted in Edward Rosen, "Harriot's Science: The Intellectual Background," in Shirley, *Thomas Harriot, Renaissance Scientist*, p. 4.

26. Donald Friedman, private correspondence. Friedman continues: "A point that follows is that Harriot's awareness of 'subversion' might, by this token, be cast in the mode of 'what else can you expect of heathen?' "

27. Francis Bacon, *The New Organon*, bk. 1, aphorism 129, in *Francis Bacon: A Selection of His Works*, ed. Sidney Warhaft (New York: Odyssey, 1965), p. 373. I am indebted for this reference to James Carson.

28. For a further instance of the term *juggler* used of English technology in the New World, see William Wood, *New Englands Prospect* (London, 1634), p. 78; quoted in Karen Ordahl Kupperman, "English Perceptions of Treachery, 1583–1640: The Case of the American 'Savages,' " *Historical Journal* 20 (1977): 263–87.

29. In Spenser, this primitive propensity toward idolatrous worship plays into the wicked hands of the Catholic church, and there may be some echoes of this preoccupation in Harriot's text where it would provide further insulation against awareness of a radical self-indictment. The fetishism of religious objects, the confusion of the spiritual and the material, is a frequent Protestant accusation against Catholicism, as is the charge that subtle priests cynically foster idolatry to control the people. In his notes to the White illustrations, Harriot remarks that the Algonquians sometimes have two or three "idols in their churches . . . which they place in a dark corner where they show terrible"; he notes that the priest who guards the bones of the dead chieftains "mumbleth his prayers night and day"; and he describes the posts around which the Indians dance as "carved with heads like to the faces of Nuns covered with their veils" (De Bry, pp. 71–72). This is the familiar language of Protestant polemics, and it may imply that the English will be saving the Algonquians not only from their own false worship but from the oddly cognate false worship spread by the Catholic Spanish and French. But it should be noted that Harriot does not push the resemblance between Indian and Catholic priests very hard.

30. John Calvin, *Institutes of the Christian Religion*, 2 vols., ed. John T. McNeill, trans. Ford Lewis Battles, Library of Christian Classics, vols. 20–21 (Philadelphia: Westminster Press, 1960), 1:1.3.2, pp. 44–45. I am indebted for this and the following reference to John Coolidge.

31. Richard Hooker, *Works*, 3 vols., ed. John Keble (Oxford: Oxford University Press, 1836), 2:5.1.3, p. 21.

32. J. G. A. Pocock, *The Machiavellian Moment: Florentine Political Thought and the Atlantic Republican Tradition* (Princeton: Princeton University Press, 1975).

33. Cf. Walter Bigges's narrative of Drake's visit to Florida in 1586: "The wilde people at first comminge of our men died verie fast and saide amongest themselues, It was the Inglisshe God that made them die so faste" (in Quinn, *The Roanoke Voyages* 1:306).

34. The search for atheists offers a parallel: atheism is the cause of treason, and the occurrence of treason is itself evidence for the existence of atheism.

35. We should note, however, that the conception of "invisible bullets" implies intention and hence morality.

36. Guido Calabresi and Philip Bobbitt, *Tragic Choices* (New York: W. W. Norton, 1978), p. 195. The term *tragic* is misleading, I think, since the same strategies may be perceived in situations that do not invoke the generic expectations or constraints of tragedy.

37. John Upton, *Critical Observations on Shakespeare* (1748), in *Shakespeare: The Critical Heritage*, ed. Brian Vickers, vol. 3, *1733–1752* (London: Routledge and Kegan Paul, 1975), p. 297; Maynard Mack, introduction to the Signet Classic edition of *1 Henry IV* (New York: New American Library, 1965), p. xxxv.

38. Who is the "we" in these sentences? I refer both to the stage tradition of the play and to the critical tradition. This does not mean that the play cannot be staged as a bitter assault upon Hal, but such a staging will struggle against the current that has held sway since the play's inception and indeed since the formation of the whole ideological myth of Prince Hal.

39. In the battle of Shrewsbury, when Falstaff is pretending he is dead, Hal, seeing the body of his friend, thinks with an eerie symbolic appropriateness of having the corpse literally emptied. As Hal exits, Falstaff rises up and protests. If Falstaff is an enormous mountain of flesh, Hal is the quintessential thin man: "you starveling," Falstaff calls him (2.4.244). From Hal's point of view, Falstaff's fat prevents him from having any value at all: "there's no room for faith, truth, nor honesty in this bosom of thine; it is all fill'd up with guts and midriff" (3.3.153–55).

Here and throughout the discussion of *1 Henry IV*, I am indebted to Edward Snow.

40. William Empson, *Some Versions of Pastoral* (London: Chatto and Windus, 1968), p. 103.

41. See S. P. Zitner, "Anon, Anon; or, a Mirror for a Magistrate," *Shakespeare Quarterly* 19 (1968): 63–70.

42. More accurately, the ratios are redistributed. For example, *Henry V* insists that the world represented in the play is extraordinarily spacious, varied, and mobile, while the stage itself is cramped and confining:

> Can this cockpit hold
> The vasty fields of France? Or may we cram
> Within this wooden O the very casques
> That did affright the air at Agincourt?
> (Prologue, 11–14)

The Chorus calls attention to this contradiction to exhort the audience to transcend it "In the quick forge and working-house of thought"(5.0.23). We have to do not with a balance of forces but with an imbalance that must be rectified by the labor of the imagination:

> Piece out our imperfections with your thoughts;
> Into a thousand parts divide one man,
> And make imaginary puissance.
> (Prologue, 23–25)

43. What we took to be the "center" may be part of the remotest periphery. More unsettling still, topographic accounts of both theater and power may be illusions: there may be no way to locate oneself securely in relation to either.

44. See, for example, Victor Turner, *Drama, Fields, and Metaphors: Symbolic Action in Human Society* (Ithaca: Cornell University Press, 1974).

45. The evidence is amply documented by Karen Kupperman, *Settling with the Indians*.

46. Thomas Harman, *A Caueat or Warening, for Commen Cursetors Vulgarely Called Vagabones* (1566), in *Cony-Catchers and Bawdy Baskets*, ed. Gamini Salgado (Middlesex: Penguin, 1972), p. 146.

47. On the problems of Elizabethan representations of the underworld, see A. L. Beier, *Masterless Men: The Vagrancy Problem in England, 1560–1640* (London: Methuen, 1985).

48. [Gilbert Walker?] *A manifest detection of the moste vyle and detestable vse of Diceplay* (c. 1552), in Salgado, *Cony-Catchers and Bawdy Baskets*, pp. 42–43.

49. Norman N. Holland, in the Signet Classic edition of *2 Henry IV* (New York: New American Library, 1965), p. xxxvi.

50. See Frank Whigham, *Ambition and Privilege: The Social Tropes of Elizabethan Courtesy Theory* (Berkeley: University of California Press, 1984).

51. The public response to betrayal is extremely difficult to measure. Lawrence Stone suggests that there is a transition in the early years of the seventeenth century: "Up to the end of the sixteenth century men saw nothing dishonorable in attacking by surprise with superior forces, and nothing in hitting a man when he was down. By the second decade of the seventeenth century, however, such behaviour was becoming discreditable and is much less frequently met with" (Lawrence Stone, *The Crisis of the Aristocracy, 1558–1641*, abridged edition [New York: Oxford University Press, 1967], p. 109).

52. The presence of the Irishman among the English forces is especially significant since as the Chorus points out, an English expeditionary army was attempting at the moment of the play to subjugate the Irish. It is not the least of the play's bitter historical ironies that in four hundred years this attempt has not become an anachronism.

53. It would not have escaped at least some members of an Elizabethan audience that an English gentleman or woman would have been far more

likely to learn French than a Frenchman English. The language lesson, Steven Mullaney suggests, is Shakespeare's "rearward glance at the improprieties that occupied the ambivalent center of Hal's prodigality." Whereas in the first and second parts of *Henry IV*, the recording of the language of the other has an element of tragedy, its equivalent in *Henry V* has only the spirit of French farce (Steven Mullaney, "Strange Things, Gross Terms, Curious Customs: The Rehearsal of Cultures in the Late Renaissance," *Representations* 3 [1983]: 63–64).

54. "This does not sound like hypocrisy or cynicism. The Archbishop discharges his duty faithfully, as it stands his reasoning is impeccable. . . . Henry is not initiating aggression" (J. H. Walter, in the Arden edition of *King Henry V* [London: Methuen, 1954], p. xxv).

55. The kill ratio is highly in the English favor in all accounts, but Shakespeare adopts from Holinshed the most extreme figure. Holinshed himself adds that "other writers of greater credit affirm that there were slain above five or six hundred" Englishmen (Holinshed, in the Oxford Shakespeare edition of *Henry V*, ed. Gary Taylor [Oxford: Oxford University Press, 1984], p. 308). Similarly, Shakespeare makes no mention of the tactical means by which the English army achieved its victory. The victory is presented as virtually miraculous.

56. In a long appendix to his edition of *Henry V*, Gary Taylor attempts to defend his emendation of "all" to "ill" in these lines, on the grounds that an interpretation along the lines of Claudius's failed repentance would be difficult for an actor to communicate and, if communicated, would make "the victory of Agincourt morally and dramatically incomprehensible" (Taylor, p. 298). The interpretive framework that I am sketching in this chapter should make the Folio's reading fully comprehensible; the effect of the victory is, by my account, intensified by the play's moral problems.

57. Taylor makes a subtle and, I think, implausible attempt to reduce the unintended irony of Gower's line, "wherefore the King, most worthily, hath caus'd every soldier to cut his prisoner's throat" (4.7.8–10): "Gower is not saying (as all editors and critics seem to have understood him) 'the king *caused* the prisoners to be executed because of the attack on the baggage train' but 'given the barbarity of the subsequent French conduct, the king *has* quite justifiably *caused* the death of his prisoners' " (Taylor, p. 243). Even were we to understand the line in Taylor's sense, it would open a moral problem still worse than the political problem that has been resolved.

58. See the illuminating discussion in Norman Rabkin, *Shakespeare and the Problem of Meaning* (Chicago: University of Chicago Press, 1981), pp. 33–62.

59. This is flattery carefully echoed in Hal's promise to his troops on the eve of Agincourt that "be he ne'er so vile, / This day shall gentle his condition" (4.3.62–63). The promise is silently forgotten after the battle.

60. For a brilliant exploration of this hypothesis, see D. A. Miller, "The Novel and the Police," in *Glyph* 8 (1981): 127–47.

61. Quoted in J. E. Neale, *Elizabeth I and Her Parliaments, 1584–1601*, 2 vols. (London: Cape, 1965), 2:119. For the complex relation between theater and absolutism, see Stephen Orgel, *The Illusion of Power: Political Theater in the English Renaissance* (Berkeley: University of California Press, 1975); Jonathan Goldberg, *James I and the Politics of Literature: Jonson, Shakespeare, Donne, and Their Contemporaries* (Baltimore: Johns Hopkins University Press, 1983); Jonathan Dollimore, *Radical Tragedy: Religion, Ideology, and Power in the Drama of Shakespeare and His Contemporaries* (Brighton: Harvester, 1983); Greenblatt, *The Power of Forms in the English Renaissance;* Steven Mullaney, "Lying like Truth: Riddle, Representation, and Treason in Renaissance England," *ELH* 47 (1980): 32–47; Paola Colaiacomo, "Il teatro del principe," *Calibano* 4 (1979): 53–98; Christopher Pye, "The Sovereign, the Theater, and the Kingdome of Darknesse: Hobbes and the Spectacle of Power," *Representations* 8 (1984): 85–106.

62. *The History of King Richard III*, ed. R. S. Sylvester, in *The Complete Works of St. Thomas More*, vol. 3 (New Haven: Yale University Press, 1963), p. 80.

63. Clifford Geertz, "Centers, Kings, and Charisma: Reflections on the Symbolics of Power," in *Culture and Its Creators: Essays in Honor of Edward Shils*, ed. Joseph Ben David and Terry Nichols Clark (Chicago: University of Chicago Press, 1977), p. 160.

64. The nameless servant in *Lear* who can no longer endure what he is witnessing and who heroically stabs his master Cornwall, the legitimate ruler of half of England, inhabits a different political world from the one sketched here, a world marked out by Shakespeare as tragic.

65. Perhaps we should imagine Shakespeare writing at a moment when none of the alternatives for a resounding political commitment seemed satisfactory; when the pressure to declare himself unequivocally an adherent of one or another faction seemed narrow, ethically coarse, politically stupid; when the most attractive political solution seemed to be to keep options open and the situation fluid.

3. Fiction and Friction

1. *Montaigne's Travel Journal*, trans. Donald M. Frame (San Francisco: North Point Press, 1983), p. 5. In his *Introdvction av traité de la conformité des merueilles anciennes auec les modernes. ov traité preparatif à l'Apologie pour Herodote* (1579), Henri Estienne recounts a similar case which he says took place some thirty years earlier: "C'est qu'vne fille natiue de Fontaines, qui est entre Blois & Rommorantin, s'estant desguisee en homme, seruit de valet d'establé enuiron sept ans en vne hostelerie du faux-bourg du Foye, puis se maria à vne fille du lieu, auec laquelle elle fut enuiron deux ans,

exerceant le mestier de vigneron. Apres lequel temps estant descouuerte la meschanceté de laquelle elle vsoit pour contrefaire l'office de mari, fut prise, & ayant confessé fut là bruslee toute viue" (pp. 94–95).

2. Michel Foucault, *The History of Sexuality*, vol. 1, trans. Robert Hurley (New York: Random House, 1978), pp. 53–73. Foucault argues for a large-scale shift in the modern period away from legal definitions of sexual roles to endlessly elaborated discursive revelations of the open secret of sexuality.

3. In one of Shakespeare's principal sources for *Twelfth Night*, Barnaby Riche tells his readers that in his story "you shall see Dame Errour so plaie her parte with a leishe of lovers, a male and twoo females, as shall woorke a wonder to your wise judgement" (*Riche his Farewell to Militarie Profession* [1581], in *Narrative and Dramatic Sources of Shakespeare*, 8 vols., ed. Geoffrey Bullough [London: Routledge and Kegan Paul, 1958–75], 2:345). "Error" has, I think, some of its etymological force of divagation, or wandering, a version of what I am calling swerving.

4. John Manningham's early seventeenth-century summary of the play mistakenly refers to Olivia as a widow—a sign, I think, of the normalization of the fantasy (in the Arden edition of *Twelfth Night*, ed. J. M. Lothian and T. W. Craik [London: Methuen, 1975], p. xxvi).

5. In the image of the cloistress, Olivia's vow picks up for Shakespeare's Protestant audience associations with life-denying monastic vows, which must be broken to honor the legitimate claims of the flesh by entering into holy matrimony. When Theseus threatens the recalcitrant Hermia with the "livery of a nun, / For aye to be in shady cloister mew'd" (1.1.70–71), we can be certain that *A Midsummer Night's Dream* will not close with her "Chaunting faint hymns to the cold fruitless moon" (1.1.73). The comedy will instead celebrate the triumph of warm blood and fruitful union. Similarly, when Isabella actively seeks the cloister, wishing only "a more strict restraint / Upon the sisterhood" (1.4.4–5), we anticipate that the play will overrule her desires. Odd as is the close of *Measure for Measure*, with the Duke's peremptory and unanswered proposal—"Give me your hand, and say you will be mine" (5.1.492)—it would be still odder in the context of English comic conventions if it consigned the heroine to the votarists of Saint Clare. And when at the start of *Love's Labor's Lost* the young French lords vow to abjure the sight of women for three years, we would be surprised if there were not an immediate announcement of the arrival of the princess and her ladies.

6. Here, as elsewhere at the opening of *Twelfth Night*, Orsino imagines a massive singleness in love, corresponding to the play's initial gambit of the union of duke and countess. And this singleness is focused conspicuously on the "rich golden shaft" that has the power to destroy all competing emotions in the beloved. If any psychological progress is sketched for Orsino, it lies in his accepting multiple emotions. It is not altogether clear that he progresses in this direction, though a skilled actor might be able to

suggest at the close that Orsino splits his desire between Cesario/Viola and Olivia.

7. The lawyer John Manningham, who saw the play in February 1602, immediately recognized several of the antecedents: "At our feast wee had a play called Twelue night or what you will. much like the commedy of errors or Menechmi in plautus but most like and neere to that in Italian called Inganni" (Arden edition, xxvi). Manningham's date "Febr:1601" is old-style. Manningham sketched the Malvolio subplot, which evidently struck him as original—"a good practise"—but said nothing further about the main plot: presumably, the simple notation of analogues seemed to him sufficient to recall the play's essential shape.

8. The modal "would" in the verb form "would have been contracted" lightly refers both to Olivia's mismatched desires and, had it not been for nature's bias, to the absurd consequences of those desires. The slight oscillation, though of miniscule dramatic effect, is worth noticing because it encapsulates the play's large-scale oscillation between will and passivity.

9. An epithalamion Donne wrote for the scandal-surrounded marriage of the Earl of Somerset to the divorced Countess of Essex (1613) includes the following stanza entitled "Equality of Persons":

> But undiscerning Muse, which heart, which eyes,
> In this new couple, dost thou prize,
> When his eye as inflaming is
> As hers, and her heart loves as well as his?
> Be tried by beauty, and then
> The Bridegroom is a maid, and not a man.
> If by that manly courage they be tried,
> Which scorns unjust opinion; then the Bride
> Becomes a man. Should chance or envy's art
> Divide these two, whom nature scarce did part?
> Since both have both th'inflaming eyes, and both the loving heart.

This miniature Shakespearean comedy would seem to be played, in part at least, for a king who had a marked erotic interest in his male favorites. (I am indebted for this reference to Paul Alpers.)

10. To Sebastian's question, "What name? What parentage?" Viola answers with the father's name (the mother in effect having no bearing on the question of parentage): "Sebastian was my father" (5.1.231–32). At the first mention of Orsino's name, Viola had remarked, "Orsino! I have heard my father name him" (1.2.28). At the play's close, when we learn that this naming must have betokened a measure of social equality, the dialogue swerves from the natural back to the social. That is, in the face of the gender confusion, attention to social conflict had apparently been deflected by a concern for the natural; now the social returns the favor by deflecting attention from the natural. The play hastens to its conclusion by matching Orsino to Viola while gesturing toward Malvolio's grievance. For a Lacanian analysis of the "Nom-du-Père" in relation to transsexualism,

see Catherine Millot, *Horsexe: Essai sur le transsexualisme* (Paris: Point Hors Ligne, 1983), esp. pp. 29–43.

11. C. L. Barber, *Shakespeare's Festive Comedy* (Princeton: Princeton University Press, 1959), p. 245.

12. Marie, subsequently renamed Marin, was a bit vague on the subject, but Jeane's recollection was that on the first night they made love four times; Jeane testified that she had more sexual pleasure—"plus grand contentement"—with Marin than with her late husband (Jacques Duval, *Des Hermaphrodits, Accouchemens des Femmes, et Traitement qui est requis pour les releuer en santé, et bien eleuer leurs enfans* [Rouen, 1603], p. 392). (The marginal note to Jeane's account of the first night is "Belle confirmation de promesse de mariage.")

13. In the only remotely comparable case that I know of, the court seemed similarly perplexed, though its decision was significantly different (and, to my knowledge, unprecedented). This was the case of Thomasine Hall, born in the 1570s near Newcastle upon Tyne. At age twelve, Thomasine was sent by her mother to live with an aunt in London, where she remained for ten years. At the time of the Cádiz action, we are told, she cut her hair, renamed herself Thomas, and enlisted as a soldier; then returned to London and resumed her life as a woman; then abandoned her needlework again and sailed as a man to Virginia; then became Thomasine once more and served as a chambermaid. Hauled before the Council and General Court of Virginia in 1629 and asked "why hee went in weomans aparell," Thomasine gave the unforgettable, if enigmatic, reply, "I goe in weomans aparell to gett a bitt for my Cat." The judges evidently felt that unresolved sexual ambiguity was more tolerable than dizzying sexual metamorphosis; they preferred a figure frozen in acknowledged androgyny to one who passed fluidly and unpredictably from one state to another. Accordingly, they ordered that it be published that Hall "is a man and a woman," and they insisted upon this doubleness in the clothes they required him to wear: "Hee shall goe Clothed in mans apparell, only his head to bee attired in a Cyse and Croscloth [?] wth an Apron before him" (*Minutes of the Council and General Court of Colonial Virginia, 1622–1632, 1670–1676*, ed. H. R. McIlwaine [Richmond, Va.: Virginia State Library, 1924], p. 195).

14. Michelle Z. Rosaldo, *Knowledge and Passion: Ilongot Notions of Self and Social Life* (Cambridge: Cambridge University Press, 1980), p. 231; see also Pierre Bourdieu, *Outline of a Theory of Practice*, trans. Richard Nice (Cambridge: Cambridge University Press, 1977):

Since the history of the individual is never anything other than a certain specification of the collective history of his group or class, *each individual system of dispositions* may be seen as a *structural variant* of all the other group or class habitus, expressing the difference between trajectories and positions inside or outside the class. "Personal" style, the particular stamp marking all the product of the same habitus, whether practices or works, is never more than a *deviation* in relation to the *style* of a

period or class so that it relates back to the common style not only by its confor-
mity . . . but also by the difference which makes the whole "manner." (86)

15. Such stories are by no means limited to literary fictions. Thus, for
example, the sixteenth-century chronicler Robert Fabian writes of three
New World savages presented to Henry VII that they "were clothed in
beasts skins, & did eate raw flesh, and spake such speach that no man
could understand them, and in their demeanour like to bruite beastes."
"Of the which upon two yeeres after," he continues, "I saw two apparelled
after the maner of Englishmen in Westminster pallace, which that time I
could not discerne from Englishmen, til I was learned what they were"
(quoted in my "Learning to Curse: Aspects of Linguistic Colonialism in the
Sixteenth Century," in *First Images of America: The Impact of the New World in
the Old*, 2 vols., ed. Fredi Chiappelli (Berkeley: University of California
Press, 1976), 2:563.

16. The modern interest, fueled by sociology, in the structures that govern individual improvisations finds its paradoxical equivalent in the Renaissance interest in prodigies: prodigies function exactly like sociological
structures—to make normative, individual variations possible. It is difficult
in an inquiry such as this to hold on to the sense that individuals are variations on (or deviations from) a set of social structures. Pierre Bourdieu:
" 'Interpersonal' relations are never, except in appearance, *individual-to-
individual* relationships and . . . the truth of the interaction is never entirely
contained in the interaction" (*Outline of a Theory of Practice*, p. 81).

Nature in Renaissance thought is not a static entity but a life force that
must constantly generate, create, reproduce individuals. If this force
should cease for an instant, all life would cease, and matter would sink
back into primal confusion and disorder. This ceaseless generativity is
epitomized in the production of prodigies, which by their very existence
affirm the variety of things and mark out ineradicable differences. At the
same time, prodigies represent the disorder that their existence helps to
negate. The monstrous is virtually defined by excess and by the improper,
disordered fashioning of matter into misshapen lumps, strange conjunc-
tions, gross and unnecessary excrescences. Hence even as they celebrate
the inexhaustible fecundity of nature in producing prodigies, Renaissance
scholars hasten to discover the principle of order that may be perceived
behind even the most uncanny oddity (see Jean Céard, *La Nature et les
prodiges: L'Insolite au 16e siècle en France* [Geneve: Droz, 1977]).

The prodigious functions as the extremest form of individuation—just
as in modern sociology the quantifiable functions as the extremest form
of the normative. This tendency of the individual, in its purest or logically extended form, to become the prodigious is supremely visible in
Shakespeare, where the prodigious taints all decisive individuation. This
is true, in different senses to be sure, in comedy as well as tragedy.
Those comic characters who achieve the greatest level of individuation in

effect pass through either a literal or metaphoric experience of the prodigious: Viola, Rosalind, Bottom the Weaver, Shylock, Falstaff, even Jaques and Malvolio. The prodigious (as physical grotesquerie, madness, or excess) is still more marked in the great tragic characters: Richard III, Macbeth, Hamlet, Othello, Antony and Cleopatra.

17. Hence the note of androgyny in Spenser's depiction of nature in the *Faerie Queene:*

> Then forth issewed (great goddesse) great dame *Nature,*
> With goodly port and gracious Maiesty;
> Being far greater and more tall of stature
> Then any of the gods of Powers on hie:
> Yet certes by her face and physnomy,
> Whether she man or woman inly were,
> That could not any creature well descry:
> For, with a veile that wimpled euery where,
> Her head and face was hid, that mote to none appear.
>
> (7.7.5)

18. Nathaniel Highmore, *The History of Generation* (London: John Martin, 1651), pp. 92–93.

19. See, for example, *The Workes of that Famous Chirurgian Ambrose Parey,* trans. Thomas Johnson (London: Thomas Cotes, 1634):

When the husband commeth into his wives chamber hee must entertaine her with all kinde of dalliance, wanton behaviour, and allurements to venery: but if he perceive her to be slow, and more cold, he must cherish, embrace, and tickle her, and shall not abruptly, the nerves being suddenly distended, breake into the field of nature, but rather shall creepe in by little and little intermixing more wanton kisses with wanton words and speeches, handling her secret parts and dugs, that she may take fire and bee enflamed to venery, for so at length the wombe will strive and waxe fervent with a desire of casting forth its owne seed, and receiving the mans seed to bee mixed together therewith. But if all these things will not suffice to enflame the woman, for women for the most part are slow and slack unto the expulsion or yeelding forth of their seed, it shall be necessary first to foment her secret parts with the decoction of hot herbes made with Muscadine, or boiled in any other good wine, and to put a little muske or civet into the neck or mouth of the wombe. (889)

This book will be referred to in the text of my essay as Paré, *Works.*

20. For an important and fascinating account of the changes in the understanding of female sexuality, see Thomas Laqueur, "Orgasm, Generation, and the Politics of Reproductive Biology," in *Representations* 14 (1986): 1–41.

21. Galen, *On the Usefulness of the Parts of the Body,* 2 vols., ed. and trans. Margaret May (Ithaca: Cornell University Press, 1968), 2:14.297, pp. 628–29.

22. *Ibid.* 2:14.297–98, p. 629. Elsewhere in his work, Galen observes that while the mole's inability to bring forth its eyes is entirely a defect, the female's comparable inability to bring forth her genitals is of great use,

since it enables her to bear children (Galen, *De semine* 2:5, in *Libri Novem* [Basel: 1536], pp. 173–74).

23. Paré, *Works*, p. 128. It is important to grasp that Paré does not connect his two explanations and argue for a "providential defect." Instead the contradictory theories exist side by side and speak to different aspects of the same problem.

24. Ambroise Paré, *On Monsters and Marvels* (1573), trans. Janis L. Pallister (Chicago: University of Chicago Press, 1982), pp. 31–32.

25. *Montaigne's Travel Journal*, p. 6. Montaigne (or his secretary) adds, "They say that Ambroise Paré has put this story into his book on surgery."

26. Hence Duval's fascination with Marin expresses his own uneasiness with the inherited medical traditions that Marin seems at once to confirm and to push toward grotesquerie.

27. The clitoris is, Duval says, such a violent source of sexual pleasure that even the most modest of women will, if once they agree to allow it to be touched by a finger's end, be overcome with desire: "amorcées & rauies, voire forcées au deduit venereén" (*Des Hermaphrodits*, p. 63). ("Donnant l'exact sentiment de cette partie, pour petite qu'elle soit, vne tant violente amorce au prurit & ardeur libidineux, qu'estant la raison surmontee, les femelles prennent tellement le frain aux dents qu'elles donnent du cul à terre, faute de se tenir fermes & roides sur les arcons" [63–64].) Hence in French, Duval writes, the clitoris is popularly called "tentation, aiguillon de volupté, verge femininine [*sic*], le mespris des hommes: Et les femmes qui font profession d'impudicité la nomment leur *gaude mihi*" (64).

On the displacement of the structural homology from the uterus to the clitoris, see Ian Maclean, *The Renaissance Notion of Woman: A Study in the Fortunes of Scholasticism and Medical Science in European Intellectual Life* (Cambridge: Cambridge University Press, 1980), p. 33.

28. *Aristotle's Master-piece or the Secrets of Generation Displayed* (London, 1690), p. 15. The first known English edition of this incessantly reprinted anonymous work is 1684, though the work was probably circulated in English considerably earlier; it was still circulated widely in the nineteenth century.

29. The notion of the enlarged clitoris is alive and well in the seventeenth and early eighteenth centuries: "Sometimes it grows so long," writes the midwife Jane Sharp in 1671, "that it hangs forth at the slit like a Yard, and will swell and stand stiff if it be provoked, and some lewd women have attempted to use it as men do theirs . . . but I never heard but of one in this Country" (quoted in Audrey Eccles, *Obstetrics and Gynaecology in Tudor and Stuart England* [Kent, Ohio: Kent State University Press, 1982], p. 34). See also Hilda Smith, "Gynecology and Ideology in Seventeenth-Century England," in *Liberating Women's History: Theoretical and Critical Essays*, ed. Berenice A. Carroll (Champaign: University of Illinois Press, 1976), pp. 97–114.

30. The interest and complexity of this account depends on the lovers' looking at the other as they strive to re-create images of themselves; or perhaps they are simultaneously looking at the other and at their own reflection in each other's eyes. In either case, the representation of oneself— one's reproduction and hence triumph over death—depends upon self-abandonment, upon giving oneself over to the image of the other. One might recall the moment in Milton when God draws Eve away from her narcissism—that is, her potentially dangerous and prodigious individuation—toward a proper bonding with another. The narcissism is symbolized by her peering in the water at her reflection, unstable and perpetually unsatisfying, and the proper bonding by her steady gazing into the face of another—Adam—and by the production of other images in the offspring they will generate.

31. The medical literature offers considerable speculation on the place of the imagination in the process of sexual consummation and conception, in the work of the German physician Paracelsus, for example, especially "Das Buch von der Gebärung der empfindlichen Dinge in der Vernunft" (c. 1520), in Theophrastus von Hohenheim gen. Paracelsus, *Medizinische Naturwissenshaftliche und Philosophische Schriften*, ed. Karl Sudhoff (Munich: Otto Wilhem Barth Verlag, 1925), 1:243–83. I owe this fascinating reference to Jane O. Newman.

32. John McMath, *The Expert Midwife* (1694), quoted in Eccles, *Obstetrics and Gynaecology*, p. 40.

33. Thomas Vicary, *The Anatomie of the Bodie of Man*, ed. Frederick J. Furnivall and Percy Furnivall, Early English Text Society, Extra Series 53 (London, 1888), p. 79. I should add, of course, that there are endless references in the erotic poetry of the period to this heat, for example, in Marlowe's *Hero and Leander:*

> She, fearing on the rushes to be flung,
> Striv'd with redoubled strength; the more she strivèd,
> The more a gentle pleasing heat revivèd,
> Which taught him all that elder lovers know.
> And now the same 'gan so to scorch and glow,
> As in plain terms (yet cunningly) he craved it.
>
> (2.66–71)

Similarly, the whole of Shakespeare's *Venus and Adonis* is dominated by the language of heat.

34. We might find in Hobbes a theoretical equivalent, outside the medical tradition, of Duval's sense of the importance of friction in the origin of human differentiation. For Hobbes all human thought emerges from sense, and sense emerges from what I have been calling chafing: "The cause of Sense is the External Body, or Object, which presseth the organ proper to each Sense, either immediatly, as in the Tast and Touch; or mediately, as in Seeing, Hearing, and Smelling; which pressure, by the mediation of Nerves, and other strings, and membranes of the body,

continued inwards to the Brain, and Heart, causeth there a resistance, or counter pressure, or endeavour of the Heart, to deliver it self" (*Leviathan* 1:1).

If the sense of outward forms originates for Hobbes in "counter-pressure," then the sense of "inward forms" likewise originates in this experience.

35. I borrow the term *commotion* from Leo Bersani, "Representation and Its Discontents," in *Allegory and Representation*, ed. Stephen Greenblatt (Baltimore: Johns Hopkins University Press, 1981), pp. 145–62. "How are cultural activities," Bersani asks in another essay, " 'invested' with sexual interests?" His answer, following Melanie Klein, is that there is in sexual excitement a supplement that exceeds any particular representation attached to it and that therefore becomes "as it were, greedily, even promiscuously, available to *other* scenes and *other* activities" (Leo Bersani, " 'The Culture of Redemption' : Marcel Proust and Melanie Klein," *Critical Inquiry* 12 [1986]: 410).

36. On the feminization of the male subject, see Terry Eagleton, *The Rape of Clarissa* (Minneapolis: University of Minnesota Press, 1982), pp. 13ff.; Anne Douglass, *The Feminization of American Culture* (New York: Knopf, 1977); George S. Rousseau, "Nerves, Spirits, Fibres: Towards the Origins of Sensibility," in *Studies in the Eighteenth Century III: Proceedings of the David Nichol Smith Conference*, ed. R. F. Brissenden and J. C. Eade (Canberra: Australia University Press, 1976), pp. 137–57; John Mullan, "Hypochondria and Hysteria: Sensibility and the Physicians," *Eighteenth Century: Theory and Interpretation* 25 (Spring 1984): 141–74; and now Terry Castle, "The Female Thermometer," *Representations* 17 (1987):1–27. I am indebted to Castle's article for several of these references.

The feminization of the male subject is linked with a change in the conception of homosexuality, or rather with the development of the whole category of homosexuality as a distinct sexual status out of (and ultimately opposed to) earlier notions of unnatural acts. Unnatural acts—perversion—become explicable as inversion: the deviant performance of the inner nature, which is feminine. Important work in progress by Christopher Craft has helped to illuminate this conceptual shift.

37. I think Shakespeare first realized the erotic energy of chafing in the wooing scene in *Richard III*. In *The Rape of Lucrece* and *The Taming of the Shrew*, he went on to explore (and exploit) this energy in the form of violence and aggression, but the aggression is itself tamed in *A Midsummer Night's Dream* and *Much Ado about Nothing*.

38. The phrase "Venus' Palace" is from Philip Stubbes, *The Anatomie of Abuses* (London, 1595), p. 104. On attacks on the theater, see Jonas Barish, *The Antitheatrical Prejudice* (Berkeley: University of California Press, 1981), chapters 3–6.

39. *The Anatomical Lectures of William Harvey*, ed. and trans. Gweneth Whitteridge (Edinburgh, 1964), p. 175. For Harvey the beauty conferred by

sex is something man shares with the rest of the animal world. Harvey's own great work on roosters and hens began the shift, after Shakespeare's lifetime, toward an understanding of the ovum, yet even his account of animal behavior conveys a sense of both the sexual energies that I find transfigured in the comedies and the melancholy darkness that lies just beyond the transfiguration:

When males prepare themselves for coitus and, swelling with desire, are stimulated by the fire of venery, how wondrously does Cupid reigning within them heighten their inflamed spirits! how proudly do they parade themselves, bedecked with ornaments, how vigorous they are and how prone to do battle! But when this office of life is once ended, alas! how suddenly does their vigor subside and their late fervour cool, their swelling sails hang loose, and they lay aside their late ferocity. Indeed, even while this gay dance of Venus yet lasts, the males are straightway sad after coitus, and are seen to be submissive and pusillanimous as if mindful that, while they are bestowing life on others, they are hastening apace to their own decease. Only our cock, full of seed and spirits, lifts himself with greater sprightliness, and with beating wings and triumphant voice sings his hymeneal at his own nuptials. Yet even he flags after long use of venery, and like a soldier time expired grows weary, and the hens too, like plants, become past laying and are exhausted. (William Harvey, *Disputations Touching the Generation of Animals,* trans. Gweneth Whitteridge [Oxford: Blackwell Scientific Publications, 1981], p. 151)

40. The English stage, unlike the Chinese or Japanese, never developed a tradition of adult female impersonation; only boys could, as it were, naturally play the woman's part. (Or perhaps—and, if so, equally significant—the English called anyone who played a woman's part a boy.)

41. For a similar argument about stories of cross-dressing in medieval saints' lives, see Caroline Walker Bynum, "Women's Stories, Women's Symbols: A Critique of Victor Turner's Theory of Liminality," forthcoming in *Anthropology and the Study of Religions,* ed. Frank E. Reynolds and Robert Moore. See also the suggestive observations in Nancy K. Miller, " 'I's in Drag: The Sex of Recollection," *Eighteenth Century* 22 (1981): 47–57.

42. For the idea of the "open secret" I am indebted to a superb essay on *David Copperfield* by D. A. Miller: "Secret Subjects, Open Secrets," *Dickens Studies Annual* 14 (1985): 17–38. This essay will appear as a chapter in Miller's forthcoming *The Novel and the Police,* to be published by the University of California Press.

There is a further, paradoxical, function to the open secret of theatrical cross-dressing since the all-male cast is used to excuse the theater from any imputation of erotic *reality:* all of the wooing has been an imaginary pageant since the "natural" end of that wooing—the union of a man and a woman and the generation of offspring—is impossible.

4. Shakespeare and the Exorcists

1. Samuel Harsnett, *A Declaration of egregious Popish Impostures, to withdraw the harts of her Maiesties Subiects from their allegeance, and from the truth of*

Christian Religion professed in England, vnder the pretence of casting out deuils (London: Iames Roberts, 1603). Harsnett's influence is noted in Lewis Theobald's edition of Shakespeare, first published in 1733. Shakespeare is likely to have known one of the principal exorcists, Robert Dibdale, the son of a Stratford Catholic family linked to the Hathaways.

On the clandestine exorcisms I am particularly indebted to D. P. Walker, *Unclean Spirits: Possession and Exorcism in France and England in the Late Sixteenth and Early Seventeenth Centuries* (Philadelphia: University of Pennsylvania Press, 1981).

2. A major exception, with conclusions different from my own, has recently been published: John L. Murphy, *Darkness and Devils: Exorcism and "King Lear"* (Athens: Ohio University Press, 1984). Murphy's study, which he kindly allowed me to read in galleys after hearing the present chapter delivered as a lecture, argues that exorcism is an aspect of clandestine political and religious resistance to Queen Elizabeth's rule. For thoughtful comments on Murphy's book by an expert on Harsnett, see F. W. Brownlow's review in *Philological Quarterly* 65 (1986): 131–33. See also, for interesting reflections, William Elton, *"King Lear" and the Gods* (San Marino, Calif.: Huntington Library, 1966). For useful accounts of Harsnett's relation to *Lear*, see *Narrative and Dramatic Sources of Shakespeare*, 8 vols., ed. Geoffrey Bullough (London: Routledge and Kegan Paul, 1958–75), 7:299–302; Kenneth Muir, "Samuel Harsnett and *King Lear*," *Review of English Studies* 2 (1951): 11–21, and Muir's edition of *Lear*, New Arden text (Cambridge, Mass.: Harvard University Press, 1952), pp. 253–56.

3. Michel de Montaigne, "Apology for Raymond Sebond," in *Complete Essays*, trans. Donald M. Frame (Stanford: Stanford University Press, 1948), p. 331.

4. Edward Shils, *Center and Periphery: Essays in Macrosociology* (Chicago: University of Chicago Press, 1975), p. 257.

5. Peter Brown, *The Cult of the Saints: Its Rise and Function in Latin Christianity* (Chicago: University of Chicago Press, 1981), p. 107.

6. Sebastian Michaelis, *The Admirable Historie of the Possession and Conversion of a Penitent Woman*, trans. W. B. (London: William Aspley, 1613), p. 21. Mass exorcism was a particularly important phenomenon in sixteenth- and early seventeenth-century France. See Michel de Certeau, *La Possession de Loudun*, Collection Archive Series no. 37 (Paris: Gallimard, 1980); Robert Mandrou, *Magistrats et sorciers en France au XVIIe siècle* (Paris: Seuil, 1980); Robert Muchembled, *La Culture populaire et culture des élites* (Paris: Flammarion, 1977); Jonathan L. Pearl, "French Catholic Demonologists and Their Enemies in the Late Sixteenth and Early Seventeenth Centuries," *Church History* 52 (1983): 457–67; Henri Weber, "L'Exorcisme à la fin du seizième siècle, instrument de la Contre Réforme et spectacle baroque," *Nouvelle Revue du seizième siècle* 1 (1983): 79–101. For a comparison between exorcism in France and in England, see D. P. Walker, *Unclean Spirits*, and my own article, "Loudun and London," *Critical Inquiry* 12

(1986): 326–46. I have incorporated some pages from this article in the present chapter.

7. *A Booke Declaringe the Fearfull Vexasion of one Alexander Nyndge. Beynge moste Horriblye tormented wyth an euyll Spirit* (London: Thomas Colwell, 1573), p. Biiii^r.

8. Carlo Ginzburg, *I benandanti: Recerche sulla stregoneria e sui culti agrari tra cinquecento e seicento* (Turin: Einaudi, 1966).

9. For Harsnett's comments on witchcraft, see *Declaration*, pp. 135–36. The relation between demonic possession and witchcraft is complex. John Darrel evidently had frequent recourse, in the midst of his exorcisms, to accusations of witchcraft whose evidence was precisely the demonic possessions; Harsnett remarks wryly that "of all the partes of the tragicall Comedie acted between him and *Somers*, there was no one Scene in it, wherein *M. Darrell* did with more courage and boldnes acte his part, then in this of the discouerie of witches" (*A Discovery of the Fraudulent Practises of J. Darrel . . . concerning the pretended possession and dispossession of W. Somers, etc.* [1599], p. 142). There is a helpful discussion of possession and witchcraft, along with an important account of Harsnett and Darrel, in Keith Thomas, *Religion and the Decline of Magic* (London: Weidenfeld and Nicolson, 1971).

10. I borrow the phrase "central zone" from Edward Shils, for whom it is coterminous with society's central value system, a system constituted by the general standards of judgment and action and affirmed by the society's elite (*Center and Periphery*, p. 3). At the heart of the central value system is an affirmative attitude toward authority, which is endowed, however indirectly or remotely, with a measure of sacredness. "By their very possession of authority," Shils writes, elites "attribute to themselves an essential affinity with the sacred elements of their society, of which they regard themselves as the custodians" (5).

11. Brown, *Cult of the Saints*, pp. 109–11.

12. Thomas, *Religion and the Decline of Magic*, p. 485. "This effectively put an end to the practice," Thomas writes, "at least as far as conforming members of the Anglican Church were concerned."

13. S. M. Shirokogorov, *The Psycho-Mental Complex of the Tungus* (Peking: Routledge, 1935), p. 265.

14. Brown, *Cult of the Saints*, p. 110.

15. Michael MacDonald, *Mystical Bedlam* (Cambridge: Cambridge University Press, 1981). See also MacDonald's "Religion, Social Change, and Psychological Healing in England, 1600–1800," in *The Church and Healing*, ed. W. J. Shiels, Studies in Church History 19 (Oxford: Basil Blackwell, 1982); H. C. Erik Midelfort, "Madness and the Problems of Psychological History in the Sixteenth Century," *Sixteenth Century Journal* 12 (1981): 5–12.

16. *A Report Contayning a brief Narration of certain diuellish and wicked witcheries, practized by Olisse Barthram alias Doll Barthram in the Country of Suffolke*, bound with *The Triall of Maist. Dorrell, or A Collection of Defences against Allegations not yet suffered to receiue convenient answere* (1599), p. 94.

17. Iohn Swan, *A Trve and Briefe Report. of Mary Glovers Vexation* (1603), p. 42.

18. *The Triall of Maist. Dorrell*, p. 29.

19. Quoted in [John Darrel,] *A Briefe Narration of the possession, disposses-sion, and repossession of William Sommers* (1598), pp. Diiv, Ciiiiv.

20. *The Triall of Maist. Dorrell*, p. 8.

21. John Deacon and John Walker, *A Summarie Answere to al the material points in any of Master Darel his bookes* (London: George Bishop, 1601), pp. 237–38.

22. Harsnett sees this argument as a variant on the exorcists' general rule that "when the deuilles are cast out of man, they endeuoure by all the means they can, to perswade, that hee was neuer in them: that so the partie being vnthankefull to God for his deliuerance, they might the better reenter into him" (*Discovery*, p. 72). Harsnett cites the important exorcism manual by R. F. Hieronymus Mengus [Girolamo Menghi], *Flagellum Daemonum* (Bologna, 1582).

23. In 1524 Erasmus satirized exorcism by depicting it not simply as a fraud but as a play in five acts (*Exorcismus, sive spectrum*, in *The Colloquies of Erasmus*, trans. Craig R. Thompson [Chicago: University of Chicago Press, 1965], pp. 231–37). The play, in Erasmus's account, is an elaborate practi-cal joke played on a character called Faunus, a gullible and pretentious parish priest who is cleverly induced to be an unwitting actor in an outland-ish and grotesque theatrical performance. The representation of the de-monic is spurious, but its effect on the victim of the joke is alarmingly real: "So thoroughly did this fancy obsess him that he dreamt of nothing but specters and evil spirits and talked of nothing else. His mental condition carried over into his very countenance, which became so pale, so drawn, so downcast that you would have said he was a ghost, not a man" (237). A successful demon play can fashion the dreams of its victims, and illusions can inscribe themselves in the very bodies of those who believe in them.

The colloquy ostensibly celebrates the histrionic cunning of the jokers, but Erasmus makes it clear that there are larger institutional implications: a gifted director, an unscrupulous actor who has "perfect control of his expression," and a few props suffice not only to create an intense illusion of the demonic among large numbers of spectators but also to entice the gullible into participating in a play whose theatricality they cannot ac-knowledge. The defense against such impostures is a widespread public recognition of this theatricality and a consequent skepticism: "Up to this time I haven't, as a rule, had much faith in popular tales about appari-tions," one of Erasmus's speakers concludes, "but hereafter I'll have even less" (237).

24. See Edmund Jorden, *A briefe discourse of a disease Called the Suffocation of the Mother* (London, 1603).

25. *A Report Contayning a brief Narration of certain diuellish and wicked witcheries*, pp. 99–100.

26. [Richard Baddeley,] *The Boy of Bilson, or A True Discovery of the Late Notorious Impostvres of Certaine Romish Priests in their pretended Exorcisme, or expulsion of the Diuell out of a young Boy, named William Perry, sonne of Thomas Perry of Bilson* (London: F. K., 1622), p. 51. Baddeley is quoting from the Catholic account of the events, which, in order to dispute, he reprints: *A Faithfull Relation of the Proceedings of the Catholicke Gentlemen with the Boy of Bilson; shewing how they found him, on what termes they meddled with him, how farre they proceeded with him, and in what case, and for what cause they left to deale further with him* (in Baddeley, pp. 45–54).

27. In both England and France the reliability of the devil's testimony was debated extensively. "We ought not to beleeue the Diuell," writes the exorcist and inquisitor Sebastian Michaelis, "yet when hee is compelled to discourse and relate a truth, then wee should feare and tremble, for it is a token of the wrath of God" (*Admirable Historie of the Possession and Conversion of a Penitent Woman*, p. C7v). Michaelis's long account of his triumph over a devil named Verrine was published, the translator claims, to show "that the Popish Priests, in all Countries where men will beleeue them, are vniforme & like vnto themselues, since that which was done couertly in England, in the daies of Queene *Elizabeth*, by the Deuils of *Denham* in *Sara Williams* and her fellowes, is now publikely taken vp elsewhere by men of no small ranke" (A4r). This seems to me a disingenuous justification for publishing, without further annotation or qualification, over five hundred pages of Catholic apologetics, but obviously the Jacobean licensing authorities accepted the explanation.

28. [Darrel,] *A Briefe Narration of the possession, dispossession, and repossession of William Sommers*, p. Biiv.

29. "Let him be brought before some indifferent persons, let the depositions be read, and let him act the same in such maner, and forme as is deposed, by naturall, or artificiall power, then Mr. Dorrell will yeeld that he did conterfeit. It he cannot, (as vndoubtedlie he cannot,) then pleade no longer for the Deuill; but punish that imp of Satan as a wicked lier, and blasphemer of the mightie worke of God" (*Briefe Narration*, p. Biiv).

30. *Booke of Miracles*, quoted in Harsnett, *Declaration*, pp. 113–14.

31. In Haiti, for example, an individual possessed by a *loa*, or spirit, is led to the vestry of the sanctuary, where he chooses the costume appropriate to the particular spirit that has possessed him; dressed in this costume—for Baron Saturday, a black suit, starched cuffs, top hat, and white gloves; for the peasant god Zaka, a straw hat, pouch, and pipe; and so forth—he returns to the clearing and performs for the assembled crowd the appropriate mimes, monologues, and dances (Alfred Metraux, "Dramatic Elements in Ritual Possession," *Diogenes* 11 [1964]: 18–36). In Sri Lanka, exorcisms integrate feasting, the making of ritual offerings, dancing, the singing of sacred texts, drumming, masking, and the staging of improvised, frequently obscene, comedies. The comedies are at once explicitly theatrical and integral to the healing process.

In a major study of exorcism rituals performed in and near the town of Galle in southern Sri Lanka, Bruce Kapferer observes that demons in Sinhalese culture are understood to operate by means of illusions; the disorder and suffering that these illusions occasion are combated by spectacular demystifying counter-illusions. Hence exorcists "consider their healing rites to be elaborate tricks which they play on demons": to induce demons to treat the illusory as reality is to gain control over them (Bruce Kapferer, *A Celebration of Demons: Exorcism and the Aesthetics of Healing in Sri Lanka* [Bloomington: Indiana University Press, 1983], p. 112). Demonic possession has disturbed a hierarchical order that must be restored by humiliating the demons and returning them to their rightful subordinate position in the order of things. This restoration is achieved through ceremonies that "place major aesthetic forms into relation and locate them at points when particular transformations in meaning and experience are understood by exorcists to be occurring or are to be effected" (8). The ceremonies transform demonic identity into normal social identity; the individual is returned to himself and hence to his community whose solidarity is not only mirrored but constituted by the aesthetic experience. Exorcists then are "the masters of illusion" (113), and their histrionic skills do not arouse doubts about their authenticity but heighten confidence in their powers.

For further reflections on demonic possession, see Ernst Arbman, *Ecstasy or Religious Trance* (Norstedts: Svenska Bokforlaget, 1963), 3 vols., esp. chapter 9; *Disguises of the Demonic: Contemporary Perspectives on the Power of Evil*, ed. Alan M. Olson (New York: Association Press, n.d.); I. M. Lewis, *Ecstatic Religion: An Anthropological Study of Spirit Possession and Shamanism* (Harmondsworth: Penguin, 1971).

32. Michel Leiris, *La Possession et ses aspects théâtraux chez les Ethiopiens de Gondar* (Paris: Plon, 1958).

33. This argument has the curious effect of identifying all exorcisms, including those conducted by nonconformist preachers, with the pope. On attacks on the Catholic church as a theater, see Jonas Barish, *The Antitheatrical Prejudice* (Berkeley: University of California Press, 1981), pp. 66–131 passim.

34. At least since Plato there has been a powerful tendency to identify the stage with unreality, debased imitation, and outright counterfeiting. Like the painter, says Socrates in the *Republic*, the tragic poet is an imitator of objects that are themselves imitations and hence "thrice removed from the king and from the truth" (597e). Though this position had its important Christian adherents, it is not, of course, the only intellectual current in the West; not only do medieval mystery plays depend upon a conviction that dramatic performance does not contradict religious truth, but the Mass itself appears to have been conceived by several important medieval thinkers as analogous to theatrical representation. For further discussion, see my "Loudun and London," pp. 328–29.

35. *Discovery*, p. A3r. As Catholic priests "have transformed the cele-

brating of the Sacrament of the *Lords supper* into a *Masse-game,* and all other partes of the *Ecclesiasticall service* into *theatricall sights,"* writes another sixteenth-century Protestant polemicist, "so, in steede of *preaching the word,* they caused it to be played" (John Rainolds, cited in Barish, *The Antitheatrical Prejudice,* p. 163).

36. Harsnett was not alone, of course. See, for example, John Gee: "The Jesuits being or having Actors of such dexterity, I see no reason but that they should set up a company for themselves, which surely will put down The Fortune, Red-Bull, Cock-pit, and Globe" (John Gee, *New Shreds of the Old Snare* [London, 1624]). I owe this reference, along with powerful reflections on the significance of the public theater's physical marginality, to Steven Mullaney.

37. This sentiment could serve as the epigraph to both of Harsnett's books on exorcism; it is the root perception from which most of Harsnett's rhetoric grows.

38. Stephen Gosson, *Plays Confuted in Five Actions* (c. 1582), cited in E. K. Chambers, *The Elizabethan Stage,* 4 vols. (Oxford: Clarendon, 1923), 4:215.

39. These lines were included in the quarto but omitted from the folio. For the tangled textual history, see Michael J. Warren, "Quarto and Folio *King Lear,* and the Interpretation of Albany and Edgar," in *Shakespeare: Pattern of Excelling Nature,* ed. David Bevington and Jay L. Halio (Newark: University of Delaware Press, 1978), pp. 95–107; Steven Urkowitz, *Shakespeare's Revision of "King Lear"* (Princeton: Princeton University Press, 1980); and Gary Taylor, "The War in *King Lear,"* *Shakespeare Survey* 33 (1980): 27–34. Presumably, by the time the folio appeared, the point of the allusion to Harsnett would have been lost, and the lines were dropped.

40. John Bunyan, *Grace Abounding to the Chief of Sinners,* ed. Roger Sharrock (London: Clarendon Press, 1966), p. 15.

41. Edgar's later explanation—that he feared for his father's ability to sustain the shock of an encounter—is, like so many explanations in *King Lear,* too little, too late. On this characteristic belatedness as an element of the play's greatness, see Stephen Booth, *"King Lear," "Macbeth," Indefinition, and Tragedy* (New Haven: Yale University Press, 1983).

42. On "counterfeit miracles" produced to arouse awe and wonder, see especially Harsnett, *Discovery,* Epistle to the Reader.

43. Words, signs, gestures that claim to be in touch with super-reality, with absolute goodness and absolute evil, are exposed as vacant—illusions manipulated by the clever and imposed on the gullible.

44. This is, in effect, Edmund Jorden's prescription for cases such as Lear's, in *A briefe discourse of a disease.*

45. "It is even possible," writes Peter Milward, S.J., "that the lot of such priests as Weston and Dibdale provided Shakespeare with a suggestion for his portrayal of Edgar in hiding" (*Shakespeare's Religious Background* [London: Sidgwick and Jackson, 1973], p. 54). But I cannot agree with

Milford's view that Shakespeare continually "laments 'the plight of his poor country' since the day Henry VIII decided to break with Rome" (224).

46. On the Yorkshire performance, see John Murphy, *Darkness and Devils*, pp. 93–118.

47. In willing this disenchantment against the evidence of our senses, we pay tribute to the theater. Harsnett has been twisted around to make this tribute possible. Harsnett several times characterizes exorcism as a "tragicomedy" (*Discovery*, p. 142; *Declaration*, p. 150). On Harsnett's conception of tragicomedy, see Herbert Berry, "Italian Definitions of Tragedy and Comedy Arrive in England," *Studies in English Literature* 14 (1974): 179–87.

48. O. B. Hardison, Jr., *Christian Rite and Christian Drama in the Middle Ages: Essays in the Origin and Early History of Modern Drama* (Baltimore: Johns Hopkins University Press, 1965), esp. pp. 220–52.

49. C. L. Barber, "The Family in Shakespeare's Development: Tragedy and Sacredness," in *Representing Shakespeare: New Psychoanalytic Essays*, ed. Murray M. Schwartz and Coppélia Kahn (Baltimore: Johns Hopkins University Press, 1980), p. 196.

50. Richard Hooker, *Laws of Ecclesiastical Polity*, 1:582–83. This truth, which is the triumph of the metaphorical over the literal, confers on the church the liberty to use certain names and rites, even though they have been abolished. The entire passage in Hooker is powerfully suggestive for understanding the negotiation between the domain of literature and the domain of religion:

They which honour the Law as an image of the wisdom of God himself, are notwithstanding to know that the same had an end in Christ. But what? Was the Law so abolished with Christ, that after his ascension the office of Priests became immediately wicked, and the very name hateful, as importing the exercise of an ungodly function? No, as long as the glory of the Temple continued, and till the time of that final desolation was accomplished, the very Christian Jews did continue with their sacrifices and other parts of legal service. That very Law therefore which our Saviour was to abolish, did not *so soon* become unlawful to be observed as some imagine; nor was it afterwards unlawful *so far*, that the very name of Altar, of Priest, of Sacrifice itself, should be banished out of the world. For though God do now hate sacrifice, whether it be heathenish or Jewish, so that we cannot have the same things which they had but with impiety; yet unless there be some greater let than the only evacuation of the Law of Moses, the names themselves may (I hope) be retained without sin, in respect of that proportion which things established by our Saviour have unto them which by him are abrogated. And so throughout all the writings of the ancient Fathers we see that the words which were do continue; the only difference is, that whereas before they had a literal, they now have a metaphorical use, and are so many notes of remembrance unto us, that what they did signify in the letter is accomplished in the truth. And as no man can deprive the Church of this liberty, to use names whereunto the Law was accustomed, so neither are we generally forbidden the use of things which the Law hath; though it neither command us any particular rite, as it did the Jews a number and the weightiest which it did command them are unto us in the Gospel prohibited. (4.11.10)

For the reference to Hooker I am indebted to John Coolidge.

51. "Truth to tell," writes Barthes, "the best weapon against myth is

perhaps to mythify it in its turn, and to produce an *artificial myth:* and this reconstituted myth will in fact be a mythology" (Roland Barthes, *Mythologies*, trans. Annette Lavers [New York: Hill and Wang, 1972], p. 135).

5. Martial Law in the Land of Cockaigne

1. "First Sermon on the Lord's Prayer," in *The Works of Hugh Latimer*, 2 vols., ed. George Elwes Corrie, Parker Society (Cambridge: Cambridge University Press, 1844), 1:335. Though her mother was a near relation of Catherine of Aragon, the duchess of Suffolk was a staunch Protestant who went into exile during the reign of Mary Tudor.

Latimer's rhetorical occasion for relating this story is an odd one: he is commenting on the appropriateness of addressing God as "our father," since God "hath a fatherly and loving affection towards us, far passing the love of bodily parents to their children." Latimer then cites a passage from Isaiah in which the prophet asks rhetorically, in speaking of God's love, "Can a wife forget the child of her womb, and the son whom she hath borne?" Isaiah uses the image of a wife, Latimer remarks, "because women most commonly are more affected towards their children than men be." He then recalls with horror that under the devil's influence some women have in fact killed their own children, but he warns his listeners not to believe every story of this kind that they hear. And he proceeds to support this warning with the story of the Cambridge woman.

2. Alternatively, we might say that Latimer occupies a peculiarly intermediate position, anticipating that occupied by the players: at once free and constrained, the strutting master of the scene and the social inferior, the charismatic object of intense cathexis and the embodiment of dependence.

3. The closest parallel, I suppose, would be nocturnal emissions, about which there is a substantial literature in the Middle Ages and early modern period, but I am not sure a story about them would have been suitable for the duchess of Suffolk.

4. The gap is, at this point, a very small one, and on her release from prison the woman may well have been sent back to her husband. Latimer does not bother to say, presumably because the woman's fate was irrelevant to his homiletic point.

5. Though the justification for a transfer (as opposed to a simple elimination) is left vague, perhaps to spare the sensibility of the duchess of Suffolk, Latimer may believe that for some time after childbirth the woman's body is tainted—hence "a green woman," as in green or tainted meat—and that in the interest of public health she should not be permitted contact, in particular sexual contact, with others. Or perhaps he simply believes that a woman still weakened from the ordeal of childbirth—hence a different meaning for "green woman," as in a green or fresh wound— should be spared the normal demands on her energies.

6. See similarly Spenser's account of Duessa (*Faerie Queene* 1.8.46–48).

There are many medical as well as literary and theological reflections on the innate filthiness of women.

7. The sermon is probably not a source for *Measure for Measure*, though it is intriguing that another, more famous, sermon by Latimer—the first of the "Sermons on the Card"—includes an emblematic story that bears a certain resemblance to Shakespeare's play. The king in Latimer's fable accepts into his favor "a mean man," "not because this person hath of himself deserved any such favour, but that the king casteth this favour unto him of his own mere motion and fantasy." The man thus favored is appointed "the chief captain and defender of his town of Calais," but he treacherously violates his trust (*The Works of Hugh Latimer* 1:4–5).

8. Although one can readily imagine a detached response to a Shakespearean comedy, such a response would signal the failure of the play to please or a refusal of the pleasure the play was offering.

9. This is, however, only a *working* distinction, to mark an unstable, shifting relation between anxiety and pleasure. Anxiety and pleasure are not the same, but they are not simple opposites. Anxiety in the presence of real bodies put at real risk is a source of pleasure for at least some of the spectators, whereas in the theater pleasure in imaginary situations is not entirely unmixed with (and does not entirely absorb and transform) anxiety. Even if we discount the rhetorical exaggerations of that anxiety in a literary criticism that often speaks of the excruciating pain and difficulty of spectatorship (or reading), we must acknowledge that Shakespeare often arouses considerable anxiety. Still, we must also acknowledge that for the collective body of spectators the ratio of anxiety to pleasure in the theater was likely to have differed from that outside its walls.

10. Theatrical anxiety must not only give pleasure in the theater but generate a longing for the theater in those who have left its precincts. If large numbers of potential spectators feel they can get what they need in other places, they will not take the trouble to return. The point is obvious but still worth remarking, since we are likely to forget, first, that Elizabethan and Jacobean public theaters had extremely large capacities (as high as two thousand spectators) and hence expected to draw substantial crowds and, second, that it was by no means simple to attend most of the theaters. A trip to the Globe took a good part of the day and involved considerable expense, including transportation by boat and refreshments. The theater had to contrive to make potential spectators think, and think frequently, "I wish I were at the theater." To do so, it could advertise through playbills and processions, but it could also count on deep associations: that is, certain anxieties would remind one of the theater where those same anxieties were turned to the service of pleasure.

11. The very point of theatrical anxiety may be that it is not "real"—that is, we are not threatened, there are no consequences in the real world to fortune or station or life, and so forth. But this formulation is at best only a half-truth, since at the level of feelings it is not always so easy to distin-

guish between the anxiety generated by a literary experience and the anxiety generated by events in one's own life.

12. He does, however, in some sense tell the story for his hearers' pleasure as well as instruction, and I think it is important to resist making too sharp a distinction between the purely theatrical uses of anxiety and the uses elsewhere in the culture. The distinction is practical and relative: no less important for that, but not to be construed as a theoretical necessity.

13. His strategy may also derive from a late-medieval clerical preoccupation with the distinction between *attrition* and *contrition*. The former was a change in behavior caused by the buffets of fortune and the hope of escaping punishment through a prudent repentance; the latter was a more authentic repentance rooted not in calculation but in grief. Latimer may have felt that only when the woman was at the point of death could she experience a genuine contrition. I discuss below an instance of this distinction in *Measure for Measure*.

14. It is worth reflecting on the implications of this casual remark: "the people" appear to believe that there is an inverse relation between the severity of the punishment and the heinousness of the crime.

15. For an account of the scene, see Catherine Drinker Bowen, *The Lion and the Throne: The Life and Times of Sir Edward Coke* (Boston: Little, Brown and Company, 1956), pp. 220–22.

16. For the text of James's letter, see *Letters of King James VI and I*, ed. G. P. V. Akrigg (Berkeley: University of California Press, 1984), pp. 218–19.

17. James himself was one of the most notoriously anxious monarchs in British history, and with good reason. In the event, his son, as well as his mother and father, met a violent end.

18. Dudley Carleton's letter, dated December 11, 1603, is reprinted in Thomas Birch, *The Court and Times of James the First*, 2 vols. (London: Henry Colburn, 1849), 1:27–32. Carleton suggests that Sir Walter Ralegh, who had also been convicted in the Bye Plot, was the particular object of the king's techniques of anxiety arousal. Ralegh was to be executed on the following Monday and was watching the scene on the scaffold from a window in his cell. "Raleigh, you must think," writes Carleton, "had hammers working in his head, to beat out the meaning of this strategem" (31). In a comparable last-minute reprieve, James suspended Ralegh's execution as well; Ralegh was kept prisoner (and was considered to be legally dead) for thirteen years until, in the wake of the Guiana fiasco, he was executed (technically on the original charge from 1603) in 1618.

19. Their popularity as spectacle suggests that the fear was to some degree pleasurable to the onlookers, whether, as Hobbes argued, because they delighted in not being themselves the victims or, as official spokesmen claimed, because the horror was produced by a higher order whose interests it served. In either case, the experience, it was assumed, would make the viewers more obedient subjects.

20. Quoted in my *Renaissance Self-Fashioning: From More to Shakespeare* (Chicago: University of Chicago Press, 1980), p. 103.

21. Durandus of St. Pourçain, quoted in Thomas N. Tentler, *Sin and Confession on the Eve of the Reformation* (Princeton: Princeton University Press, 1977), p. 251. Tentler observes that this psychologizing of the distinction is not characteristic of the medieval *summae* for confessors; the crucial distinction rather was between sorrow that was imperfect and sorrow that had been formed by grace and hence was perfect. In either case the limitation—and perhaps the cunning—of the distinction is that it is virtually impossible to establish with any confidence.

22. Recall Carleton's description of the expression on the faces of the Bye Plot conspirators as they were assembled together on the scaffold.

23. On the significance of pardon as a strategy in Renaissance monarchies, see Natalie Zemon Davis, *Fiction in the Archives* (Stanford: Stanford University Press, forthcoming). Davis's wonderful book, which she graciously allowed me to read in manuscript, shows that the system of pardons in France generated a remarkable range of narratives. Though the English legal system differed in important ways from the French, pardon played a significant, if more circumscribed, role. Shakespeare seems to have deliberately appropriated for *The Tempest* the powerful social energy of princely pardons.

24. In this regard Prospero resembles less a radical reformer like Latimer than a monarch like Queen Elizabeth: a ruler who abjured the complete inquisitorial control of the inner life and settled when necessary for the outward signs of obedience.

For a brilliant discussion of Prospero's relations with Antonio, see the introduction to the Oxford Shakespeare edition of *The Tempest*, ed. Stephen Orgel (Oxford: Oxford University Press, 1987). Throughout this chapter, I have profited from Orgel's introduction, which he kindly showed me in advance of its publication.

25. I am trying to resist here the proposition that Latimer's story is the actual practice that is then represented in works of art, and hence that in it we encounter the basis in reality of theatrical fictions. Even if we assume that the events in Cambridge occurred exactly as Latimer related them— and this is a large assumption based on a reckless act of faith—those events seem saturated with narrative conventions. It is not only that Latimer lives his life as if it were material for the stories he will tell in his sermons but that the actions he reports are comprehensible only if already fashioned into a story.

26. On Strachey's career, see S. G. Culliford, *William Strachey, 1572–1621* (Charlottesville: University Press of Virginia, 1965). See also Charles Richard Sanders, "William Strachey, the Virginia Colony, and Shakespeare," *Virginia Magazine* 57 (1949): 115–32. Sanders notes that "many of the eighteenth and nineteenth century Stracheys became servants of the East India Company" (118).

27. William Strachey, in Samuel Purchas, *Hakluytus Posthumus or Pur-*

chas His Pilgrimes, 20 vols. (Glasgow: James Maclehose and Sons, 1905–7), 19:5–72. It seems worth remarking the odd coincidence between this circumstance and Latimer's presenting his sermon also to a noble lady. Men in this period often seem to shape their experiences in the world to present them as instruction or entertainment to powerfully placed ladies. The great Shakespearean exploration of this social theme is *Othello*.

28. On joint-stock companies in the early modern period, see William Robert Scott, *The Constitution and Finance of English, Scottish, and Irish Joint-Stock Companies to 1720*, 3 vols. (Cambridge: Cambridge University Press, 1912). On the theater and the marketplace, see the excellent book by Jean-Christophe Agnew, *Worlds Apart: The Market and the Theater in Anglo-American Thought, 1550–1750* (Cambridge: Cambridge University Press, 1986).

29. Indeed the demand for such connections, a demand almost always frustrated in the early modern period, has strengthened the case for the formalist isolation of art.

30. Charles Mills Gayley, *Shakespeare and the Founders of Liberty in America* (New York: Macmillan, 1917); William Strachey, *The Historie of Travell into Virginia Britania* (1612), ed. Louis B. Wright and Virginia Freund, Hakluyt Society 2d ser., no. 103 (London, 1953), p. xix.

31. Detestation of the sailors is a common theme in the travel literature of the period. One of the strongest elements of an elitist utopia in *The Tempest* is the fantasy that the sailors will in effect be put to sleep for the duration of the stay on the island, to be awakened only to labor on the return voyage.

32. Quoted in the introduction to *The Historie of Travell into Virginia Britania*, p. xxv.

33. I quote these lines because they may have caught Shakespeare's attention: "What have we here?" asks Trinculo, catching sight of Caliban, "a man or a fish? dead or alive? A fish, he smells like a fish" (2.2.24–26). Prospero in exasperation calls Caliban a tortoise (1.2.316).

34. The promotional literature written on behalf of the Virginia Company prior to the voyage of 1609 makes it clear that there was already widespread talk in England about the hardships of the English colonists. No one on the *Sea Venture* is likely to have harbored any illusions about conditions at Jamestown.

35. The office of governor was created by the royal charter of 1609. The governor replaced the council president as the colony's chief executive. He was granted the right to "correct and punishe, pardon, governe, and rule all such the subjects of us . . . as shall from time to time adventure themselves . . . thither," and he was empowered to impose martial law in cases of mutiny or rebellion (quoted in *The Three Charters of the Virginia Company of London, with Seven Related Documents, 1606–1621*, ed. S. F. Bemiss, Jamestown 350th Anniversary Historical Booklet 4 [Williamsburg, Va., 1957], p. 52). See Warren M. Billings, "The Transfer of English Law to Virginia, 1606–1650," in *The Westward Enterprise: English Activities in Ireland, the Atlan-*

tic, and America, 1480–1650, ed. K. R. Andrews, N. P. Canny, and P. E. H. Hair (Liverpool: Liverpool University Press, 1978), pp. 214ff.

36. Leaving the island is not in itself, as is sometimes claimed, an abjuration of colonialism: as we have seen in the case of Bermuda, the enforced departure from the island signals the resumption of the colonial enterprise. On the other hand, insofar as *The Tempest* conflates the Bermuda and Virginia materials, the departure for Italy—and by implication England—would necessitate abandoning the absolute rule that had been established under martial law.

37. The noblemen's pride is related to the gentlemanly refusal to work that the leaders of the Virginia Company bitterly complained about. The English gentlemen in Jamestown, it was said, preferred to die rather than lift a finger to save themselves. So too when the boatswain urges Antonio and Sebastian to get out of the way or to work, Antonio answers, "We are less afraid to be drown'd than thou art" (1.1.44–45).

38. For acute observations on the parallels with Sycorax, see Stephen Orgel, "Prospero's Wife," *Representations* 8 (1985): 1–13; among the many essays on Caliban is one of my own: "Learning to Curse: Aspects of Linguistic Colonialism in the Sixteenth Century," in *First Images of America: The Impact of the New World on the Old,* 2 vols., ed. Fredi Chiappelli (Berkeley: University of California Press, 1976), 2:561–80.

39. Quoted in Nicholas Canny, "The Permissive Frontier: The Problem of Social Control in English Settlements in Ireland and Virginia, 1550–1650," in *The Westward Enterprise,* p. 36.

40. William Crashaw, *A sermon preached in London before the right honorable the Lord Lawarre, Lord Governour and Captaine Generall of Virginia . . . at the said Lord Generall his leave taking of England . . . and departure for Virginea, Febr. 21, 1609* (London, 1610), pp. H1v–H1r. The British Library has a copy of Strachey's *Lawes Diuine, Morall and Martiall* with a manuscript inscription by the author to Crashaw; see Sanders, "William Strachey, the Virginia Colony, and Shakespeare," p. 121.

41. William Strachey, *For the Colony in Virginea Britannia. Lawes Diuine, Morall and Martiall, &c.* (London: Walter Burre, 1612), in Peter Force, *Tracts and Other Papers, Relating Principally to the Origin, Settlement, and Progress of the Colonies in North America, from the Discovery to the Year 1776,* 4 vols. (Washington, D.C., 1836–46), 3:67.

42. In our century the market for Shakespeare as book has come to focus increasingly upon adolescents in colleges and universities who are assigned expensive texts furnished with elaborate critical introductions and editorial apparatus. On the ideological implications of Shakespeare in the curriculum, see Alan Sinfield, "Give an account of Shakespeare and Education, showing why you think they are effective and what you have appreciated about them. Support your comments with precise references," in *Political Shakespeare: New Essays in Cultural Materialism,* ed. Jonathan Dollimore and Alan Sinfield (Manchester: Manchester University Press, 1985), pp. 134–57.

43. But if Shakespeare's works have become a fetish, they are defined for their possessors not by their magical power to command but by their freedom from the anxieties of rule. They are the emblems of cultivation, civility, recreation, but they are not conceived of as direct agents in the work of empire.

44. Henry M. Stanley, *Through the Dark Continent*, 2 vols. (New York: Harper and Brothers, 1878), 2:384–86. I owe this story to Walter Michaels, who found it quoted by William James in a footnote. James's interest was aroused by what he saw as primitive literalism. The natives' oral culture makes it impossible for them to understand writing. They cannot distinguish between books that are reproducible and books that are unique, or for that matter between fiction and field notes, and because of this inability they cannot identify what was at least the immediate threat to their culture. In making the book a fetish they fail to make the necessary distinction between fantasy and truth, a distinction whose origins reside in texts like *The Tempest*, that is, in texts that thematize a difference between the island of art and the mainland of reality.

It is difficult to gauge how much of this analysis is only James's own fantasy. The natives may not actually have been incapable of making such a distinction. It is interesting, in this regard, that they are said to be carrying muskets, so there must already have been a history of involvement with Arabs or Europeans, a history that Stanley, making much of his role as explorer, represses. It is noteworthy too that as Stanley warms to his story, his natives increasingly speak in the racist idiom familiar from movies like *King Kong:* "M-m. No, no, no." And it is also possible, as I have already suggested, to see in Stanley the actual fetishism of the book: the attribution of power and value and companionship to the dead letter. In Stanley's reverie Shakespeare becomes a friend who must be sacrificed (as Stanley seems prepared to sacrifice Safeni) to protect the colonial project. Shakespeare is thus indispensable in two ways—as a consolation in the long painful trials of empire and as a deceptive token of exchange.

45. *The Exploration Diaries of H. M. Stanley,* ed. Richard Stanley and Alan Neame (New York: Vanguard Press, 1961), p. 187. Many of the journal entries that Stanley professes to transcribe in *Through the Dark Continent* are in fact invented: "The so-called 'extracts from my diary' in *Through the Dark Continent,*" the editors remark, "are hardly more than a device for varying the typeface, for they are quite as deliberately composed as the rest of the narrative" (xvi). I should add that the day after the burning of his "genial companion," Stanley lost his close friend and associate Frank Pocock, who drowned when his canoe overturned. There is an odd sense of a relation between the loss of these two friends, as if Stanley viewed the burning of the one and the drowning of the other as linked sacrifices for the cause of empire.

Index